Gregor von Bochmann

Concepts for Distributed Systems Design

With 107 Figures

Springer-Verlag
Berlin Heidelberg New York 1983

Professor Dr. Gregor von Bochmann

Université de Montréal, Faculté des arts et des sciences
Département d'informatique et de recherche opérationnelle,
(I.R.O.), Case postale 6128, Succursale "A",
Montréal, P.Q., H3C 3J7, Canada

ISBN-13:978-3-642-68853-9   e-ISBN-13:978-3-642-68851-5
DOI: 10.1007/978-3-642-68851-5

Library of Congress Cataloging in Publication Data. Main entry under title:
Bochmann, Gregor von, 1941 – Concepts for distributed systems design.
Bibliography: p. Includes index. 1. Electronic data processing – Distributed
processing. 2. System design. I. Title QA76.9.D5B64 1983 OO1.64 83-574

This work is subject to copyright. All rights are reserved, whether the whole
or part of the material is concerned, specifically those of translation,
reprinting, re-use of illustrations, broadcastening, reproduction by photo-
copying machine or similar means, and storage in data banks. Under § 54
of the German Copyright Law, where copies are made for other than private
use, a fee is payable to 'Verwertungsgesellschaft Wort', Munich.

© Springer-Verlag Berlin Heidelberg 1983
Softcover reprint of the hardcover 1st edition 1983

The use of registered names, trademarks, etc. in the publication does not
imply, even in the absence of a specific statement, that such names are
exempt from the relevant protective laws and regulations and therefore free
for general use.

Preface

This book is written for computer programmers, analysts and scientists, as well as computer science students, as an introduction to the principles of distributed system design. The emphasis is placed on a clear understanding of the concepts, rather than on details; and the reader will learn about the structure of distributed systems, their problems, and approaches to their design and development. The reader should have a basic knowledge of computer systems and be familiar with modular design principles for software development. He should also be aware of present-day remote-access and distributed computer applications.

The book consists of three parts which deal with principles of distributed systems, communications architecture and protocols, and formal description techniques. The first part serves as an introduction to the broad meaning of "distributed system". We give examples, try to define terms, and discuss the problems that arise in the context of parallel and distributed processing. The second part presents the typical layered protocol architecture of distributed systems, and discusses problems of compatibility and interworking between heterogeneous computer systems. The principles of the lower layer functions and protocols are explained in some detail, including link layer protocols and network transmission services. The third part deals with specification issues. The role of specifications in the design of distributed systems is explained in general, and formal methods for the specification, analysis and implementation of distributed systems are discussed. We consider in particular a general state transition model and its use for the description of communication services and protocols.

This text does not give the description of any particular distributed system, nor does it discuss the advantages and disadvantages of distributed computer applications, such as for banking transactions or distributed data bases. We have given extensive references to more detailed descriptions of the topics discussed, to complementary articles, and to explanations of certain prerequisite concepts, most readers will be familiar with.

This book is largely based on the "Architecture of Distribute Computer Systems" which appeared in the series of Lecture Notes in Computer Science. The different chapters have been largely revised, and two new chapters on formal description techniques have been added. The Lecture Notes were originally written in 1977-78 for a one-semester course ("troisième cycle") given at the Ecole Polytechnique Fédérale de Lausanne, Switzerland. I would like to thank the Département de Mathématiques of the Ecole Polytechnique, and in particular Professor G. Coray, for my pleasant stay in Lausanne. For the preparation of this text, I have profited from many discussions, in particular with J. Gecsei, D. Gurtner, M. Raynal, C. Sunshine and F. Vittoz. I thank S. Waddell for suggesting many improvements of previous versions of this manuscript, Ch. Luyet, D. Salconi and H. Collerette for the careful typing, and R. Fortier for the drawing of the figures. Last, but not least, I thank my wife, Elise, for her patience and moral support.

Table of Contents

PART I: THE NATURE OF DISTRIBUTED SYSTEMS   1

1. Distributed systems: examples and definition
   1.1 Distribution of control and data in existing systems   2
       1.1.1 Systems distributed over long distance   2
             1.1.1.1 Remote access   2
             1.1.1.2 Computer networks   7
             1.1.1.3 Systems for distributed processing   10
       1.1.2 Locally distributed systems   14
       1.1.3 Multi-processor systems   19
       1.1.4 Virtual distribution   20
   1.2 Classification of distributed systems   21
       1.2.1 Degree of coupling   22
       1.2.2 Interconnection structure   22
       1.2.3 Interdependence of components   25
       1.2.4 Synchronization between components   26
   1.3 Definition of "distributed system"   26
2. Parallelism
   2.1 Parallel processes and applications   32
   2.2 Constraints on independence   34
   2.3 Modular system structure and abstraction   38
3. Common problems
   3.1 Cooperation   43
       3.1.1 Compatibility   43
       3.1.2 Synchronization   44
   3.2 Distributed resource sharing   44
   3.3 Naming and addressing   45
       3.3.1 Search strategies for link editors   45
       3.3.2 Naming of I/O flows   45
       3.3.3 Addressing scheme of telephone networks   46
       3.3.4 Process addressing by ports   46

	3.4	Protection	49
		3.4.1 Protection in distributed systems	50
	3.5	Error recovery	51
		3.5.1 Error detection	51
		3.5.2 Recovery by retry	52
		3.5.3 Redundant hardware	52
		3.5.4 The design principle of recovery blocks	53
	3.6	Real time considerations	54
		3.6.1 Time-outs	55
		3.6.2 Clock synchronization in distributed systems	55

PART II: DISTRIBUTED SYSTEM ARCHITECTURE AND COMMUNICATION PROTOCOLS — 59

4.	Architecture of distributed systems		60
	4.1	Layered hierarchical system structure and physical distribution	61
	4.2	Typical structure of a distributed system	72
		4.2.1 Communication over a dedicated circuit	73
		4.2.2 Communication through a network	76
		4.2.3 A uniform transport service	77
		4.2.4 Higher level protocols	79
	4.3	Compatibility and interworking issues	82
		4.3.1 Requirements for compatibility	83
		4.3.2 Network interconnection	84
		4.3.3 System interworking and adaptation	88
5.	Message transport requirements and data transmission networks		93
	5.1	Message transport requirements	93
	5.2	Data transmission services	95
		5.2.1 Dedicated circuits	95
		5.2.2 Switching	96
		5.2.3 Circuit and packet switching	96
	5.3	The transport protocol	97
6.	Link protocols		99
	6.1	Transmission of bits	100
		6.1.1 Interface procedures	100

		6.1.2 Physical **transmission media**	101
		6.1.3 Bit synchronization	103
	6.2	Transparency and framing	106
		6.2.1 Bit-oriented method	107
		6.2.2 Character-oriented method	108
		6.2.3 Method based on envelope transmission	109
	6.3	Transmission error detection and correction	109
		6.3.1 Principles	109
		6.3.2 Error detecting codes	113
		6.3.3 Error correcting codes	116
	6.4	Retransmission protocols	116
		6.4.1 Principles	116
		6.4.2 The "alternating bit" protocol	119
		6.4.3 The HDLC classes of procedures	122
		6.4.4 Multiplexing	128
7.	Technological developments and standards	134

PART III: FORMAL DESCRIPTION TECHNIQUES   137

8.	Role of specifications in the design of distributed systems	138
	8.1 Specification of different scope and detail	139
	8.1.1 The "reference model"	140
	8.1.2 Service specifications	140
	8.1.3 Protocol specifications	143
	8.1.4 Implementation specifications	143
	8.2 System design validation	144
	8.3 Protocol implementation assessment	146
	8.4 Protocol implementation	148
9.	A state transition formalism for the description of systems	151
	9.1 The basic model	151
	9.1.1 Transition systems	151
	9.1.2 Operations	152
	9.1.3 Transitions and relations between states	152
	9.1.4 Abstraction	155
	9.1.5 Parallelism and functionality	157

9.2	Reachability and execution sequences	159
	9.2.1 Possible operation sequences	159
	9.2.2 Liveness	161
	9.2.3 Equivalence between systems	162
9.3	Synchronization mechanisms	162
9.4	Non-instantaneous operations	166
	9.4.1 Mutual exclusion	166
	9.4.2 Queueing condiserations and scheduling	168
9.5	Processes	169
	9.5.1 The concept	170
	9.5.2 Cooperation	171
	9.5.3 Mutual exclusion	176
9.6	The induction principle	178
9.7	Distinction between "control structure" and "interpretation"	179
9.8	Assertions	183
9.9	Formalized specification methods for systems with parallelism	186
10.	**A formal description technique for distributed systems**	190
10.1	Discussion of specification concepts	190
	10.1.1 Components and their interactions	190
	10.1.2 Ports and interconnections	191
	10.1.3 Elements of a specification	193
10.2	A transport service specification	194
	10.2.1 Ports and interaction primitives	195
	10.2.2 Local rules for a service access point	197
	10.2.3 Specification of the service provider component	199
10.3	Step-wise refinement of specifications	202
	10.3.1 The internal structure of components: examples	202
	10.3.2 Comments on component substructure	205
	10.3.3 Port refinements	206

References	210
Annex: Possible approaches to stepwise refinement, protocol specification and implementation	221
Annex 1: A general transition model for protocols and communication services (G.v. Bochmann)	222
Annex 2: Development and structure of an X.25 implementation (G.v. Bochmann and J. Tankoano)	230
Annex 3: Structured specification of communicating systems (G.v. Bochmann and M. Raynal)	238

Part I
The Nature of Distributed Systems

The chapters I through III give an introduction to the nature of distributed computer systems, their problems and some of the possible solutions. In chapter I, the architectures of typical distributed systems are considered, and different schemes for distributing control and data are explained. The notion of parallel processing is explored in chapter II, as it relates to computers, as well as to other kinds of systems. Special attention is given to the concept of processes, process cooperation, and modular system description. Chapter III, finally, reviews some well-known problem areas usually encountered during the design of computer application systems, and discusses possible solutions, some of which specific to distributed systems.

1. Distributed Systems: Examples and Definition

What is a distributed system ? - Most data processing systems are of a distributed nature, and most computer systems can be considered as being distributed under certain aspects. This chapter presents some common examples of data processing and computing systems and discusses in particular the aspects of parallelism and distribution of control and data. Some classification schemes are explained, and a definition of "distributed systems" is attempted.

1.1. DISTRIBUTION OF CONTROL AND DATA IN EXISTING SYSTEMS

The following examples of existing systems demonstrate how control information and data may be distributed over the different components of a data processing system, which may imply distributed processing and decisions, as well as distributed algorithms.

1.1.1. *Systems distributed over long distance*

1.1.1.1. *Remote access*

With the advent of multi-programming systems, which provide data processing services to several applications simultaneously, it became desirable to obtain access to such facilities from terminals at different locations. It has become common practice to exchange data between terminals and computer systems through telephone circuits, as shown in figure 1.1, using modems for the adaptation of the digital interfaces of the terminals and computer systems to the analogue nature of the telephone transmission facility. Leased circuits, providing a dedicated connection between two or more system components, are often used as an economic alternative to frequent connections established through the public switched telephone system.[1]

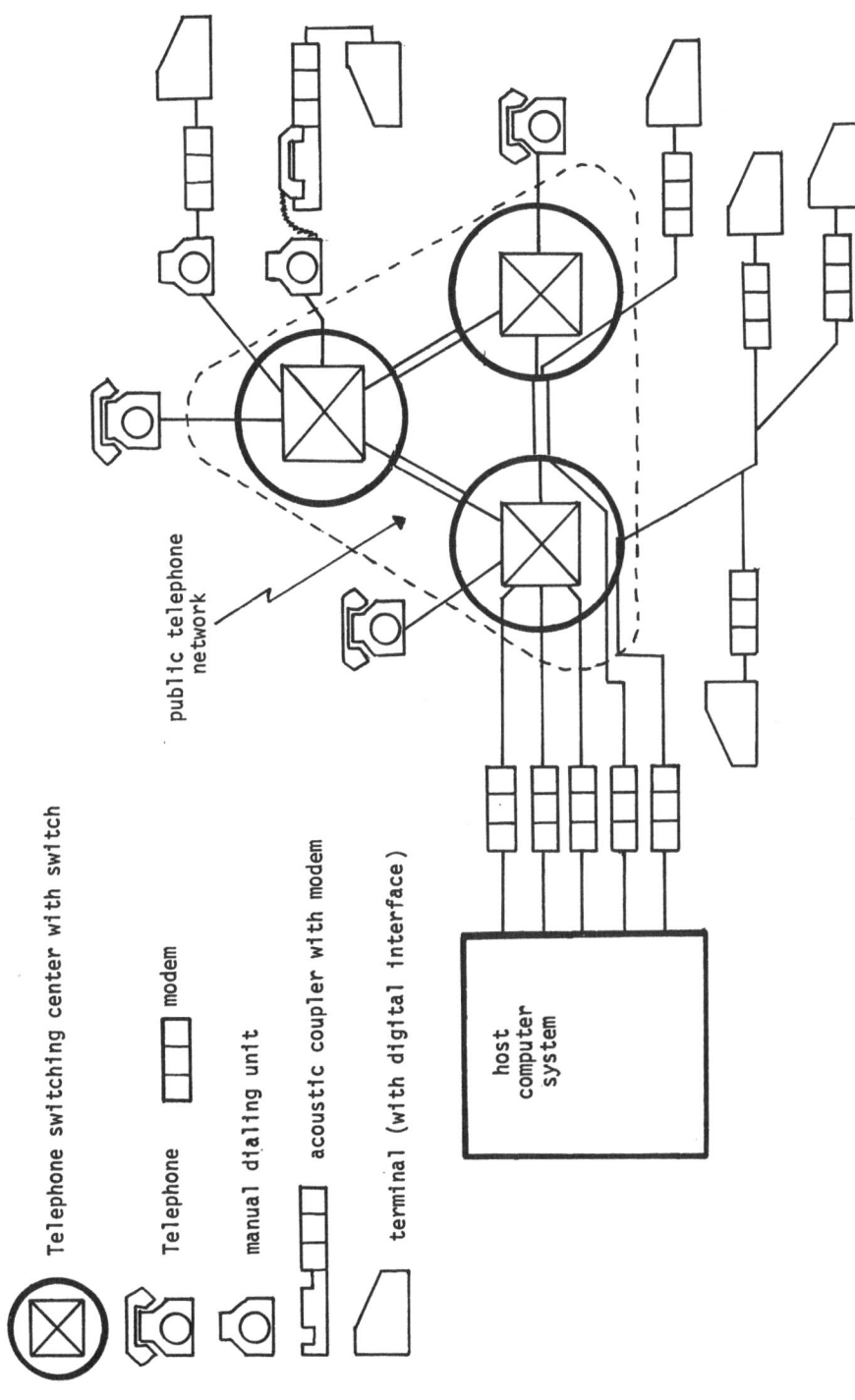

FIGURE 1.1: Use of the telephone network for data transmission

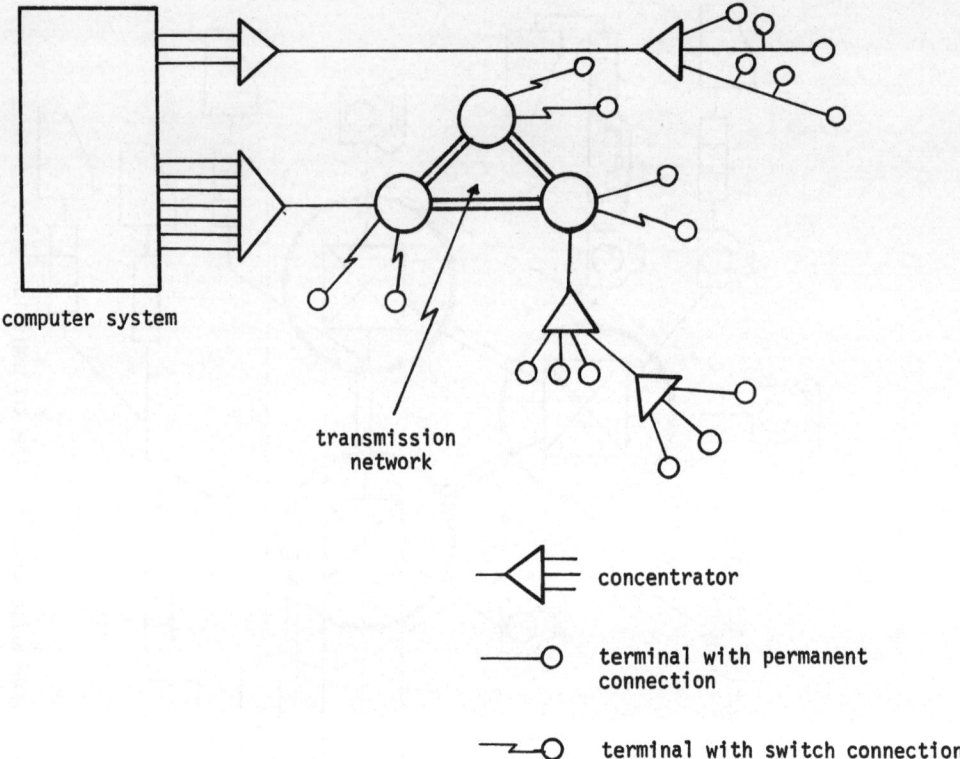

FIGURE 1.2: Multiplexing and concentration

Typical terminals used for remotely accessing a computer system are interactive terminals and remote batch terminals, consisting essentially of a card reader and line printer for the remote submission of batch jobs (remote job entry, RJE). The interactive terminals range from simple character oriented teletypes to intelligent terminals providing local data processing, such as text editing, execution of programs written in some high-level language, such as BASIC or PASCAL, and local file storage on magnetic cassettes or floppy disks. Data entry and transaction terminals are widely used classes of terminals of intermediate complexity, usually providing local editing on a line or page basis.[2]

To avoid excessive long distance transmission costs, concentrators are used when several terminals in one area communicate with a computer or terminals in another, distant, area. A concentrator shares a given transmission path between several, independent, logical communications. Systems involving concentration at several hierarchical levels, as shown in figure 1.2, are very frequent. Some of the levels of concentration may be implemented inside the transmission network without the knowledge of the subscriber. For example, the wide-band trunk lines between the telephone switching centers are shared among a large number of simultaneous long distance switched telephone connections and leased telephone circuits. Similar configurations are used with the new public data networks providing permanent (leased) or switched (possibly virtual) circuits, based on digital transmission technology with lower error rates.[3]

Two different kinds of concentration may be distinguished for data transmission.[4] The simplest method is known as "multiplexing" (frequency division multiplexing for analogue transmissions, such as telephony, and time division multiplexing for digital transmission). In this case, the available transmission capacity of the shared channel is divided in a <u>fixed ratio</u> among a certain number of secondary channels.

A more flexible method is known as "statistical multiplexing" or "concentration". In this case, the available capacity is allocated to the different channels in a varying ratio depending on the demand. Data is transmitted in the form of blocks (packets or messages) each containing same control information, which is used in particular to identify the secondary channel to which the data belongs. Because of the varying transmission demands of the different secondary channels, data blocks may be put on a queue, to await transmission at the earliest possibility. Depending on the amount of data traffic and the capacity of the shared channel, this queuing introduces an additional, statistically varying transmission delay.[5]

Statistical multiplexing is usually implemented on minicomputer systems. Often these systems also provide for the adaptation of the terminals, which are connected on to the secondary channels, to the data transmission facility and the communication protocols of the distant host computer system. This function is called "terminal handling", and consists mainly of the assembly (and disassembly) of characters exchanged with the terminal into (from) data blocks exchanged over the shared channel with the distant host.

The host computer system is closely related to the design of the remote access communication system. In many cases, the communication system was built around existing host computer systems, and the latter had a strong impact on the design of the former. In particular, the following parts of the host operating system have a counterpart in the distributed communication system :

- The handling of interactive terminals in the operating system and the remote concentrators is related.
- The handling of files by the operating system and the operation of remote job entry stations is related.

- The concentration protocol used over the shared access lines must be implemented in the concentrators and the operating system of the host.

Often, in order to reserve the processing power of the host computer for the application program, many of the communication functions of the operating system are realized in a specialized front-end mini-computer.

Some well-known applications of remote access systems as described above are :
- passenger reservation systems for air travel,
- banking systems,
- sale and inventory systems for warehouses and super-markets,
- computer applications service companies, etc.

1.1.1.2. Computer networks

While the systems discussed above provide access to a single host computer, computer networks provide access from terminals to several host computers, and also communication between application programs residing in different computers. The main reasons for the construction of computer networks are[6]

(1) to provide remote access to a variety of resources, for example normal data processing, special facilities such as high power numerical calculations, graphical applications, etc., access to data bases, a facility for exchanging personal messages, etc.;

(2) to share these resources among a large number of users;

(3) to provide back-up facilities in the case of the failure of one of the resources;

(4) to provide a reliable communication medium for the remote accessing of resources and for distributed processing involving several resources.

The experimental networks Arpanet[7] (in the US) and Cyclades[8] (in France) were developed in the late sixties and early seventies to gain experience with computer networks. The architecture of these networks is shown in figure 1.3. The data transmission sub-network is responsible for the exchange of data between the connected computers and terminals. An irregular topology with multiple paths between any two network nodes provides for reliable service, even in the case of occasional failures of transmission circuits and intermediate nodes.

The concept of "packet switching" is used in these networks, which means that the data exchanged among the computers and terminals is transmitted through the sub-network in the form of data packets with a typical length of about one line of text or up to some thousand bits. The individual packets are transmitted through the sub-network more or less independently of each other, depending on the design of the network.

The sharing of transmission circuits between different applications is realized at several levels. The access circuit between a computer and the sub-network is usually shared among a large number of communications involving this computer and several terminals and other computers. The high-speed transmission circuits between the nodes of the sub-network are shared between the data traffic of all users and some control traffic of the sub-network. Since statistical multiplexing is used, the end-to-end transmission delay for data packets varies and is usually of the order of several hundred milliseconds, sufficiently short for interactive applications, but noticeably longer than the delay over dedicated or switched circuits.

After the pioneering work of Arpanet and Cyclades, many private computer networks have been built using similar approaches. Also, some of the communications software packages provided by computer manufacturers for their systems provide similar functions. Most of these systems and networks use as their

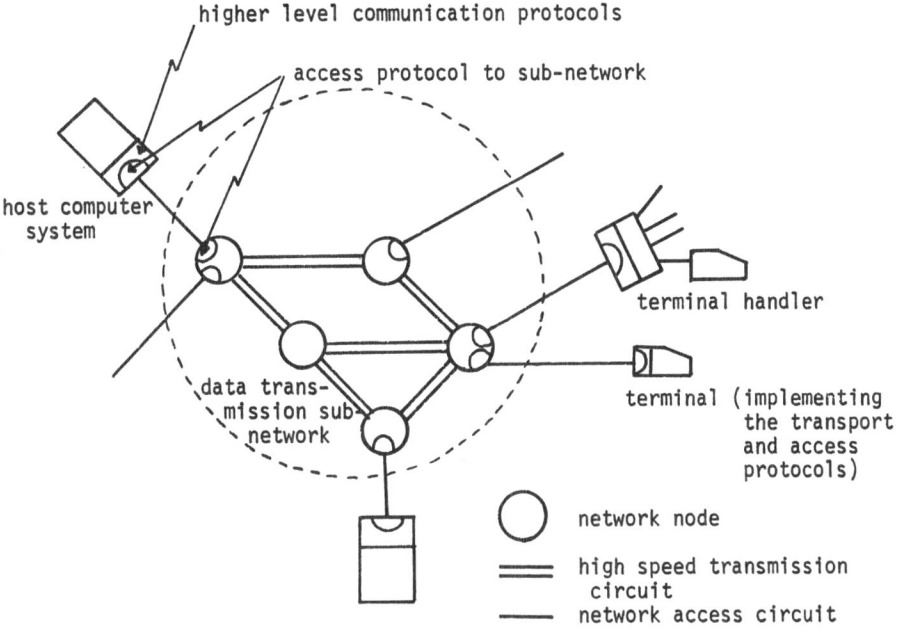

FIGURE 1.3: Typical architecture of a computer network

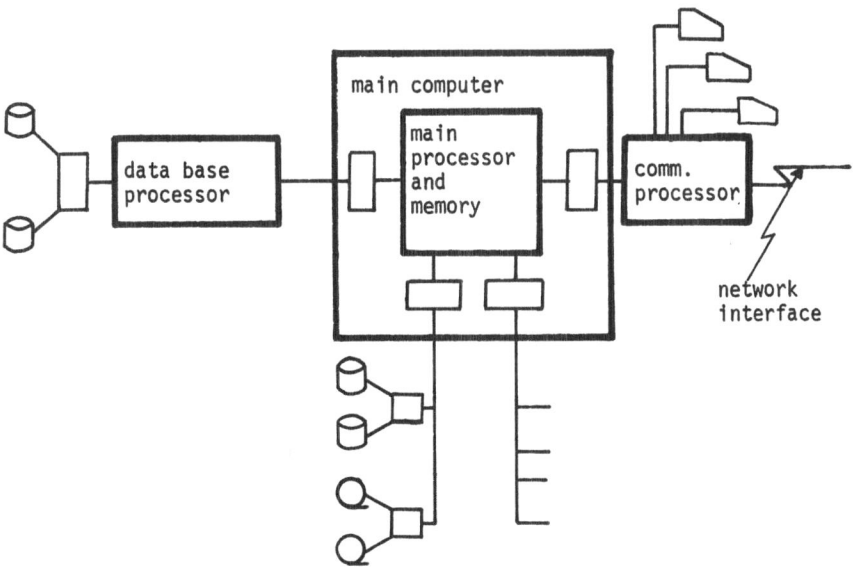

FIGURE 1.4: Local distribution in a computer system

transmission facility the public service of leased circuits
provided by common carriers. More recently, some common carriers
have introduced public data transmission facilities based on
packet switching. These public packet-switched data networks,
similar to the data transmission sub-networks of Arpanet and
Cyclades, are used for remote access to host computers and
computer-computer communications.[9]

An important aspect of the Arpanet and Cyclades computer
networks is the "heterogenity" of the connected host computers and
their operating systems. Realizing meaningful communications between application programs, terminals, files and data bases on
different computers requires some agreement on so-called higher
level protocols. These protocols, implemented in the communication software of the connected computers and terminals, provide
end-to-end data transport between the communicating entities,
and access to terminals, files, etc.. It is clearly very important to develop protocol standards which are suitable for future
systems and allow for easy adaptation of the conventions used in
present operating systems. Some higher-level protocol standards
are being developed in the so-called framework of "Open Systems
Interconnection"(OSI).[10]

As long as such standards are not available, it is difficult to implement communications between heterogeneous computer
systems, either within a computer network or directly. This is
why most private computer networks are homogeneous systems where
all host computers belong to the same family.

1.1.1.3. Systems for distributed processing

In this section we consider systems in which the processing of a given task is not limited to one host computer, but
distributed over several computers at different locations.

One principle of distributed processing is to do the
processing where the data is. Since the data usually enters the
system at many different locations, this means that the data

processing is distributed. Examples of this principle are local text editing, and validation of data entry close to the terminal. In the case of a distributed data base, i.e. a data base with data stored at different locations, a query may give rise to searches through the stored data at several locations. Again, the processing is done where the data is. This principle leads to a reduction of the data communications traffic, since data processing usually involves data reduction.

A second principle of distributed processing is redundancy. Since the processing is performed at several locations, it is often not too difficult to organize the system such that the different processing centers can replace one another in performing the required work. This leads to very resilient systems characterized by "graceful degradation" in the case of failures, which means that the failure of a processing center does not imply a failure of the overall system, but only results in a reduced processing capacity.

A third principle that can be applied to distributed processing is the construction of dedicated systems. Instead of using a general purpose computer system for executing a variety of necessary tasks, the different components of a distributed processing system could each be specialized to do a particular task. This simplifies the design of each component. Note that this is a very important consideration since complexity means high development costs, software errors and high maintenance costs.

At the time of writing, the field of distributed processing is an area of intensive research and development, and cannot be considered as being completely understood. In the following we give some points for illustration.

(a) A distributed algorithm

Consider the problem of finding a strategy for routing data packets through a transmission sub-network from the source to the destination node. We suppose that the packet contains a field indicating the destination node. Each node has a so-called routing table which indicates, for each destination node, the next inter-node circuit over which the packet should be sent. How can the routing tables be established ?

A centralized approach to this problem is possible. It consists of collecting at a given node, or at the network control center, the necessary information, including present failures of nodes and inter-node circuits, queuing delays over the operational circuits, etc. Based on this information, relatively optimized routing tables can be calculated by a relatively complex algorithm, and the results are subsequently sent to all operational nodes for updating the tables. To adapt to the changing environment, this algorithm should be executed as often as possible.

A distributed algorithm was first adopted in the Arpanet[11], and similar algorithms have subsequently been used in many other networks. Again, the routing tables must be updated as often as possible. For each update, the new table values are calculated at each node separately, using the previous table values and information obtained from the immediately neighbouring nodes. Since the calculations of each node are not based on a global knowledge of the network, but only on information about the immediately surrounding region, the resulting tables are clearly not as optimal as centrally determined tables can be. We note, however, the following advantages of the distributed approach :

(1) The algorithm executed at each node is very simple.

(2) Less control packets have to be exchanged.

(3) The complexity of the calculation is independent of the network topology and size.

(4) The danger that the control center of a centralized system may fail is eliminated. The failure of a node is automatically dealt with by the distributed nature of the algorithm.

We note that the routing problem for data networks is one of the few areas for which distributed algorithms have been studied extensively[12]. For most other applications, only few distributed algorithms are known.

(b) Distributed data bases

Following the first principle mentioned above, different parts of a data base are often located at different processing locations. For example, the data base of a bank may be distributed over several centers in different cities, where each center contains the data base information on the clients in that geographical area. Then most transactions can be processed locally.

In other cases, the same information may be contained in several redundant copies at different locations. This has the advantage that the different copies can be used as back-ups for one another. For the information needed frequently at many places, an access to the closest copy reduces the communication costs. Finally, complicated queries may be processed in parallel at several locations, which may reduce the response time.

The above considerations give some reasons for distributing data bases over several locations. Such a distribution introduces many problems for which, at present, practical solutions have been found for some, but not all[13].

1.1.2. *Locally distributed systems*

In contrast to the systems considered above, involving long distance data communications, usually over public data transmission facilities, we consider in this section systems using local data transmission facilities, often privately owned, and suitable for distances up to about thousand meters. Over such distances, high speed transmission facilities can be built relatively cheaply, which allows for a closer integration of the different components of the distributed system. We note that similar transmission facilities are available over long distances, too, but at a greater cost.

The reasons for distributing the processing in a local system over several components are those outlined in section 1.1.1.3 : processing where the data is, increasing system reliability and availability by redundancy, and specialization of the components. The last reason seems to be the most important for locally distributed systems. Instead of sharing a central processing unit between the different activities to be performed by the system, relatively independent processing units are provided for each of these activities. This allows for a simple design for each processing unit and their optimization, taking advantage of their specialization.

Typical examples of locally distributed systems are those derived from centralized computer systems by the addition of specialized mini-computers. Figure 1.4 shows a computer system with distinct communications and data base processors. The former implements the protocols to be followed for the communication with distant terminals and other computers over dedicated circuits and a network, and the latter manages a data base and processes logical requests for enquiry and update. This approach of separating certain functions of an operating system and implementing them on a distinct processor can be pushed further. It leads to a computing system consisting of a number of mini- or micro-computers

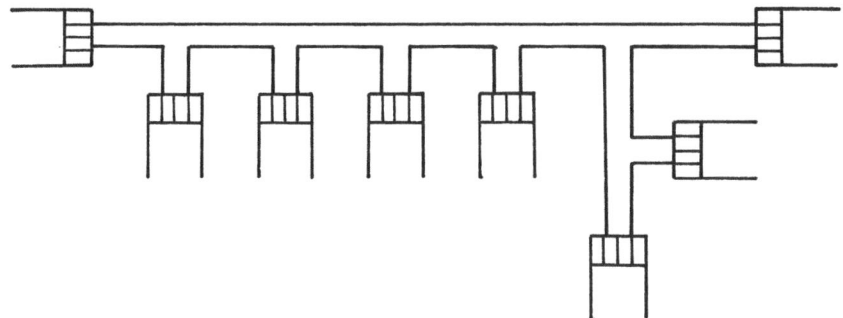

FIGURE 1.5: Shared bus

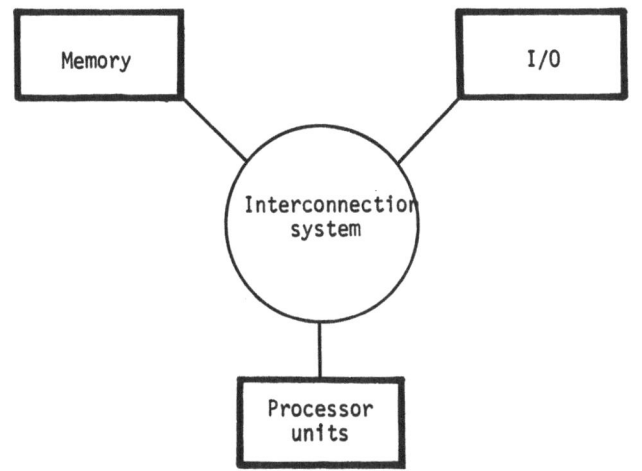

FIGURE 1.6: Basic multiprocessor organisation

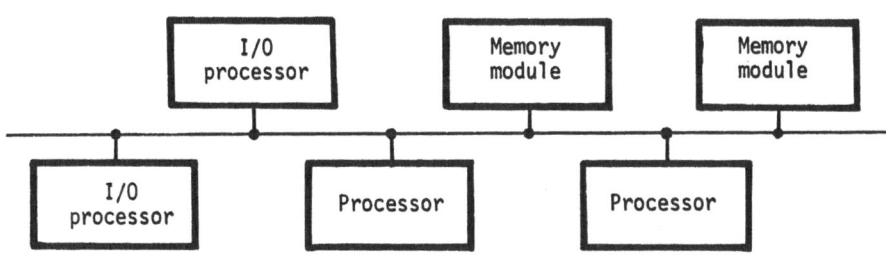

FIGURE 1.7: Time-shared common bus system organization - single bus

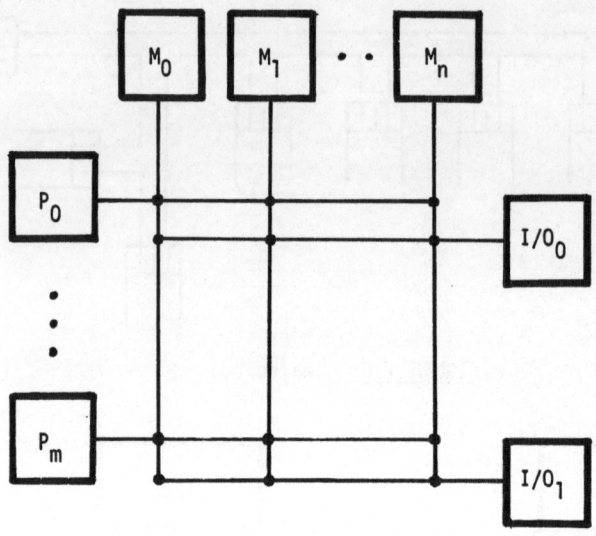

FIGURE 1.8: Crossbar (nonblocking) switch system organisation

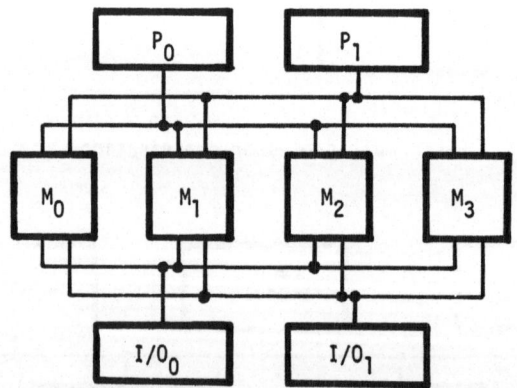

FIGURE 1.9: Multiport-memory system organization - basic organization

each realizing a specific function of the system or handling a specific input-output or storage device.[14]

Whereas the examples above illustrate the distribution of activities of a given system onto separate processors, locally distributed systems are also obtained when initially independent elements are integrated into an organized system by the provision of an appropriate communication scheme. This is illustrated by certain systems for real-time process control, and by systems for office automation where each person may use a personal computer, and intelligent terminals, typewriters, filing systems etc. are interconnected and integrated.

The communication between the different processors of a locally distributed system is often realized by a local area network in the form of a data transmission "bus". It consists of one or several ("parallel bus") signaling circuits shared between the communicating processors, as shown in figure 1.5. All connected processors see the same signals on the bus. Therefore it is important to avoid conflicting write accesses to the bus by different processors. This is the reason for introducing an appropriate discipline for sharing the bus, called the bus access protocol[15].

There are two basic approaches to the sharing of a bus : centralized control and distributed control. In the case of centralized control, one of the connected processors is identified as the bus controller, or primary station, and all other processors play a secondary role. The latter are not allowed to write on the bus, unless they are invited by the primary to do so, i.e. unless they are "polled".

If all connected processors are to have the same rights to the use of the bus, either a centralized bus controller is added which polls all processors in turn, or a distributed bus control is implemented in the processors. In the latter case, "contention" may occur, when several processors try to write on the bus simultaneously. Therefore a distributed bus protocol has to detect contention and recover from it. Contention can usually be detected by the processors involved, which listen to the bus signals and recognize interference with another processor when the signal read is inconsistant with the signal written. Recovery is usually performed by a retry after some delay. Indefinite cycling through retries and consecutive interferences must be avoided, for example by using randomly chosen delays.

The details of the bus access protocols vary considerably between different systems. Many systems use a mixture of the centralized and distributed approaches. For example, the input-output channel interface of a computer system is usually a parallel bus over which several device control units transmit data in an order determined by the channel processor which acts as bus controller. But there is contention of the data ready signals (usually involving interrupts) from the devices which can be resolved by a priority scheme between the devices. Another example is the provision of several processors that could play the role of the centralized bus controller. At any given time, only one of them would play the primary role of the controller, whereas the others would act as secondaries. However any of them could take over the primary role after being invited to do so by the acting primary[16], or when the latter has a failure.

In the case of very high transmission capacities and/or longer distances, the propagation delay of the signals over the bus can no longer be neglected. If reflection of the propagating signals at the terminations of the circuits is avoided, one obtains a so-called multi-point circuit. Except for noticable transmission delays, it has the same characteristics as a bus. A similar transmission facility is also provided by terrestrial and satellite radio transmission. All these facilities have in common the provision of information broadcasted between all connected components, and the same principles apply to the sharing of the transmission facility.

Another kind of local area network uses a ring interconnection structure (see figure 1.12), instead of a bus. In such a ring network data packets travel around the ring. Single destination, as well as broadcast transmission can be supported. A new data packet may be sent during an empty slot; and the reception, by the sending processor, of the same packet or its acknowledgement indicates that the ring is operational and that all connected destination processors may have read the data. As in the case of a bus network, the control of the ring is partly distributed, partly centralized. The sharing of the transmission capacity is usually controlled by a distributed algorithm, and the communication controllers of all connected processors participate in the data transfer by forwarding the received packets to the next controller on the ring. However, the maintenance function is usualy implemented centrally in one of the processors, which may check whether the ring becomes disconnected (due to the failure of one of the controllers) and may remove packets that have not been collected by their respective sender or destination processors.

1.1.3. Multi-processor systems

Multi-processor systems are computer systems consisting of several closely coupled processors. The basic organization, as shown in figure 1.6, involves processors, and input-output (I/O) processors that access memory units through some kind of interconnection system. The memory units represent the central memory of the system, and in many cases the memory access is provided by a shared memory bus, as shown in figure 1.7. Other possible schemes for interconnection are a crossbar switch matrix (see figure 1.8) and an organization with multi-port memories (see figure 1.9).[17]

Reasons for introducing multiple processors into a computer system are the same as for the distribution of processing (see section 1.1.2). An additional objective is increased system performance.

Communication between the processes running on the different processors of a multi-processor system is usually realized through the access of shared memory. In this system organization, the access of memory units containing private data of a given process involves the same hardware functions as the access to shared memory used for interprocess communication. Therefore this organization allows for very close coupling between the different processes of the system.

1.1.4. *Virtual distribution*

We call "virtual distribution of control and data" the introduction of conceptually independent processes within a system whose physical realization does not correspond to this conceptual organization. A typical example of virtual distribution is an operating system, for a single processor computer, which is designed as a collection of processes, each performing a particular task and interacting through a given communication mechanism. The system software is usually structured into several hierarchical layers, where the first layer (directly on the hardware level) provides the multiplexing of the available (hardware) processors among the processes of the system and the inter-process communication mechanism. If the adopted interprocess communication mechanism resembles a message system, the overall system design may easily be adapted to a physically distributed system.[18]

The main reason for the distribution of processing between several virtual processes is to obtain a modular system design.[19] The introduction of a process for each activity in the system seems to simplify the overall system design and to lead to simple interaction between the different parts of the system.

Since virtual distribution is realized through software support, the communication mechanism provided to realize the interaction between the different system components may be adapted to particular requirements. As a consequence, this mechanism varies considerably from one system to another. Certain primitives for inter-process communications have been incorporated into system programming languages. The following list presents the most important concepts.

(a) Process creation :

- coroutines,[20]
- static declarations of parallel processes,[21]
- fork and join primitives for evoking parallel execution of statements,[22]
- dynamic process creation and management, possibly with hierarchical inter-process dependencies[23] (a "father" process creates and supervises its "son" processes).

(b) Mutual exclusion[24]

- critical regions for accessing shared variables,
- conditional critical regions.

(c) Explicit process scheduling

- semaphores,[25]
- event signaling and waiting.[26]

(d) Message queues

- fixed message queues between pairs of processes,[27]
- mailboxes, one for each process,[28]
- exchange of command-response messages.[29]

1.2. CLASSIFICATION OF DISTRIBUTED SYSTEMS

Distributed systems may be classified according to many different aspects. In the following we consider four aspects that seem particularly useful for a classification of distributed systems. We base our discussion on a system model consisting of several system components which interact through some communication mechanism, as shown in figure 1.10.

1.2.1. *Degree of coupling*

The degree of coupling between two system components may be defined informally as the ratio between the amount of data exchanged between these components per amount of local processing performed. Taking the degree of coupling as a criterion for a classification leads to the distinction between the following kinds of systems :

(a) systems with weak coupling between components, typically using communication channels of some Kbits per second, sometimes called "thin wire communication",

(b) distributed systems with strong coupling, typically using a communication channel with a capacity comparable with the transfer rate of secondary storage devices,

(c) very strongly coupled systems, for which data transfer between components is nearly as efficient as access by a component to the data it processes.

We note that this classification underlies the distinction, made in section 1.1, between (a) systems distributed over long distance, (b) locally distributed systems, and (c) multi-processor and virtually distributed systems.

1.2.2. *Interconnection structure*

Whereas the classification aspect above involves mainly the transmission capacity of the communication mecanism, the classification according to the interconnection structure involves its logical structure, and in particular the addressing and routing strategies.

The following interconnection structures may be distinguished :[30]

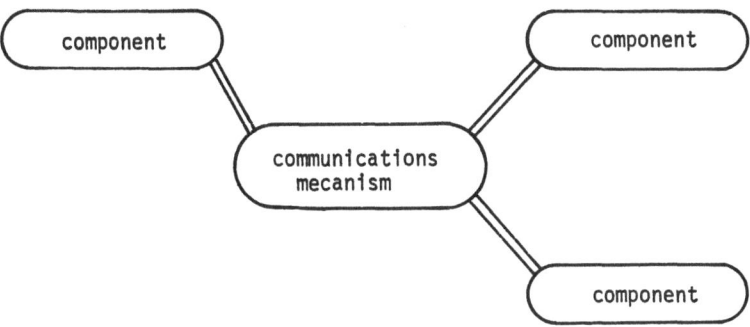

FIGURE 1.10: Communications mecanism and its users

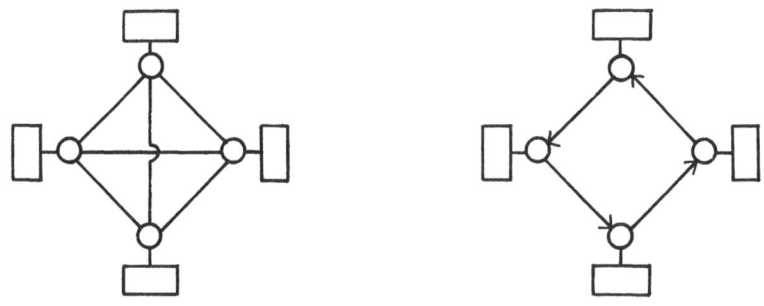

FIGURE 1.11: Complete interconnection structure

FIGURE 1.12: Loop connection structure

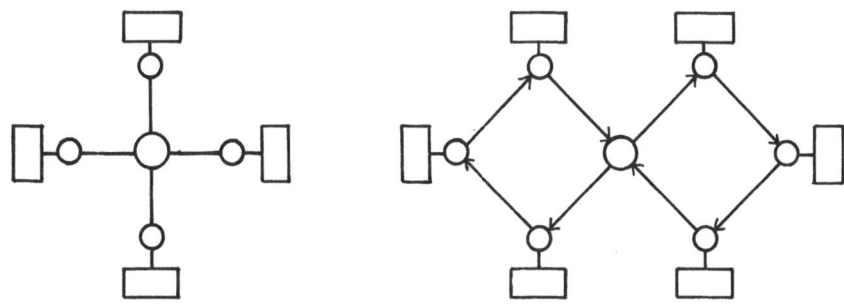

FIGURE 1.13: Star-like interconnection structures

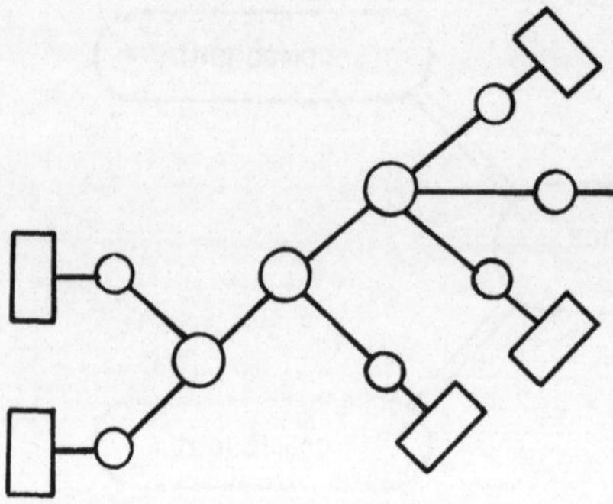

FIGURE 1.14: Tree-like interconnection structure

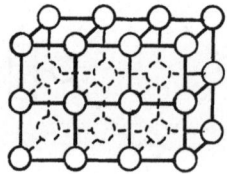

FIGURE 1.15: n-cube interconnection structure (n = 3)

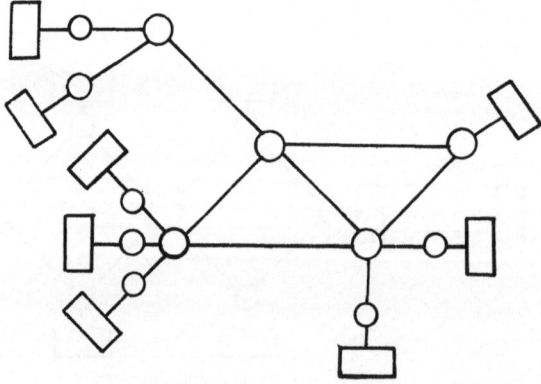

FIGURE 1.16: Irregular interconnection structure

(a) Direct interconnections between components :

- (a1) Dedicated facility for each pair of communicating components : Typical examples are complete interconnection structures as shown in figure 1.11, and loop structures as shown in figure 1.12.

- (a2) Communications facility shared between all components : Typical examples are local bus structures, as shown in figure 1.5, or radio broadcast channels. In contrast to the structures of (a1), contention among the system components must be resolved. Shared memory of multi-processor systems can also be considered in this category.

(b) Indirect interconnections between components :

- (b1) Centralized routing : Typical examples are star-like networks with a central switch where each branch may consist of a loop (see figure 1.13).

- (b2) Non-centralized routing :
  - (b2i) Networks with one possible path per pair of communicating components : Typical examples are tree-like networks, as shown in figure 1.14.
  - (b2ii) Networks with generally several possible communication paths between two components : Typical examples are networks connected as an n-cube (see figure 1.15), or irregular networks.

1.2.3. *Interdependence of components*

Whereas the classification aspects above involve mainly the characteristics of the communications medium, the following two depend on the structure of the communicating components.

Components are strongly interdependent when the operation of one component relies on the successful operation of the other component(s). On the contrary, components are weakly interdependent when the failure of one component does not jeopardize the successful operation of the others. As mentioned earlier (section 1.1.1.2), such system behavior may be obtained through redundancy, and leads to highly resilient systems with good availability and graceful degradation in the case of partial failures.

1.2.4. *Synchronization between components*

Most distributed systems are asynchronous, in the sense that each components operates at its own speed (which may vary in time) and may wait when its own operation requires information not yet available, to be provided by another component. The speed of the overall system is determined by the speed of the slowest component. For such an asynchronous system, the communication mecanism has to provide a "pacing" or "flow control" facility for correlating the effective processing speeds of the different components.

Some other distributed systems are synchronous, in the sense that there is a fixed relation between the processing speeds of the different components. The synchronization between the components is maintained by a common clock, which is usually provided through the communication medium.

1.3. *DEFINITION OF "DISTRIBUTED SYSTEM"*

We consider a "distributed system" as consisting of several interacting components, as shown in figure 1.10. The degree of coupling between the components may be weak or strong, but very strongly coupled systems, such as multi-processor systems, are excluded. All kinds of interconnection structures are considered. We are particularly interested in systems with weakly interdependent components, and in questions of compatibility which must be considered if a given component is to be replaced by another component, or one component is to communicate with a large number of different components.

We also include in our definition virtually distributed systems, i.e. systems designed with an internal structure which would allow for a distribution of functions over several physically disjoint components, but actually implemented on one physical component.

We hope to demonstrate in the following chapters that distributed systems may be designed using a specification method which is equally suitable for physically distributed implementation as for centralized implementation in one physical component. Given such a system design, it is a matter of cost and efficiency to choose the best physical distribution of functions; and this choice should be independent of the design of the logical system components.

FOOTNOTES

1. See for example [Davi 73], chapters 2 and 4.
2. Typical applications and characteristics of terminals which are used in remote access to computers are described in [Hobb 72].
3. See for example [Davi 73], chapter 7.
4. See for example [Davi 79].
5. Statistical multiplexing in data networks is an instance of resource sharing. The problems and solutions adopted are similar to those encountered in resource sharing in computer operating systems (see for example [Klei 75] or [Coff 73]). The consideration of queuing delays is crucial for the optimization of the transmission network, taking into account the network cost and the expected transmission delays.
6. See for example [Kahn 72] where possible applications for and usage of the Arpanet are described.
7. Funded by the Advanced Research Projects Agency (ARPA) of the US National Defence Department, the Arpanet was the first large scale experience with packet-switched data transmission. Still operational, it allows resource sharing between a large number of computer centers in universities and research centers. The main objectives and characteristics are described in [Robé 70].
8. Building on the experience gained with the Arpanet, the Cyclades network has much contributed to the state of the art of packet-switched data communications. Its major features are described in [Pouz 73].

9. The following packet-switched transmission services have been defined, to be provided by public data networks : (a) virtual circuits and (b) datagrams. For virtual circuits, a virtual connection must be established before packets can be exchanged, whereas datagrams are selfsufficient packets, including complete addressing information, which are sent independently of one another. The internal operation of a packet-switched network does not necessarily reflect these characteristics of the provided transmission services [Kirs 76]. Most public packet-switched networks only provide virtual circuit services.

10. An overview of the issues of standardization in data communications is given in [Boch 77c]. An overview of computer network protocols from the OSI viewpoint is given in [Gree 82]. A recent status report on this area of standardization may be found in [OSI 83].

11. See for example [Davi 79], section 3.5.

12. The particular aspect of avoiding loops, which could be introduced by a distributed algorithm using local information only, is considered in [Nayl 75] and [Merl 77].

13. The range of problems in the area of distributed databases is demonstrated by conferences, such as [Delo 80]. Problems of concurrency control are discussed in [Bern 81].

14. See for example [Prob 77].

15. Many different bus-oriented local area networks have been designed. Standards for local area networks are being developed [IEEE 82]. The design principles of a typical system (Ethernet) are described in [Metc 76]. It is important to note that baseband or broadband physical transmission technology may be used over a coaxial cable bus network. In the latter case, usually based on cable TV technology, the available frequency channels can be shared for digital data transmission and the transmission of analogue video signals.

16. A bus discipline for a parallel bus with possibly several alternating primary processors is exemplified by the IEEE standard 488 (originally Hewlett-Packard [Knob 75]).

17. A more detailed discussion of multiprocessor systems can be found in [Ensl 77].

18. The design of a computer operating system based on parallel processes communicating through the exchange of messages is described, for example, in [Brin 70]. "Message driven" processes were adopted for the software design of the public data network Datapac [DATAPAC] as described in [Mell 77] and [Cunn 77]. The network system is implemented on several geographically distributed special-purpose multi-processor systems. Operating system kernels facilitating the design of such systems have been developed (see for example [Rash 81]).

19. [Horn 73] describes a formalized concept of "processes" which is used for structuring complex systems into simpler modules.

20. Coroutines are provided by Simula. See for example [Dahl 72].

21. As for example in Concurrent Pascal [Brin 75] and Modula [Wirt 77b]. ADA (see for example [Ichb 79] also allows dynamic process creation.

22. See for example in [Karp 69].

23. See for example [Sevc 72], [Cunn 77], or [Jamm 77]. Hierarchical process dependencies in a distributed environment are discussed in [Mart 77].

24. See for example [Brin 73], sections 3.3 and 3.4.

25. See for example [Dijk 68].

26. Semaphores can be used for explicit scheduling. The combination of shared variables with mutually exclusive access through a predetermined set of procedures, together with event queues for explicit scheduling of processes has been called a monitor (see for example [Hoar 74]).

27. See for example [Kahn 74] or [Ridd 72]. The case of direct exchange without queuing, sometimes called "rendezvous" interaction, is also often considered (see for example [Boch 78], [Hoare 78], [FDT 82b], the ADA programming language [Ichb 79] or section 9.5.2).

28. See for example [Brin 70].

29. See for example [Goos 72], [Cheri 79].

30. A similar classification is proposed in [Ande 75].

2. Parallelism

What is the meaning of "parallism" and "parallel" when applied to processes ? The origin of these terms lies outside the field of computer science. Parallel processes are found in the world for which the computer analysts build application systems or simulation models. The mastery of system complexity is closely related to the concept of parallelism. The scope of a process within a system depends on the level of abstraction from which the system is considered, and the more the processes are independent of one another the more decomposition of a system into parallel processes is useful.

2.1. PARALLEL PROCESSES AND APPLICATIONS

By now it is common place to consider data processing and other computer application systems, as a collection of communicating parallel processes. This is by analogy to many biological, social and industrial systems, which have a much longer history. It is not clear whether this similarity stems from the human inability to think in terms different from those he is used to, or is an indication that these concepts are essential for building complex systems. In many cases, the processes within a computer application system are related to the processes of the environment for which the computer system is built. As examples, we may consider interactive systems, real-time control systems, and simulation systems.

In the case of interactive systems, the system's environment consists essentially of the human users that communicate with the system through terminals. Typical examples are the computing facility of a software house or university, an interactively used

data base, computer aided instruction and learning, or real-time
control of complex systems by humans, such as pilots, etc. Usually, in each of these applications, many operators use the same
system. As shown in figure 2.1, the system usually contains at
least two processes for each human user : (i) a "user process",
usually implemented in a "host computer", which is responsible
for executing the operations the user wants to the system to perform, and (ii) a "terminal process", often implemented in an
intelligent terminal, which is responsible for the communication
with the user, via displays, keyboards and other devices suitable
for human interaction, and for converting this communication into
a form suitable to the user process.

In the case of a real-time control system, the environment
consists essentially of the physical devices to be controlled. In
the particular case of a computer's operating system, these devices
are disks, tape units, printers, interactive terminals, as well as
central memory and processing units. Other examples are systems for
data acquisition and supervision of scientific experiments, space
flights, etc., or industrial systems for verifying the quality of
manufactured products or for supervising an automated production
process. Sometimes the environment covered is widely distributed,
as for instance for systems supervising pipelines. As shown in
figure 2.2, the control system usually contains one process associated directly with each external device controlled, or group of
devices which logically form an external process. Within the control system, which may contain other processes as well, these processes "represent" the external devices they are associated with,
and they communicate with the latter by appropriate input-output
devices, often involving digital-analogue conversion.

In the case of simulation systems, it is natural to represent each physical process to be simulated by a simulating process
in the simulation system. In addition, the system will contain
processes for supervising the simulation process and obtaining
the desired results. An example is shown in figure 2.3, which

represents a manufacturing process, where some raw material, stored in P_7, is used by the processes P_1 through P_5 to build semi-finished products, which are stored in P_8, P_9 and P_{10} respectively, and which are assembled by process P_6 into two types of finished products and one type of defective product. The storing processes, P_7 through P_{10}, are of a particular type. Except for possible product degradation during storage, they may be considered passive processes, exchanging products with the other processes P_1 through P_6, considered active.

We note in closing that the term "process" is different from the term "processor". The latter is applied to the hardware device which makes the execution of processes possible. Usually, a given processor is responsible for executing several (logical) processes, sometimes in collaboration with other processors.

2.2. CONSTRAINTS ON INDEPENDENCE

Different processes within a given system are usually considered as being relatively independent of one another. Complete independence is usually excluded, because it would lead to unrelated subsystems. Usually, the different processes are considered independent of one another[1] except for certain explicitely introduced dependencies. Different kinds of process interdependencies may be considered ; they are usually related to the mutual exclusion of several processes during the access of shared resources, or to process cooperation involving the exchange of data.

If several processes access a shared resource which may only be accessed by one process at a time, it may occasionally be necessary to delay any processes that want to access the resource, when it is being accessed by another process. As an example, we assume that the processes P_2 and P_3 of figure 2.3 share a common tool for their operation so that they may have to wait for one another. If the processing time of P_2 and P_3 is short compared to

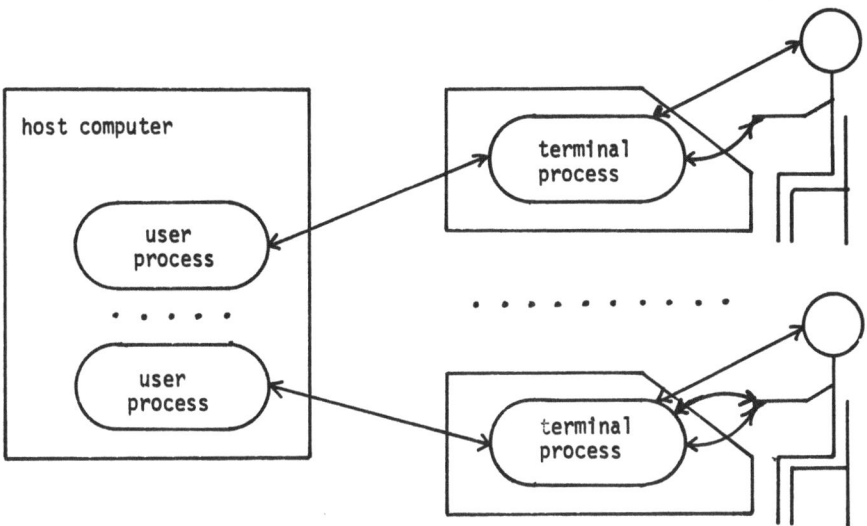

FIGURE 2.1: Processes in a computer application system

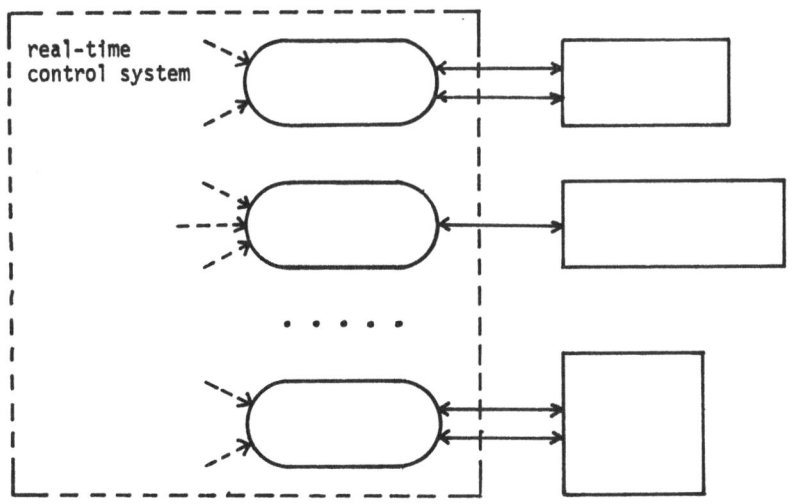

Figure 2.2: Processes in a real-time control system

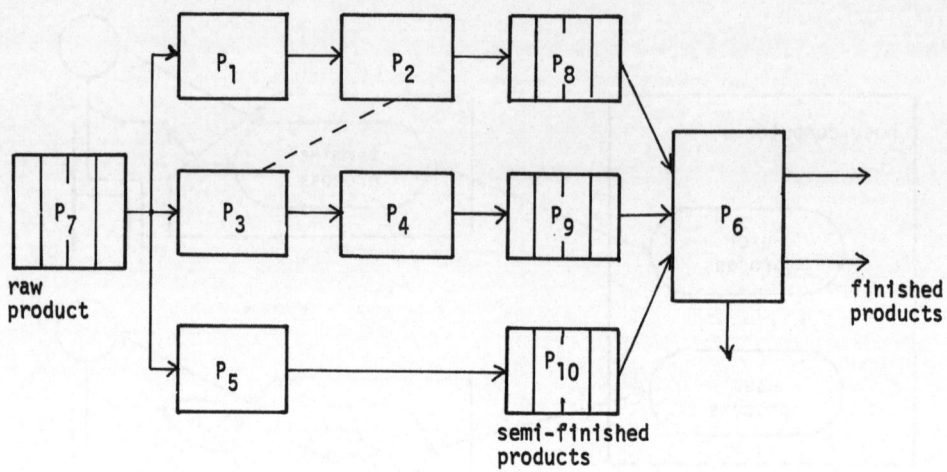

FIGURE 2.3: Processes in a manufacturing plant

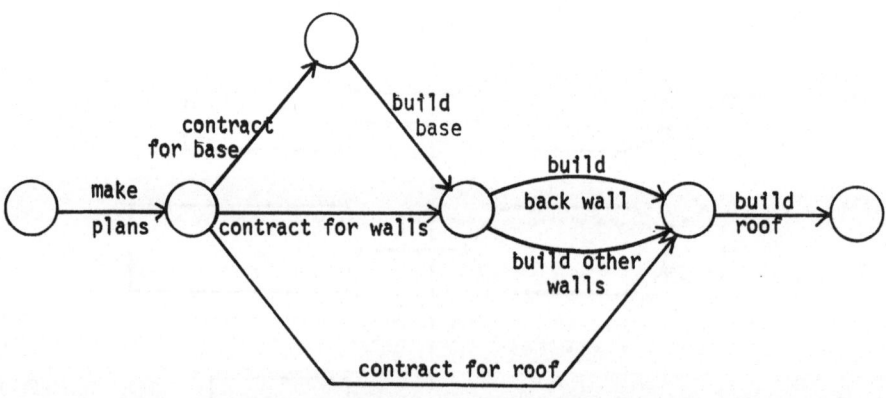

FIGURE 2.4: Example of PERT scheduling

the time needed by the processes P_1 and P_4 such waiting would be very infrequent and have a negligeable effect on the overall system operation. For highly used resources, on the contrary, many processes may be waiting[2], and the average waiting time may be sufficiently long to significantly degrade the overall performance.

Figure 2.3 also shows an example of process cooperation. In this instance, the product of process P_1 serves as the input of process P_2. This is a producer-consumer relationship between two processes, which implies that P_2 has to wait for the termination of P_1. Here the coupling of the processes is direct : since no intermediate storage is available, P_2 has to start executing as soon as P_1 has finished. A similar producer-consumer relationship exists between P_2 and P_6, except that the intermediate storage process P_8 allows for a certain time lag between the two processes. Other examples of process cooperation, also involving a sequence in which certain operations must be executed, are given by the PERT project scheduling method (see figure 2.4), or by systems in which the different processes communicate through the exchange of messages, where, clearly, the message reception always comes after the sending.

The synchronization rules implied by process interdependency, such as mutual exclusion and cooperation, are in general not sufficient to completely determine the relative execution speed and order between the processes of a system. Additional synchronization decisions are usually taken by a scheduling algorithm which, in a sense, supervises the whole system. This algorithm has to avoid deadlocks[3], where several processes wait upon each other, thus preventing any progress, and insure that the schedule is fair for all processes. A scheduling algorithm may be called "fair" in respect to a process p if the time that the process is waiting for its next steps of execution while all conditions depending on other processes and resources are satisfied is always finite.

2.3. MODULAR SYSTEM STRUCTURE AND ABSTRACTION

Most systems are too complex to be understood as a whole by the human mind. Therefore, it is necessary to introduce a structure subdividing a system into several more or less independent subsystems, processes[4], or modules. Such a structure allows each subsystem to be understood individually, the interaction of the subsystems leading to the understanding of the system as a whole.

The interaction between the subsystems is related to their interdependency and may be characterized by the assumptions each given subsystem must make about its environment, i.e. the other subsystems. As discussed in section 2.2, three levels of interdependence may be distinguished :

(a) No interaction between certain subsystems, such as for processes P_1, P_4 and P_5 in figure 2.3, i.e. no interdependence.

(b) Implicite interaction between certain subsystems due to scheduling constraints for shared resources. This interaction is not explicitely visible to the subsystems involved, but may nevertheless influence their operation[5].

(c) Explicit interaction involving cooperation between a certain number of subsystems. This kind of interaction usually involves the exchange of messages and/or one subsystem performing work for another one. This necessitates agreement on the meaning of the messages or procedure parameters exchanged between the subsystems.

A basic design principle favors a system structure with infrequent and simple subsystem interactions. The "interface" between two interacting subsystems may be defined as the set of assumptions each subsystem must make about the operation of the other. Such an interface must specify _what_ each subsystem does, as seen from the outside, but not (necessarily) _how_[6].

Opposite to the division of a system into subsystems is
the abstraction which consists of considering the collection of
subsystems with their interactions as a whole, ignoring the subsystem structure, and considering the interaction of this system
with its environment. For example, figure 2.5 shows a structure of
subsystems which realizes process P_6 of figure 2.3. In figure 2.3
abstraction is made from the details of P_6's structure shown in
figure 2.5. If the interface of P_6 with its environment is well
defined, the internal structure of P_6, as shown in figure 2.5, is
irrelevant to the operation of the whole system, as shown in figure 2.3.

Clearly, system subdivision or abstraction may be performed
at several levels as indicated in figure 2.6, giving rise to a
hierarchy of system descriptions. This principle is not only useful for the design of computer systems[7], but also for the understanding of complex biological and social systems[8]. It is important
to note that the amount of parallel activity found in any given system depends on the level of detail (or abstraction) on which the system is considered. For example in figure 2.3, the operation of process P_6 is considered as a whole (no parallelism), whereas the consideration of figure 2.5 introduces some parallel activity between
the subsystems of the process. Another example is shown in figure
2.7, where different levels of detail (or abstraction) are considered for the query handling process of an interactive data base.

It follows from the above considerations that the understanding of a system at different levels of details (or abstraction)
is a basic tool for the design of complex systems. This aspect of
system design should be supported by the system specification method (or programming language) used during the design[9].

It is important to note that the term "abstraction" is
often used in a meaning opposite to step-wise refinement[10]; and
refinement does not necessarily imply a decomposition into subsystems. Sometimes a refined system description simply provides
certain details which are left undefined in a more abstract
description. An example is the distinction between a protocol
specification and a description of a corresponding protocol
implementation, as discussed in section 8.2.

FIGURE 2.5: A more detailed description of process P_6 of figure 2.3

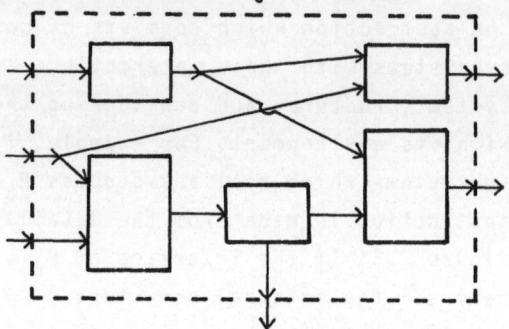

FIGURE 2.6: A given system specified in three different levels of details (or abstraction)

Explanations:

↑
⋮   abstraction
⋮   (less details)
⋮
⋮   subdivision
↓   (more details)

↑
↕   interaction between subsystems
↓

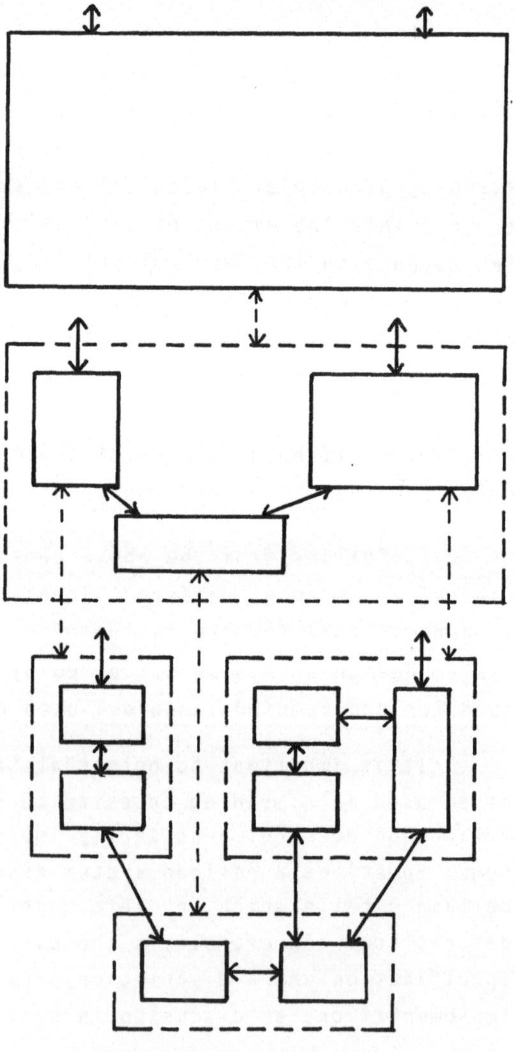

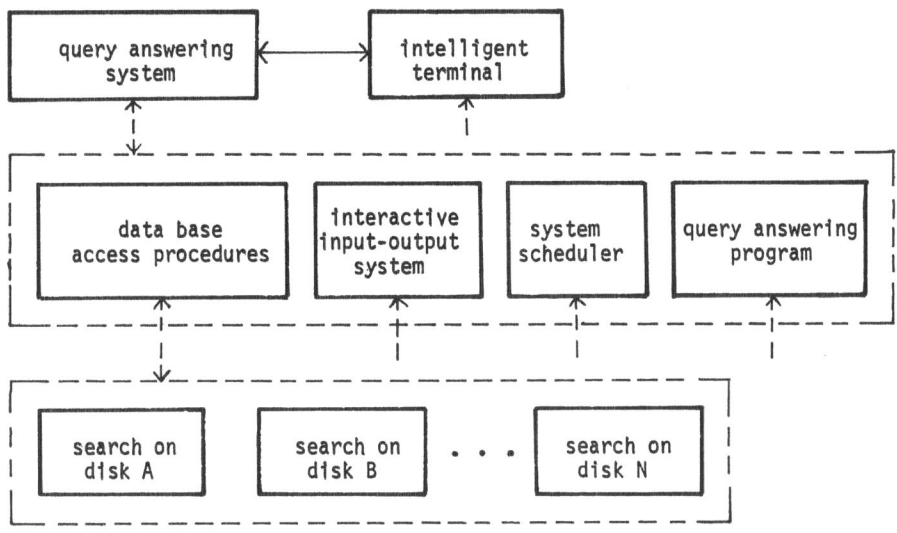

FIGURE 2.7: Description of a query answering system in different levels of detail (incomplete)

FOOTNOTES

1. Complete independence leads to functional behavior, as discussed in [Brin 73], section 3.

2. The processes waiting for a resource are usually organized in a queue. Sometimes several queues, corresponding to different service priorities, are associated with a resource. The queuing analysis of such systems is important for determining the overall performance of the system. See for example [Klei 75].

3. See for example [Coff 73], section 2.3.

4. Some examples of operating systems structured as a collection of several processes are described in [Brin 70], [Goos 72] and [Mell 77]. Communication software is often implemented as a collection of processes (see for example [Boch 79b]). Structuring principles based on the concept of processes are described in [Horn 73].

5. Implicit interaction also leads to protection problems, as exemplified by information leak through so-called covered channels [Lamp 73].

6. For a more detailed discussion, see for example [Parn 77].

7. See for example [Dijk 68b]. The concept of nearly completely decomposable systems has also been explained in [Cour 77] and applied to performance analysis.

8. [Simo 62].

9. The concepts of *class* [Dahl 72] or abstract data types [Lisk 75, Gutt 77] are provided in certain programming languages for providing a means for abstraction. In ADA [Ichb 79] they are called "packages". Language constructs for hierarchical process structures are for example discussed in [LeGu 80] and [Boch 83].

10. For a discussion of different meanings of "abstraction" see for example [Parn 74].

3. Common Problems

This chapter reviews some well-known problem areas encountered during the design of a computer application system. These problems are not specific to distributed systems. They were first studied in the framework of single processor computer systems, their operating systems, and application programs. However, some of the solutions to these problems are specific to distributed systems. Without claiming complete coverage of the subject, this chapter presents some example problems and a few possible solutions.

We believe that these problems should not be considered independently of one another, but a system design method, or particular system design should be chosen such that all these problems are solved, in so far as possible, simultaneously by the same approach, tool or mechanism. In this chapter, the problems are presented separately in order to simplify the discussion.

3.1. COOPERATION

3.1.1. Compatibility

Cooperation between several system components is only possible if the interfaces of the components are compatible. There are two levels of compatibility :

(a) If <u>functional compatibility</u> does not exist, cooperation is not possible. Consider for example a standard alpha-numeric terminal to be used for displaying arabic text, or a 6 Mbyte disk to store a 60 million character text file.

(b) If <u>procedural compatibility</u> does not exist, but the components are functionally compatible, cooperation can only be obtained by introducing a suitable adaptation module which translates between the communication procedures used by the different components. For example, alpha-numeric text can be translated between different character codes, or virtual circuit data communication can be operated through the X.25 or an HDLC interface.[1]

3.1.2. *Synchronization*

An example of a synchronous system is an assembly line where all workers work at the same speed. An example of an asynchronous system is a job shop where different processes work at independent speeds and semi-finished products are stored between the different steps of the processing.

3.2. *DISTRIBUTED RESOURCE SHARING*

Resource sharing is one of the main problems in the design of computer operating systems. Most resources impose restrictions (for example mutual exclusion) as to when they can be accessed by the different processes in the system. Scheduling algorithms have to maintain these restrictions for each resource. Such algorithms have been extensively studied for a centralized environment, where the scheduling decisions for the whole system are made by a centralized scheduler.

For a distributed system, the following three approaches may be taken :

(a) <u>centralized scheduling</u> : one component, the scheduler, is responsible for scheduling all resources in the system ;

(b) <u>scheduling at the resource</u> : a scheduling module is associated with each sharable resource. It processes requests for resource access coming from all components of the system ;

(c) <u>distributed scheduling algorithm for a given resource</u> : all processes competing for a resource execute a distributed algorithm which determines the schedule.

Considering only one resource, the approaches (a) and (b) are quite similar. However, the avoidance of deadlocks in the presence of several resources, seems to be more difficult in the case of approach (b).[2]

The approach (c) seems to be appropriate if the resource is not localized in one component, so that approach (b) is not applicable.[3]

3.3. NAMING AND ADDRESSING

The following examples demonstrate the wide variety of naming and addressing problems and approaches to their solution.

3.3.1. *Search strategies for link editors*

Each link editor or operating system has a strategy for identifying and locating object program modules to satisfy the external references of a load module. Given a reference name, such a strategy finds, if possible, a corresponding program module by searching through the provided input file, private object files, public program libraries and execution support modules. This is analogous to an addressing scheme.

3.3.2. *Naming of input-output flows*

A given input or output flow, for example the input character stream from an interactive terminal to the application program in a computer system is identified in many different ways, depending on the frame of reference within the system structure. For instance from the point of view of the terminal driver, the terminal is usually identified by an integer value, sometimes

called the I/O address, and usually a physically fixed value. For
the scheduler of the operating system, the input stream could be
identified by a port number associated with the application program, or the address in central memory of a file control block
which contains the control information of the stream. For the
control command interpreter, the input stream is usually characterized by a file name, such as INPUT. The application program,
finally, may use another name, such as USER-TERMINAL, to identify
the same file.

3.3.3. *The addressing scheme of telephone networks*

The addressing scheme of telephone networks is hierarchical, as shown in figure 3.1. In the case that the different telephone sets of an organization share the access to the public network, each telephone set is identified by an internal number within
the range of the office exchange. The office exchange is identified
by a local number within the range of the local telephone exchange,
etc. For establishing a connection with a telephone set connected
to the same office exchange, dialling the internal number is sufficient, as shown in figure 3.2a. To establish a connection outside
the range of the office exchange, the dialling sequence must start
with a local escape number which is interpreted as such by the office exchange of the originating party. An example of long distance
dialling is shown in figure 3.2b .

3.3.4. *Process addressing by ports*

Like a telephone set on a public telephone network, a computer system connected to a data network is usually identified by
a number which identifies the link between the network and the computer, i.e. its address. In order to distinguish between the different processes, within the computer system, that communicate with
other processes or terminals through the network, the concept of
ports has been proposed.[4] Each process has a certain number of

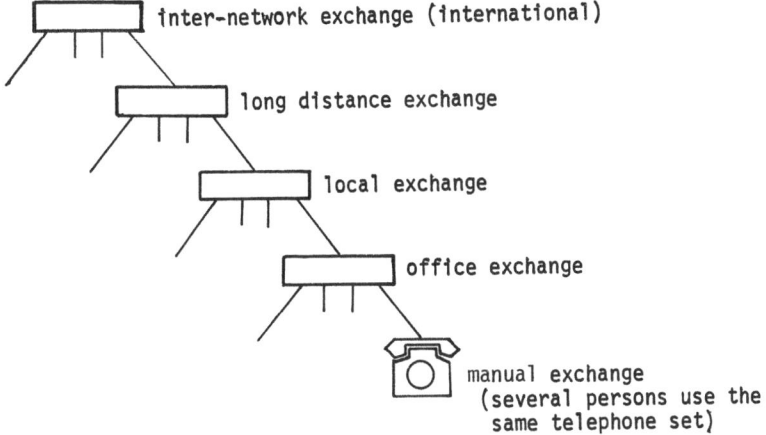

FIGURE 3.1: Hierarchical addressing scheme of telephone networks

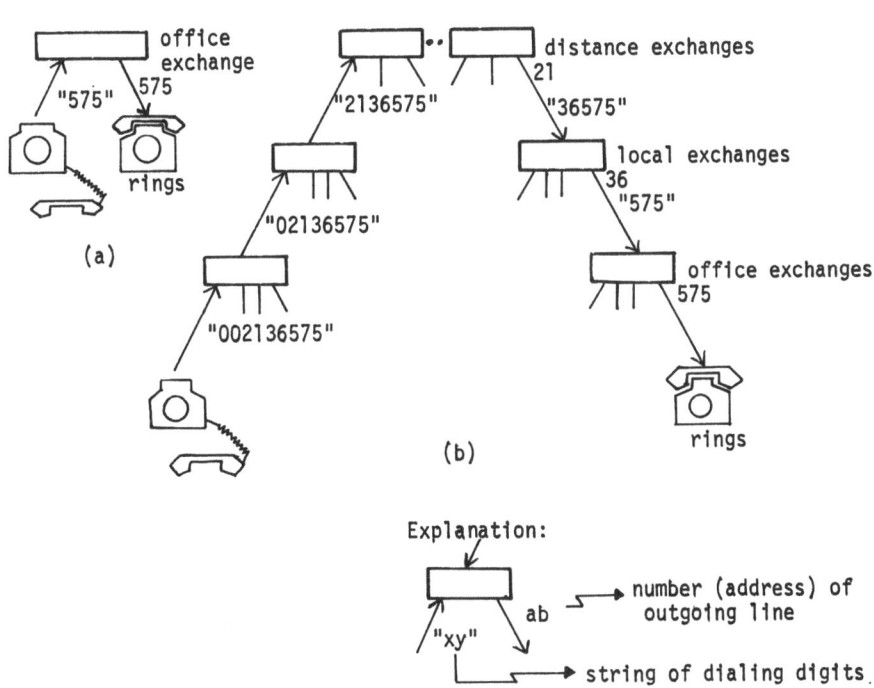

FIGURE 3.2: Telephone call establishment and addressing information

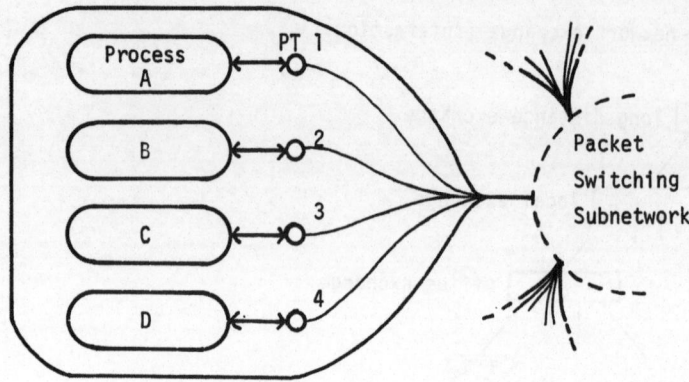

FIGURE 3.3: A Transport Station is a collection of Ports

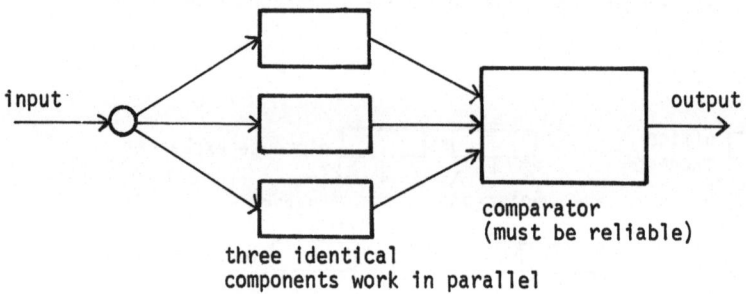

FIGURE 3.4: Reliability obtained through hardware redundance

A fault-tolerant sort program

<u>ensure</u> sorted (S) ∧ (sum(S) = sum(<u>prior</u> S))
<u>by</u> quickersort (S)
<u>else by</u> quicksort (S)
<u>else error</u>

Note: Rather than incur the cost of checking that the elements are a permutation of the original items, it merely requires the sum of the elements to remain the same.

FIGURE 3.5: Example of a recovery block

ports through which it communicates with other processes or terminals, as shown in figure 3.3. For establishing a connection through the network with a particular process in the host computer, it is therefore necessary to indicate the address of the host plus the appropriate port number of the process.

Well known services provided by the computer system, such as a particular data base, a Fortran compiler, or a general log-in facility to the operating system, may be assigned fixed port numbers, which are known to the user community. However, the majority of port numbers may not be permanently assigned, but used on a temporary basis by the user created processes. The available ports (or port numbers) are shared among the processes that reside in the computer system.

Instead of using numbers, within a fixed range, to identify the available ports within a host, one may allow for alpha-numeric names to identify ports. For example, a process may inform the operating system that it wishes to open a port and receive all incoming messages addressed to the port DATABASE (we assume that this process is the query manager of a database). Except for the "well known" ports, the name of a port used by a process for communication may be changed dynamically by the latter.[5]

Extending the scope of the port names from one host computer to the whole network yields a system where the user, which communicates with a given port name, need not be aware of the physical location of the process which serves this port.[6]

3.4. PROTECTION

We consider here the protection of system integrity against hardware faults and software bugs, as well as inadvertant users and those persons that try to obtain information they are not supposed to obtain. It is important to distinguish between the mechanisms that provide this protection and the security policy implemented in the system which determines the access rights and capabilities of the different processes and users.[7] The following points provide protection mechanisms :

(a) A modular system design using extended type objects as system modules, combined with small protection domains placed around these modules prevents unanticipated or undesirable actions of a module from disturbing other parts of the system.[8]

(b) The distribution of the different system modules onto several physically disjoint components increases the independence between the modules and eliminates unwanted interferences between the modules.[9]

(c) Physical control over the hardware of the system is a means of avoiding physical infractions.

(d) Identification of users is a means of protection at the system-user interface. Possible methods are the use of passwords, signatures, identification cards, etc.[10]

(e) Identification of terminals and other physical devices in distributed systems is useful as an additional check on the integrity of the communications medium, and make sure that some remote device has not been replaced by some other unauthorized item.

3.4.1. *Protection in distributed systems*[11]

The physical security (point (c) above) is not always attainable in distributed systems. For example, radio communication channels and circuits for accessing telephone or data networks can be tapped without any impact on the communication channel. It is also possible to falsify the data exchanged, or to introduce additional data into an ongoing exchange, provided the system is well enough known to the intruder. It is therefore impractical to physically secure the privacy and integrity of the information exchanged between distant system components.

A possible approach to protection is the use of encryption. For better protection, encryption may be used independently at different levels in the system. For example, a distributed system using a communication sub-network, independent encryption may be used for each process to process communication, and additionally and independently over each link between a system component and the sub-network.

Most encryption techniques use matching keys at each end of the encrypted communication path.[12] A pair of keys must be agreed upon prior to the communication.[13]

3.5. ERROR RECOVERY[14]

3.5.1. *Error detection*

Before error recovery can be performed, the occurrence of an error must be detected. Error detection is common practice in data transmission and storage techniques, where error detecting codes are used. The principle is the addition of redundant information which must agree with the original data to be transmitted or stored. During the reception or reading from storage, the consistancy can be checked and possible errors are detected with high probability.

Frequently used error detecting codes are the following :

(a) parity bit : the addition of one redundant bit such that an even (or uneven) parity is obtained for each character or memory word (single bit errors are detected, errors involving an even number of bits are not detected) ;

(b) checksum : the addition, to a block of data, of a redundant octet (or word) containing the modulo sum of all octets (words) of the block ;

(c) longitudinal parity, and

(d) polynomial or cyclic codes : similar to (b) .

The polynomial or cyclic codes present the best error detection characteristics.[15]

For errors involving only a few bits, redundant codes can be used which not only detect possible errors, but are also able to determine the original data, i.e. they are "error correcting codes".

3.5.2. *Recovery by retry*

One of the simplest forms of error recovery is recovery by retry, which consists of reperforming the operation which lead to the error condition. In the case of transmission errors, or read or write errors on magnetic surfaces, the operation will usually perform correctly the second time. A certain number of retries are usually admitted, and failure to perform the operation is declared in the case that none of the retries was successful.

If the error is due to a persistant hardware fault or a software bug, repeated execution of the same operation will usually not change the error condition. For these kinds of errors, the recovery strategy by retry is not appropriate, but one of the strategies described below may be used.

3.5.3. *Redundant hardware*

The provision of redundant hardware makes it possible to recover from hardware faults of a limited nature. Different degrees of redundancy may be foreseen, depending on the desired reliability of the system. In decreasing order of reliability, we mention the following approaches :

(a) Three identical components operate in parallel, as shown in figure 3.4. A majority vote among the three determines the correct result and detects any errors in one component.

(b) Two identical components operate in parallel and any error of one component is detected by a discrepancy of the results. If a possible malfunction of one component can be detected by itself, the other component can be used as stand-by.

(c) Only one component operates, but similar components are available in the case of a failure of the former. Either one component is identified as the back-up, or several identical components share the processing load, as long as they are operational.

3.5.4. *The design principle of recovery blocks*

The concept of recovery blocks has been proposed as a design principle for building reliable and resilient systems.[16] It is intended as a method for specifying recovery mechanisms for software bugs, as well as for spurious or persistant hardware errors. For software bugs, the methods of retry or hardware (and software) duplication clearly do not work as long as the input data do not change.

The principle consists of subdividing the system into modules which are the units of error recovery, i.e. the recovery blocks. For error detection, a verification condition is associated with each module. Depending on the output result parameters of the module, the condition must be satisfied after each execution of the module. (The presence of such a condition represents a certain redundancy in the values of the output parameters). The verification condition is used to detect errors.

The operation of the module is specified in several (different) program versions. When the module is executed, the first version is executed and the verification condition is tested. If it is satisfied, it is assumed that the result is correct and the execution of the module ends. If it is not satisfied, an error has occurred and the second program version is executed, which is followed by another test of the verification condition. If the program versions are sufficiently different from one another,

there is a good chance that the second version works correctly
after the first one failed. If all program versions fail to check
the verification condition, then the module, as a whole, is considered to have failed.

It seems that this approach to error recovery is of general applicability. An example is shown in figure 3.5.

3.6.   REAL TIME CONSIDERATIONS

It is useful to distinguish the following three levels of real time constraints[17] :

(a) No real time constraints :
    termination within finite time : typical for batch applications ;

(b) Probabilistic real time constraints :
    termination within a given time with a given probability (real time constraint on average execution time, but no definite time limit) : typical for real time systems for interactive applications ;

(c) Real time constraints :
    termination within a definite time limit : typical for applications in process control etc. (real "real time" systems).[18]

Systems with real time constraints are clearly much harder to build than systems with probabilistic or no real time constraints. Therefore it seems good practice to design real time systems such that real time constraints apply for as few system modules as possible, and that for the remaining parts of the system only probabilistic constraints apply.

3.6.1. *Time-outs*

A typical application of a time-out mechanism can be found in most data transmission protocols for recovery after message loss. If, within a predetermined real time period, the sender does not receive an acknowledgement for a message sent, the message is retransmitted. If the time period elapses before the acknowledgement is received, one says "a time-out occurs".

A time-out period is related to a real time constraint. If, in the example, the message transmission and reception of an acknowledgement is always executed (except in the case of message loss) within a definite time limit, there is no problem : the time-out period will be set longer than this time limit. If, however, there is no definite, but only a probabilistic time limit for the response, then for any time-out period chosen, it may happen that the acknowledgement of the original message sent arrives after the time-out occurred and the message was retransmitted. This possibility may have implications on the system's design.[19]

3.6.2. *Clock synchronization in distributed systems*

For distributed systems with real time constraints it seems necessary to define a global real time which is known to all system components, and represents the physical time. If each component uses its own clock, there must be some algorithm for synchronizing the different clocks.[20]

Much simplicity is gained for the system if no global real time is needed. For many distributed real time applications, it is, in fact possible, to consider only a relative time which has no simultaneous global value, but which preserves the causal order of events within the system.[20]

FOOTNOTES

1. For example, the Network service used for Teletex (CCITT Recommendation S70) may be provided through a packet-switched network using X.25 or through the telephone network using HDLC procedures.

2. Distributed algorithms for deadlock detection are for example given in [Mena 79] and [PODC 82].

3. Distributed algorithms for obtaining mutual exclusion have been discussed in [Lamp 74], [Dijk 74], and [Lela 77]. A different approach to mutual exclusion is the use of time stamps for regulating the access to distributed data bases (see for example [Thom 78] or [Bern 81]).

4. See for example [Zimm 75]. The port number mentioned here corresponds to the Transport and Session sub-addresses in the OSI environment [OSI 83, Zimm 80].

5. Based on this possibility, continuous renaming of ports is proposed in [Farb 75] for obtaining protection.

6. The distinction between names, addresses and routing in a distributed computer system is explained in [Shoc 78]. The same issues also arise in the framework of distributed message systems or "electronic mail" [Schi 81]. In this context the translation from names to addresses is usually performed by databases, sometimes called "name servers", which contain for each mail subscriber the addresses of his mailbox(es) (see for example [Garc 81]).

7. [Wulf 74] elaborates on this distinction.

8. [Lind 76] gives a survey on the use of extended types, small protection domains, and capability based addressing to support security and reliable software.

9. This is a reason for building distributed operating systems where the different functions are realized on different physical components, see for example [Prob 77, Rash 81].

10. The use of encryption for authentication is discussed in [Need 78].

11. Protection issues in public data networks are discussed in [Clip 76].

12. A "Data Encryption Standard" has been defined by the US National Bureau of Standards.

13. This method is called "private key" encryption. Usually the keys are exchanged manually. Automated procedures for obtaining matching keys are considered in [Need 78]. The key distribution problem is much simplified in the case of "public key" encryption methods, where only the key for decryption is private, but the key for encryption is publicly known, (see for example [Need 78]).

14. Error recovery is related to fault-tolerance. For a review on a fault-tolerant computing see for example [Aviz 77].

15. See for example [Mart 70], section 5. The HDLC standard (see also section 6) has adopted a particular cyclic code, adding 16 bits to each block of data.

16. See for example [Rand 75] or [Hech 76]. This and other techniques for synchronization and recovery in distributed systems are discussed in [Kohl 81].

17. For a more detailed discussion, see [Wirt 77].

18. In the case of certain applications, such as the transmission of packetized voice, any operation that takes more time than foreseen by its schedule is simply aborted in order to give priority to the processing of the most recent information.

19. The verification of systems with arbitrary message delays is considered, for example, in [Schl 82]. [Boch 79] considers design constraints that make the logical behavior of a system independent of any message delays.

20. See for example [Lamp 78].

Part II
Distributed System Architecture and Communication Protocols

Chapters IV through VII deal with the architecture of distributed systems and in particular with the functions of a communication subsystem that supports distributed applications. Chapter IV presents the typical layered architecture of communication protocols, and discusses the problems of compatibility and interworking between heterogeneous computer systems. An overview of transport and network transmission services is given in chapter V. Chapter VI explains in detail the principles of synchronization, transparency, error detection and retransmission usually encountered in data link protocols for point-to-point and multipoint circuits. Chapter VII, finally, gives an outlook to the future, considering technology developments and standardization issues.

4. Architecture of Distributed Systems

Distributed systems are usually very complex. In addition to the system part which deals with the application proper, a large part of the system is concerned with the communication between the distributed components, exchanging data over great distances, and controlling the synchronization and consistency of the operations performed at different locations. This section deals in particular with this communications aspect of a distributed system.

Because of their great complexity, the design of distributed systems is usually structured into a certain number of hierarchical layers, as explained above (see section 2.3). Each layer provides some specific additional services (facilities), to be used by the next higher layer, and uses the services provided by the next lower layer. In using these services it ignores the details of their implementation in the lower layers. An example of such a layered system was first given for an operating system designed for a single computer and its peripherals[1] . In this case, the computer hardware is considered as being the lowest system layer, and the higher layers, implemented in software, each implement some particular facility needed by the operating system and its users. The lower software layers are the following :

- Allocation of the physical processors to the different logical processes in the system : the facility provided by the layer is the (quasi-) parallelism of the different processes.

- Virtual memory management : the facility provided is a large virtual memory for each process.

- Dialogue with the operator : the layer provides, independently for each process, the possibility to converse with the operator.

- Input/output stream buffering : the layer provides the higher layers with a communications facility via logical input/output streams. (This facility is comperable to the transport communication service discussed below.)

The communications part of a distributed system may also be structured into such a layered architecture, as explained in the following sections. Section 4.1 explains the layering principle for the case of distributed systems in general. Section 4.2 gives an overview of the functions found in the different communication layers of a typical distributed system. This discussion also relates to the Open Systems Interworking (OSI) standards[5] which are being developed for interworking between heterogeneous computer systems. Section 4.3, finally, discusses architectural issues related to interworking and compatibility.

4.1.   LAYERED HIERARCHICAL SYSTEM STRUCTURE AND
       PHYSICAL DISTRIBUTION

In this section we consider the communication between two processes, but the discussion also applies to the communication between more than two processes and may easily be generalized to this case.

Figure 4.1 (a) shows two directly interacting processes. We assume that, instead of directly interacting, two processes in a distributed system communicate via some subsystem providing a communication service, as shown in figure 4.1 (b). The communication subsystem is called "transparent" in as much as the direct interaction between one process and the communication subsystem appears, to the process, as a direct interaction with the other process. Possible limitations to the transparency may be due to

(a)   throughput limitations,
(b)   delay,
(c)   limitations of the available interaction primitives,
(d)   transmission errors,
(e)   loss or duplication of messages,
(f)   loss of the message sequencing,
(g)   complicated interfaces to the communication subsystem, etc.

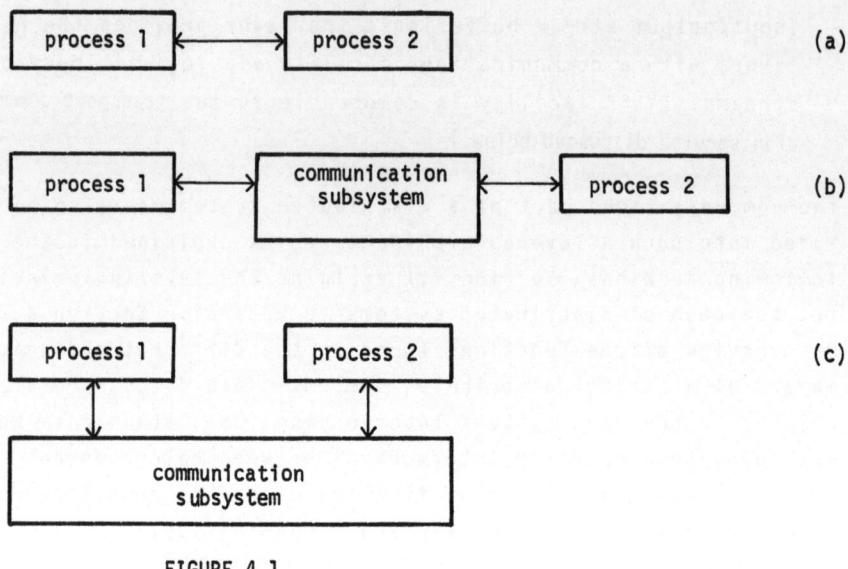

FIGURE 4.1

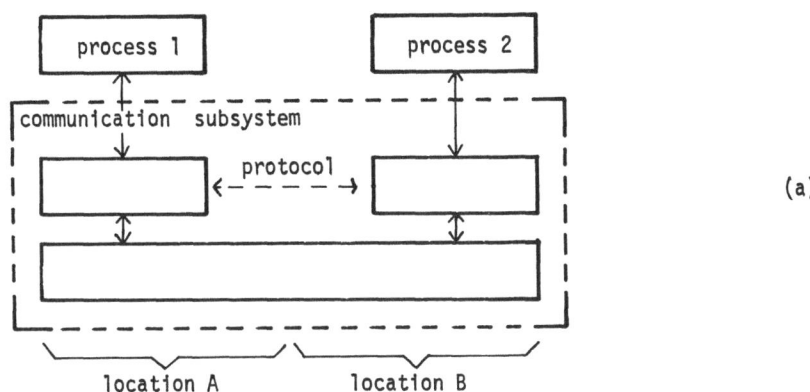

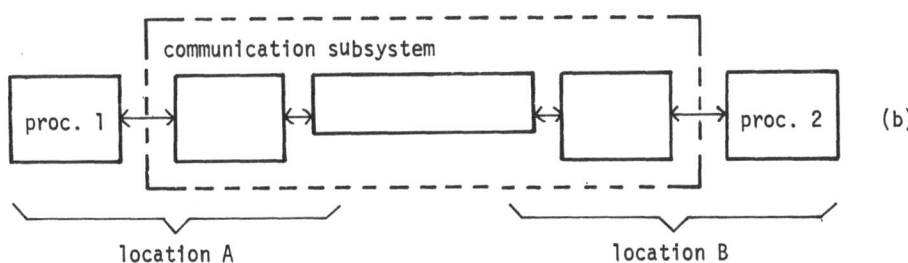

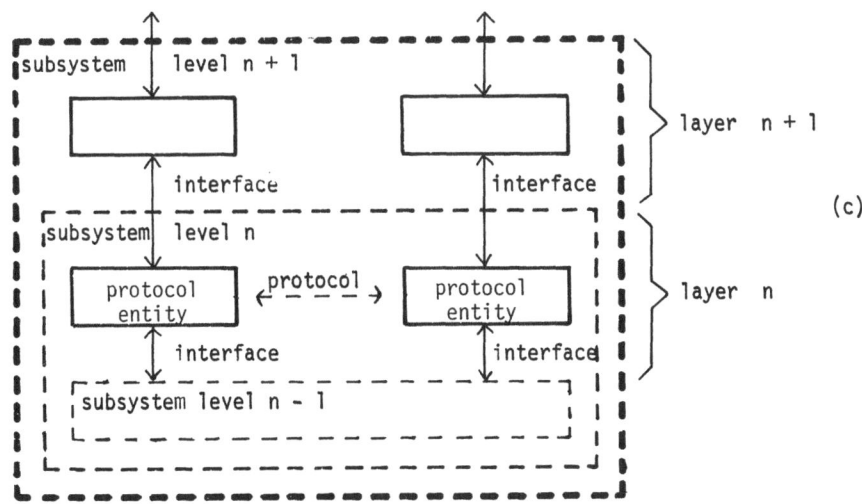

FIGURE 4.2: Layered structure of a communication subsystem

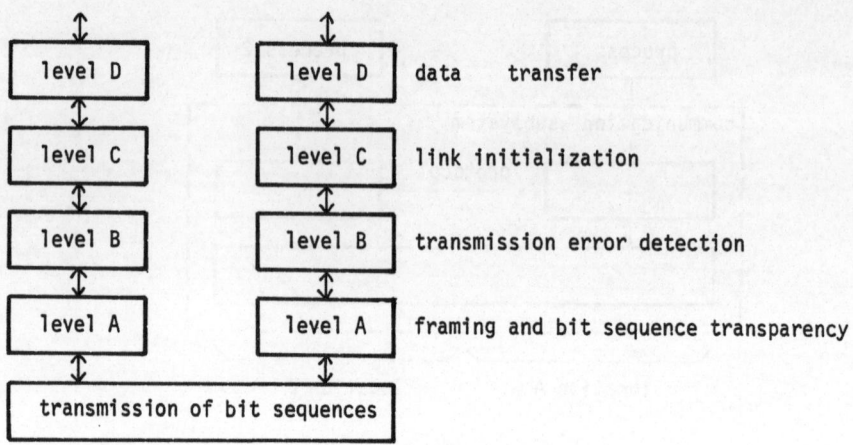

FIGURE 4.3: Functional sublayers of a link protocol

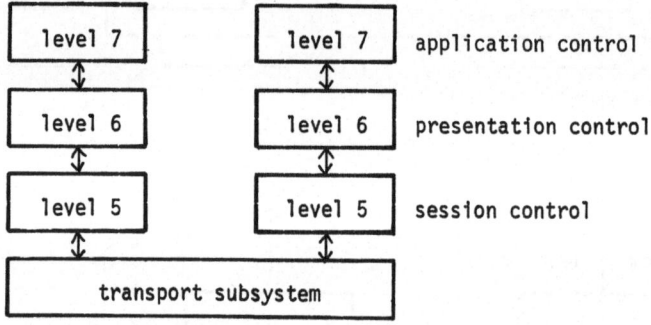

FIGURE 4.4: Higher level protocol layers

Figure 4.1 (c) is equivalent to figure 4.1 (b), but it is sometimes preferred because it shows that the communication subsystem provides a service which is used by the two processes, and that the two processes are considered as a higher layer within the hierarchical architecture of the system.

The communication subsystem itself is usually built as a hierarchical, layered system. Figures 4.2 (a) and (b) show an additional level of detail. Two system components, building the process-to-process communication service out of a more primitive communication service are shown, located with each of the communicating processes, respectively. They may be considered service processes^2 which communicate with one another via the more primitive communication service, according to a particular protocol.

Figure 4.2 (c) shows a particular layer (of level n) within the hierarchical structure of the communication subsystem. The layer consists of two components^2 providing the "level n" service to the next higher system layer. They provide this service by following the "level n" protocol and use for the communication between one another the "level n-1" communication service provided by the next lower system layer. As examples of hierarchical communication systems, we may mention the protocol layers for reliable communication over a dedicated physical circuit, and the protocol layers for Open Systems Interworking, as shown in figures 4.3, and 4.4, respectively, and explained in section 4.2.

To show how such a layered communication subsystem may be used, we consider an application program that uses a data base. If the application and the data base are implemented in the same host computer the application program may be directly coupled to the data base access procedures, as shown in figure 4.5 (a). If the application program resides in a different computer a logically identical interface between the program and the access procedures may be realized by a communication subsystem containing several protocol layers, as shown in figure 4.5 (b).

The kind of communication service required depends on the characteristics of the interfaces between the distributed components of the application system, the interface between the application program and the data base access procedures in the above example. Sometimes the exchange of individual messages between different system components is an appropriate service, sometimes it is necessary to establish a certain number of logical links between system components, over which messages are sequentially delivered[3].

So far we have assumed that all the communication protocol layers are implemented together with the communicating application components. However, this is not necessarily so. As an example, figure 4.6 (a) shows a system where the protocols of figure 4.4 are partly implemented in a front-end computer and partly together with the application in the host computer. We note that the interface between the level 6 and level 7 layers goes through the connection between the front-end and host computers. However, the communication service provided by this (physical) connection may not be appropriate for this interface, in which case an additional protocol layer between the front-end and host computer may provide an appropriate interface, as indicated in figure 4.6 (b).

A similar situation arises when data transmission networks are used for communications. In general, certain services may have to be added by an end-to-end transport protocol layer to the service provided by the network, as shown in figure 4.7, in order to obtain the transport service desired. However, the network is usually implemented by switching nodes and transmission trunk lines, and the services can only be obtained through access lines over which particular network access protocols must be followed. Therefore, these network access protocols implement the interface between the network services and the end-to-end transport protocols, which are implemented in the subscriber equipment. This is shown in figure 4.8.

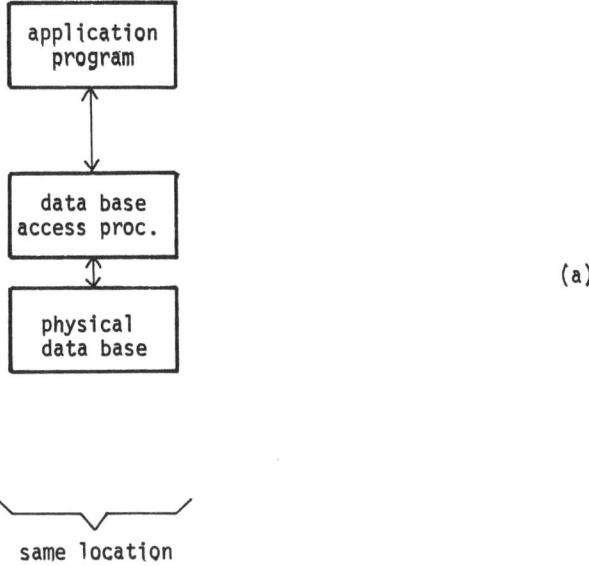

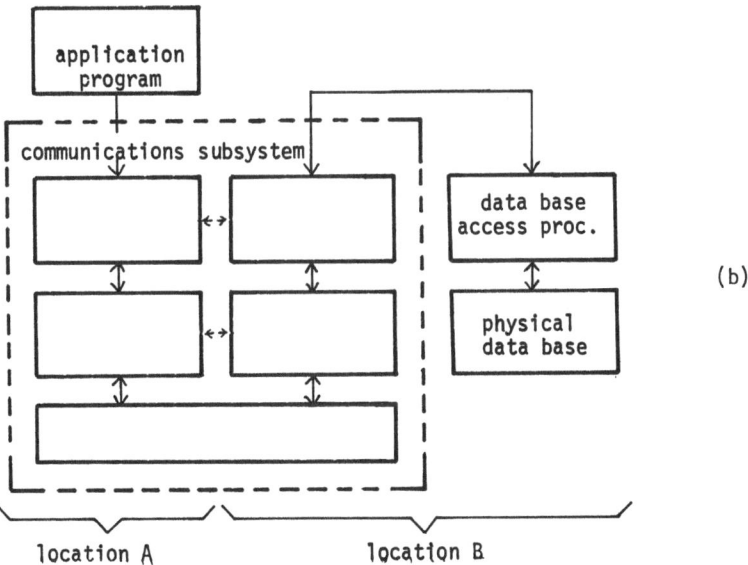

FIGURE 4.5: Local and distant communication with a data base

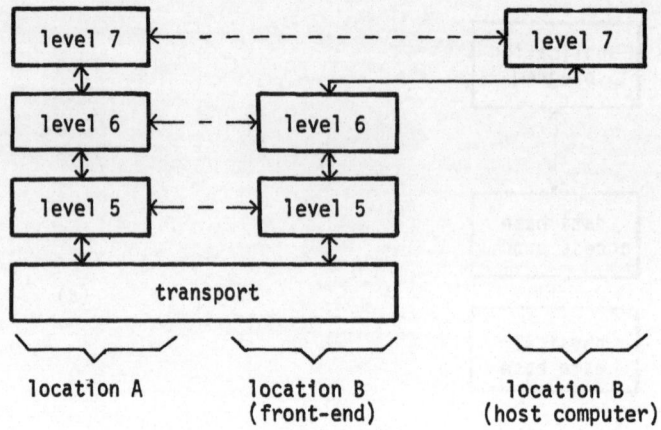

FIGURE 4.6(a): Distribution of protocol functions over front-end and host computer

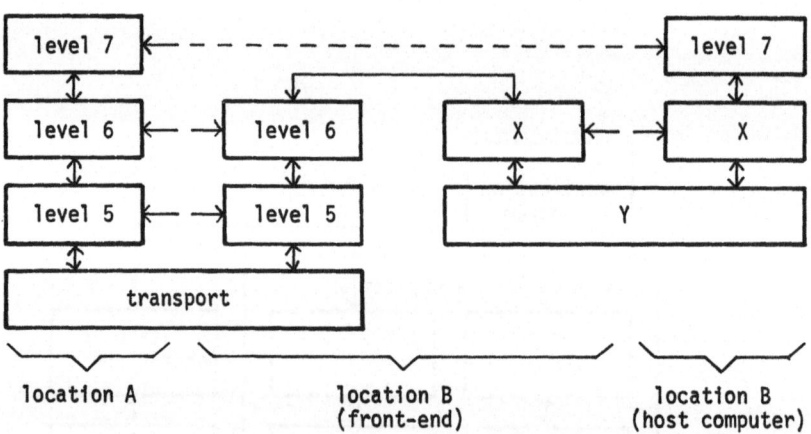

FIGURE 4.6(b): The front-end may be seen as a protocol converter

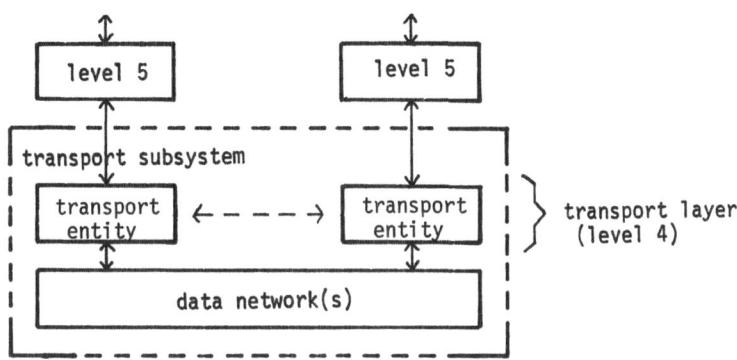

FIGURE 4.7: The transport sub-system

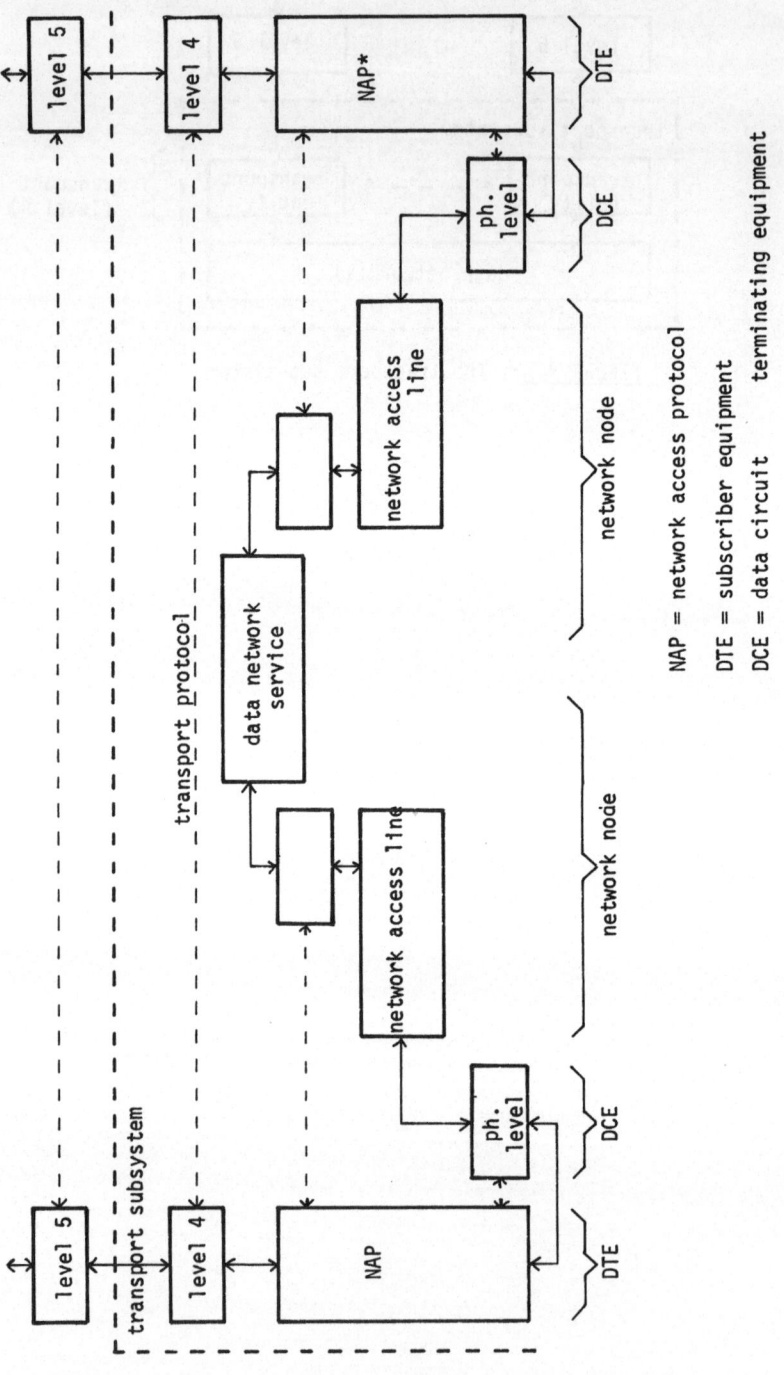

FIGURE 4.8(a): The transport subsystem:
Definition of "network access protocol" (NAP)

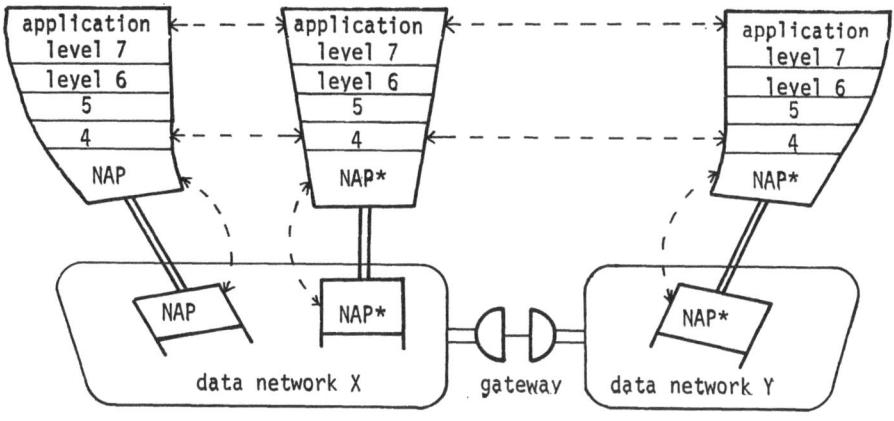

FIGURE 4.8(b): Protocols in a computer network (NAP*: the NAP for different network access lines need not necessarily be the same)

4.2. TYPICAL STRUCTURE OF A DISTRIBUTED SYSTEM

In comparing the communication functions implemented in different distributed computer systems, great similarity can be found between the problems handled in the different systems, although the methods of solving them may vary from one system to the other. Therefore, the idea of giving a typical structure of a distributed system consists of considering a layered architecture of the communication subsystem, as explained above, and indicating, for each layer, the problems handled by that layer. It seems that a similar structure applies to most distributed systems.

The interworking of different systems is clearly much simplified if their layered structure is the same and if, in addition, the same methods are used, in corresponding layers, for solving the same problems. Since interworking with other systems is an important requirement for most distributed systems, the development of standards in this area is of utmost importance[4]. National and international organizations are working on the elaboration of such standards, in particular the ISO (International Organization for Standardization) Subcommittees 6, on Data Communications, and 16, on Open System Interworking (OSI), of the Technical Committee TC 97 on Computers and Information Processing. Also the CCITT (International Telegraph and Telephone Consultative Committee of the International Telecommunications Union) is active in this area by defining standards for network access procedures for public data networks, which may also be used for private networks, and higher-level protocols for telematic services to be used over public communication networks.[5]

In the following subsections, we elaborate on the different layers of the typical structure of a distributed system. The structure of the lower layers, described in sections 4.2.1 and 4.2.2, are relatively well established. However, the higher level structure of distributed systems, especially the part corresponding to the presentation and application layers, is still a subject for research and experiment, although the overall structure, as described in sections 4.2.3. and 4.2.4, now seems to be generally accepted.[6]

4.2.1. *Communication over a dedicated circuit*

A dedicated circuit is a means of transmitting data between two fixed locations. It can be considered the lowest layer in the hierarchical structure of the communication system, and provides as service the transmission of bit sequences, as described in section 4.2.1.1 below. The provide reliable data transmission between the two locations, a so-called "link" layer protocol is usually employed. The functions of the link layer may be partitioned into several sublayers as shown in figure 4.3 and described in sections 4.2.1.2 through 4.2.1.4. A typical link protocol is HDLC. More details are given in section 6.

4.2.1.1. *Transmission of bit sequences*

We consider, as a basic communication service, the transmission of bit sequences in both directions, simultaneously or alternately, between the two locations. The service is characterized by

(a) the nominal transmission speed (in bits per second),
(b) the end-to-end delay,
(c) the transmission error characteristics,
(d) possible limitations of code transparency,
(e) reliability and availability, etc.

Such a service is provided by analogue (for instance telephone) circuits with modems, and digital circuits. It is usually accessed through a standard interface protocol[7] , often called the physical interface, as indicated in figure 4.9.

4.2.1.2. *Framing and bit sequence transparency*

The service provided by this layer is the transmission of data blocks consisting of arbitrary bit sequences (i.e. there is bit sequence transparency), usually limited to a maximum length (typically 127 octets or longer). These data blocks are coded into "frames" which are sent over the basic communication service, and interspersed with "idle" traffic when no data is available for transmission. The service may be characterized by

(a) fixed or variable data block length, and possibly a maximum data block length,

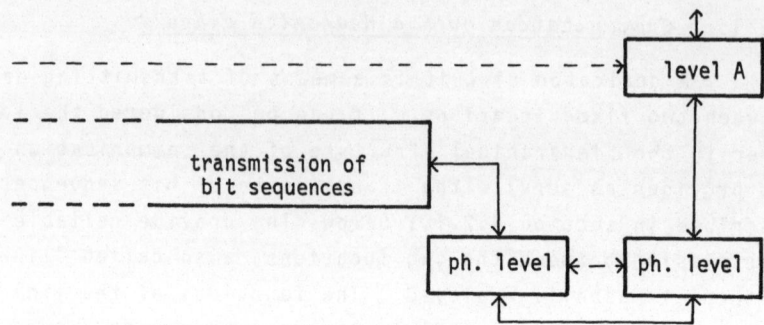

FIGURE 4.9: Physical level procedures are used to access a data transmission circuit

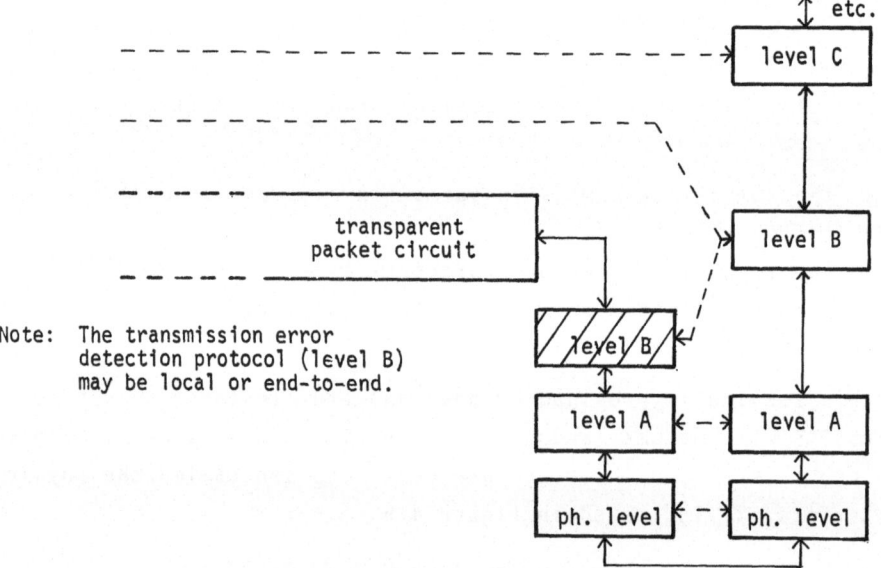

Note: The transmission error detection protocol (level B) may be local or end-to-end.

FIGURE 4.10: Local vs. end-to-end significance of link sub-layer procedures in the case of a transparent packet circuit

(b) the probability of a transmitted data block being lost,
(c) the overhead introduced, etc.

in addition to the characteristics a, b, c, and e of section 4.2.1.1 above.

When provided on a commercial basis, such a service is usually charged on the number of data blocks transmitted. It may be accessed through an interface protocol containing two layers, as shown in figure 4.10. We call such a service a "transparent packet circuit"[8].

We note that the asynchronous (i.e. start-stop) data transmission service may be considered a particular service with framing and transparency, where the data blocks have a fixed length of one octet.

4.2.1.3. Transmission error detection

The service provided by this layer is the transmission of data blocks and the detection of possible transmission errors. Some redundancy coding scheme is used to detect transmission errors. The service may be characterized by

(a) the probability of undetected transmission errors,
(b) the introduced overhead,

and the characteristics of the lower system layers (see above).

4.2.1.4. Link initialization and reliable data transfer

The link initialization layer is concerned with establishing agreement, between the communicating subsystems, on the status of the communication subsystem, its initialization, and the recovery from major faults of the layers below. The data transfer layer provides reliable data transmission by using retransmission techniques to recover from (detected) transmission errors and loss of data blocks. We note that these two aspects are not always as clearly separated into distinct layers as indicated in figure 4.3.

In addition to reliable data transfer, the following facilities may be provided :

1. Flow control, i.e. the receiver may inform the sender of its readiness to receive more data (and the sender will wait for the receiver).
2. Fragmentation, i.e. the transmission of long messages as a sequence of packets which are transmitted in individual data blocks.
3. Out of band signalling, i.e. (high priority) transmission of short information not related to the normal data flow.

We note that the service provided by this layer, with the above facilities, is similar to a (permanent) virtual circuit between the two locations, as defined by the CCITT Recommendation X.25.

4.2.2. *Communication through a network*

Compared with a dedicated circuit, communication through a network is complicated by the fact that a given subsystem may exchange information not only with one, but with a large number of different subsystems located at different places. The different subsystems connected to a network, or several different interconnected networks, are usually distinguished by network subscriber addresses. The selection of the desired destination subsystem may be made in one of the following modes :

(a) long term selection : so-called "permanent" or "dedicated" circuits are established between subscriber addresses by the network administration

(b) medium term selection : real or virtual (packet-switched) circuits are established between subscriber addresses and cleared dynamically in accordance with an established network access protocol

(c) short term selection : the address of the destination subsystem is indicated in each data packet sent through the network. The establishment of a (logical) connection between subscriber equipments is not needed prior to data transfer. This selection mode is adopted for datagrams[9].

Consequently, a network access protocol, as shown in figure 4.8, contains, in addition to a physical interface layer, a network access layer which handles the selection of the destination subsystem, and the exchange of status information between the network and the subscriber equipment. This layer also requires the framing and possibly transparency functions of the link layer. In the case of packet-switched virtual circuits, the functions of the remaining layers of figure 4.3 are also required for accessing the transmission service of these circuits.

Public data networks usually provide services for medium and long term selection: CCITT Recommendations X.21 and X.25 deal with circuit switching and packet-switched virtual circuits, respectively. In the context of local area networks, short term selection, as well as broadcast, packet transmission is often used. More details on network services and access protocols are given in section 5.2.

4.2.3. *A uniform transport service*

While data networks and dedicated lines provide data transmission between several physically distributed devices, such as terminals, data bases, host computers, etc., the transport service provides the facilities needed for communication between (logical) processes, such as application programs, terminals, host computer log-in processes, data base access procedures, etc. The communicating system components are identified not only by the network subscriber address, but also by a so-called port[10]. A host computer operating system typically provides a large number of ports, some of them "well known" to the user community, through which the processes in the host communicate with one another and with external processes and terminals, as indicated on figure 4.11.

The communication facilities provided by the transport service may include

(1) process addressing, via ports,

(2) establishment and clearing of port-to-port associations,

(3) transport of "messages"[11] (i.e. the logical units of the process communications) and short "interrupts"[12], directly between ports or through established associations,

(4) protection against transmission errors,

(5) sequencing of messages (this includes protection against message loss and duplication),

(6) flow control of messages,

(7) delivery confirmation, etc.

We note that not all of these facilities are necessarily needed by all applications.

The transport protocol layer should be designed such that
(a) it may be implemented in many different environments in order to allow for the interworking of different computer systems, and
(b) the same transport service can be provided using different network transmission services, such as dedicated or switched circuits, packet switched circuits, or datagrams.

As shown in figure 4.8 (a), the transport protocol is an "end-to-end" protocol. For example, a facility such as delivery confirmation can only be implemented when the protocol operates end-to-end between the communicating processes[13]. This is in contrast to network access protocols which have a local significance between the subscriber equipment and the closest network node. Certain special kinds of end-to-end significance provided by the service of some networks may be lost in the case of transmission through several interconnected networks. More details on the transport layer are given in sections 5.1 and 5.3.

The message-oriented communication in a distributed environment has a noticeable impact on the design of computer operating systems. For a straight-forward interworking in a distributed environment, the operating system should be message oriented[14], and the inter-process communication facilities provided within the operating system should also be available from a distance[15]. Such a design also allows the different functions of an operating system to be distributed over several micro-computers coupled over a local bus, and other computer systems at larger distances[16].

4.2.4. *Higher level protocols*

The term "higher level protocols" usually means the end-to-end layers of a distributed system. In particular, it includes the transport layer described above and some additional layers, as shown in figure 4.4. The boundary between the layers of the communication subsystem and the distributed application layers is not exactly defined. Usually, the term "higher level protocols" denotes those layers of a distributed system (from the transport layer up) which provide functions that are sufficiently general to be used by a variety of different applications. Typical examples of higher-level protocols are the following :

(a) Terminal access protocols specify the interaction between an application program and a terminal, or between two terminals. To simplify the adaptation of application programs to different types of terminals and of terminals to different kinds of computer and operating systems, standard terminal access protocols have been proposed, also called "virtual terminal" protocols. Different classes of terminal access protocols may be distinguished depending on the functions they provide. We mention, in particular, access protocols for

- line-and/or page-oriented interactive character terminals[17],
- data entry terminals, handling forms which are structured into fields of characters,
- graphics terminals[18],
- batch terminals for remote job entry.

(b) File transfer protocols specify how complete data files may be transfered from one computer system to another[19]. Such a function may be used for remote entry of batch processing jobs, and for many distributed processing applications, including local edition of files.

(c) File access protocols specify how an application program may selectively access certain elements of a file at a different location. More elaborated forms of such protocols are used for access to data bases, as for example the highest layer of the communication subsystem of figure 4.5 (b). Different classes of file access protocols may be distinguished, such as:

- file transfer, i.e. obtaining a complete copy of a distant file (see above),
- record oriented file access, i.e. selective access (read, write or update) to individual logical records of a file, in random or sequential order[20],
- structure oriented file access, i.e. retrieval and update access to structured data bases.

The identification, selection, protection, etc., of the distantly accessed file is an additional problem which closely relates to the conventions of the operating system in which the file resides.

The above protocols are also called "function-oriented" protocols, since each of them provides a particular set of functions used for obtaining access, from a distance, to a given kind of resource, such as terminals, files, data bases, etc. Many function-oriented protocols have been implemented in different distributed systems, often closely interwoven with the message transport mechanism. They are different from one another, and interworking between these different systems is very difficult. New, standard function-oriented protocols are being elaborated which could serve as the language for function-oriented interworking and be locally adapted to the different existing systems. In the development of such standards the following aspects are important :

(a) ease of adaptation to existing systems, and

(b) flexibility and open-endedness for future developments.

An agreement on standards for higher level protocols is essential for the interworking of different computer systems. The Reference Model for Open Systems Interworking[5] was elaborated by the ISO committee TC97/SC16 as a framework for the development of protocol standards for the different layers of the hierarchy. This model contains the following higher protocol layers (as shown in figure 4.4):

(a) Transport end-to-end control (as discussed in section 4.2.3).

(b) Session control : This layer is concerned with supporting structured dialogues ("sessions") between processes, such as, for example, an alternate mode of message exchange. It may also contain functions for checkpointing and recovery from message transmission errors, as well as from errors and faults of the communicating processes[21].

(c) Presentation control : This layer is concerned with the representation and coding of data.

(d) Application control : This layer is concerned with the assignment, access and release of system resources, process initiation and termination and other management functions, as well as with the application proper.

We note that the function-oriented protocols described above usually extend over several of these architectural layers. For example, a terminal access protocol includes conventions for dialogue control (session control layer), character coding (presentation control layer), and terminal reservation (application control layer). A function-oriented protocol may be considered as being implemented in the process handling the resource on the one end, and in the process using the resource on the other end. An appropriate end-to-end transport service (see sections 4.2.3) is used for the exchange of messages between these two processes.

4.3. COMPATIBILITY AND INTERWORKING ISSUES

The possibilities for interworking between different, present day computer systems are very poor. This is due to the large number of different conventions used by the different systems to provide the functions discussed above (see section 4.2). The following are some of the reasons that have contributed to this development :

(a) Different systems have grown independently of one another over long periods of time.

(b) Different systems have different communication requirements, which leads to different choices during the system design.

(c) During the initial design of a system, interworking with other systems is often not considered a requirement.

Reason (b) above shows that there are limits to compatibility and interworking. The advantages of a standard layered system structure, such as the one outlined in section 4.2, relate to the following :

- Standard protocols for a given system layer may be defined independently of the other layers.

- For each layer, different protocols may be defined corresponding to different communication requirements.

- For a given system, the protocols of each layer may be chosen independently of one another in accordance with the communications and interworking requirements.

4.3.1. Requirements for compatibility[22]

We now consider a given communications layer, as shown in figure 4.2, and ask the question : What are the points on which the subsystems of the layer must agree in order to guarantee a meaningful communication ?

There must be agreement, between the two sides, on the communication service provided at the upper interface to the next higher layer. This must be so, since the service provided over these interfaces may be used to replace a single interface between two subsystems, as indicated by figures 4.5. However, it is not necessary that the form in which this service is provided at the interfaces be the same on both sides. An example are the interfaces between the layers 6 and 7 in figure 4.6 (b).

There must also be agreement on the communication service used by the given layer (and provided by the interface with the next lower layer), but not necessarily agreement on the form in which it is accessed. (Note that this interface is the upper interface for the next lower protocol layer).

Finally, there must be a certain agreement on the way in which the two subsystems of the layer operate. The rules for their interaction through the communication service provided by the next lower layer, are called the communication protocol of the given layer. Certain aspects of the protocol are essential for the compatibility between the two subsystems, such as the meaning, format and coding of information exchanged via the lower communication layer, and certain rules about the order in which certain operations are executed in each of the subsystems. On the other hand, there are other aspects of the operation of the subsystems, also part of the protocol, which are not essential to compatibility, i.e. they may be changed in one subsystem alone without affecting the correctness of the given layer. However, these aspects have often an impact on the efficiency of the protocol. They may therefore be ajusted independently in each subsystem such that the best operating conditions be obtained.

4.3.2. Network interconnection

To allow for the interconnection of different circuits and networks and the communication between subscriber equipments connected to these different facilities, the communication service provided by these facilities is usually such that the concatenation of two or more such services, as shown in figure 4.12, results in a logically identical service, the differences being of a qualitative nature, such as delay, maximal throughput, transmission error characteristics, etc.

Therefore the data network service box in figure 4.8 (a) may, in fact, be realized by the interconnection of several networks, each providing the same service. In practice, the interconnection between two networks must be realized through some physical circuit over which appropriate access protocols must be used. Such an interconnection is called a "gateway", and its architecture may be represented as in figure 4.13. The interconnection is particularly simple in the case of dedicated physical circuits, and datagram networks, respectively, because of the simplicity of the services provided.

So far we have considered the interconnection of logically identical transmission services. Interworking between transmission services of different type is also possible. A simple way of interworking consists of adding a protocol layer on top of one of the services such that it looks like the service it is to be connected with. As an example, we consider the interworking between packet-switched virtual circuits, real circuits, and transparent packet circuits. Figure 4.14 shows the architecture of a system consisting of two networks, providing virtual circuits and transparent packet circuits respectively, which are connected through a real circuit. Subscriber equipments are also shown, connected to a net-

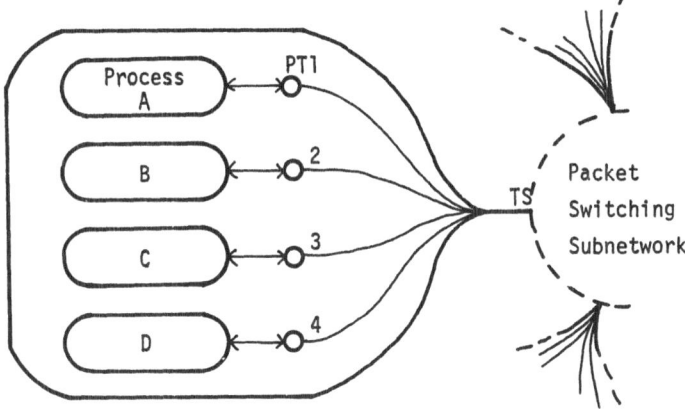

FIGURE 4.11: The concept of ports

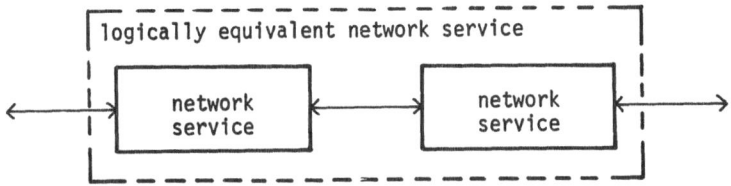

FIGURE 4.12: Concatenation of transmission services

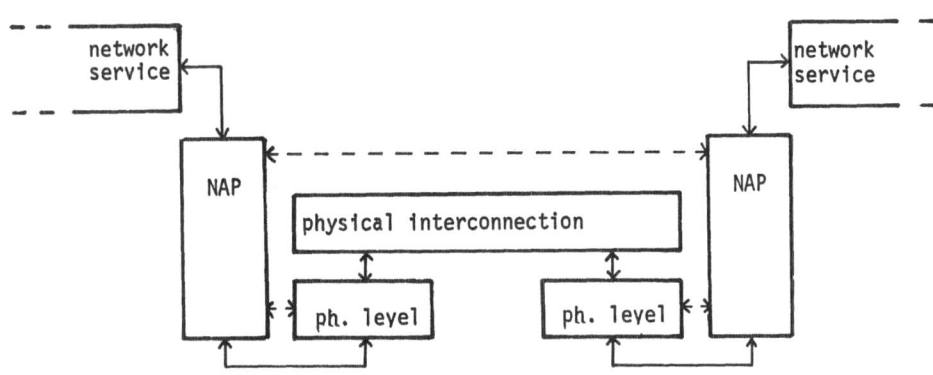

FIGURE 4.13: The structure of a gateway

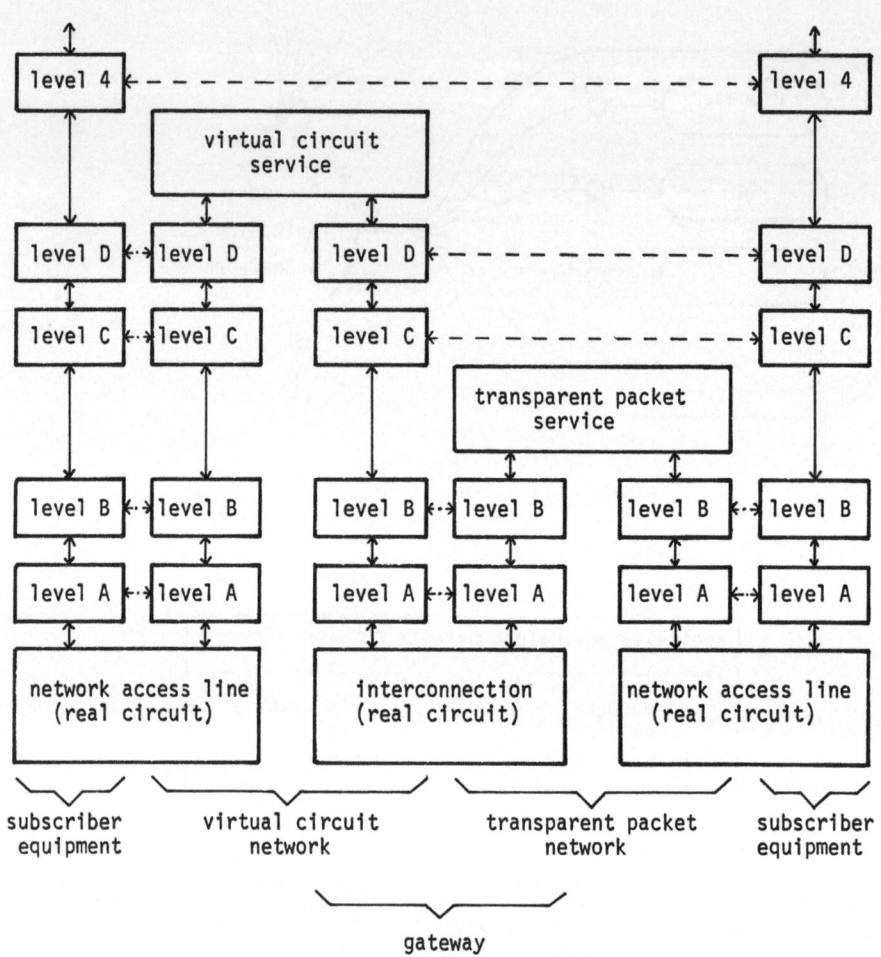

FIGURE 4.14: Interworking of virtual circuits and transparent packet services.

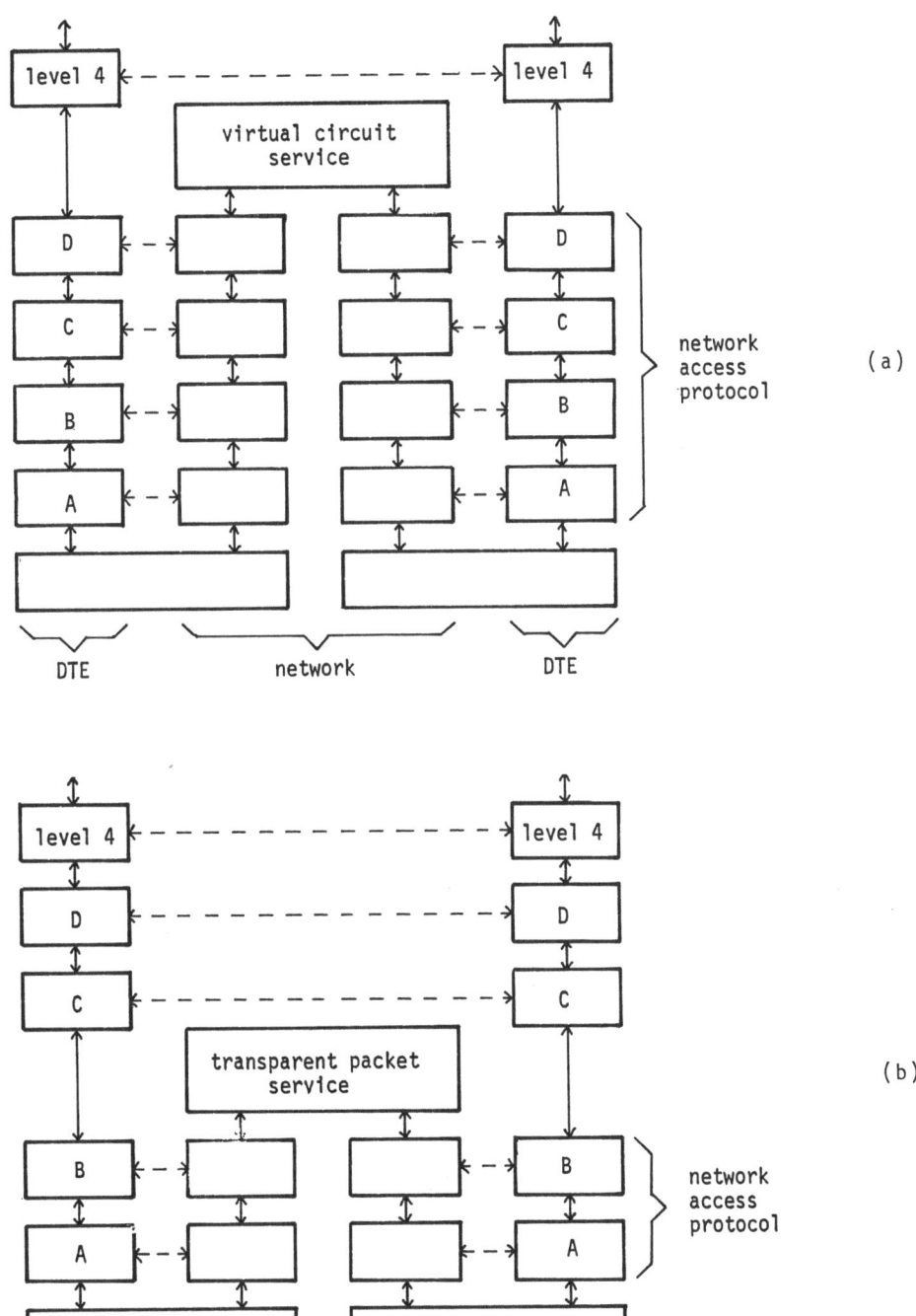

FIGURE 4.15: Communication through virtual circuits and transparent packet circuits using the same protocols

work through a real circuit, i.e. the network access line. This
example, together with figure 4.15, also demonstrates that the
same protocol layers implemented in a subscriber equipment may be
used for interworking through networks with different services, as
well as for separately accessing the different services of the
networks[23].

4.3.3. *System interworking and adaptation*

In section 4.3.1 we assumed that systems are built for
interworking, and that the compatibility requirements are taken
into account during the design. In many cases, however, this is
not true. Most present day computer hardware and software, as
well as terminals, are incompatible. Computer operating systems,
as well as sophisticated terminals incorporate parts which correspond to several layers of communication protocols, although often
not clearly identified as such. For direct interworking of the
systems, these parts would have to be changed and replaced by
mutually compatible protocols. Unfortunately, such a change is
practically impossible because of the interwoven interfaces found
in most systems.

A viable approach to the interworking of incompatible
systems is to add (hardware and/or software) modules which provide
an adaptation between the protocols of the different systems. The
architecture of an example is shown in figure 4.6 (b) where we
assume that the protocols labelled "X" are part of the usual software and hardware of the host at location B. To realize an interworking with a system at location A which uses different protocol
layers (labelled "level 5", "level 6", and "transport") for essentially the same function, a front-end computer has been added at
location B which translates the protocols of one system into those
of the other, preserving the communication service at the interface
below the layer labelled "level 7" [24].

As explained above, figure 4.6 (b) shows an example of the adaptation of higher level protocols. We note that for the interworking to be possible, there must be some compatibility at some higher level (at level 7, in the example), i.e. there must be agreement on what one system is going to do for the other. If this is the case the lower protocol layers may be translated. We note, however, that the end-to-end significance of the message exchanges may be lost. In figure 4.6 (b), the transport, level 5, and level 6 protocols operate between location A and the front-end at location B, but not the host computer ; end-to-end significance would remain at level 7 only if the box labelled "Y" included a data transmission network[25].

FOOTNOTES

1. We refer to the THE operating system [Dijk 68b].

2. In the OSI (see section 4.2 and footnote 5) terminology, they are called "entity" or "protocol entity".

3. The latter kind of service is sometimes calles "connection oriented", while the former is called "connectionless" and, for short messages, may be realized by a datagram service (see section 4.2.2).

4. For a more detailed discussion of the compatibility issues involved, see section 4.3. The need for data communication standards is also pointed out in [Sand 76] and [Boch 77c].

5. A standard "Reference Model" [OSI RM] has been elaborated by ISO TC97/SC16 and CCITT on the overall layering structure for protocols to be used in an "Open Systems" environment. Informal descriptions of the services to be provided by the different layers have also been developed. Discussions on standard protocols for the different layers are still in progress, in particular on the higher layers of the hierarchy. An overview of the OSI status may be found in [Gree 82] and [OSI 83].

6. Most protocol hierarchies for private distributed systems developed by computer manufacturers and large-scale users exhibit many similarities with the hierarchical structure explained below. More details on these protocol hierarchies may for example be found in the following references: IBM's SNA [Cyps 78]; Digital's DECNET [Weck 80]; and others [Bogg 80].

7. A status report on these interface standards may be found in [Bert 80].

8. Switched and permanent transparent packet circuits are offered, for example, in Canada by the Infocall service of the public Infoswitch data network.

9. A datagram service does not necessarily preserve the sequence of transmitted data packets, nor does it exclude the loss of data packets. See for example [Pouz 73].

10. Here it is assumed that, within the context of a subsystem identified by a given network address, a port identifies a particular process, application program or terminal. The OSI Reference Model (see footnote 5) introduces so-called Transport and Session addresses for this purpose.

11. Called "Transport service data units" in the OSI terminology.

12. Called "expedited data units" in the OSI terminology.

13. However, a basic transport service (as for instance defined for OSI [OSI TS]) may be provided by the concatenation of the transport layers of two separate systems (with possibly different protocols) through a gateway.

14. Examples of such systems are described in [Brin 70], [Goos 72], [Mell 77], and [Rash 81].

15. The design of the system may have to take into account the difference in service quality, in terms of delay and throughput, available in the local area context compared to larger distances (see for example [Bogg 80] or [Akko 74]).

16. See for example [Prob 77].

17. The role and nature of standards for access to character-oriented terminals is well described in [Barb 77].

18. A standard code for the transmission of graphic information is defined for videotex [PLP 82].

19. The basic approach to file transfer is explained in [Gien 78].

20. A standard file access service is described in [OSI FS].

21. A general approach to distributed error recovery is described in [Merl 77b]. Various protocols for transaction processing in distributed databases also deal with this problem.

22. A more detailed discussion of these issues is given in section 8.2.

23. Note that the figures do not show the protocol layer for network access. See also footnote 2 in chapter V.

24. The same principle is also applied to the interworking of different computer systems in heterogeneous computer networks (see for example [Davi 77] and the adaptation of existing start-stop terminals to packet-switched data networks and Virtual Terminal protocols (see section 4.2.4).

25. It is noted that the issue of end-to-end significance is not important for those layers in the hierarchy for which the services provided within two systems may be concatenated through a gateway in such a way that the resulting end-to-end service at that layer has the same qualitative properties as the services within each system. This is for example the case for the network service (see section 4.3.2).

5. Message Transport Requirements and Data Transmission Networks

5.1. MESSAGE TRANSPORT REQUIREMENTS

As explained in section 4.2, higher-level function oriented protocols rely on an appropriate process-to-process message transport service, which is provided at the interface of the transport subsystem. Depending on the applications, different communication requirements are encountered. These requirements may be characterized (i) by the way in which a communication partner is identified and selected, and (ii) by the following points :

(a) <u>Message sequencing</u> is provided over logical connections, also called "liaisons", which may be established between two processes. Otherwise messages are sent independently of each other, and sequencing is not guaranteed, a situation sometimes called "connectionless data transfer".

(b) A <u>maximum message length</u> may be imposed by the transport subsystem.

(c) <u>Throughput</u> may be defined as the number of message-bits transported per second.

(d) <u>Response time</u> may be defined as the delay between the submission of a message by a process and the reception of the (complete) message by the destination process, provided the latter is waiting. Short response time for long messages requires a high <u>transmission rate</u>.

(e) <u>Transmission error rates</u> may be defined as the number of bit errors in received messages per number of received message bits. Two different rates must be considered :

- rate of <u>detected errors</u> concerning errors which are not recovered by the transport service but are detected and signalled to the transport users, and

- rate of <u>undetected errors</u>, concerning errors which are not signalled to the transport user (because they are not detected by the transport subsystem).

(f) The rate of <u>message loss</u> may be defined as the number of lost messages over the number of messages sent. Usually, losses are signalled to the transport user in the case of a liaison (but only in this case).

(g) <u>Reliability</u> may be defined as the expected period for which the specified transport service is provided without interruption.

(h) <u>Availability</u> may be defined as the percentage of time the specified service is available.

(i) <u>Security</u> is the assurance that the messages sent are delivered to the right destination, and are available only to this destination, and that only authorized processes may send messages.

In the following we give a list of some typical applications of distributed systems and their message transport requirements :

(1) Transaction systems for banking, sales control, etc. : The message transport requirements are characterized by fast response time, high throughput at the processing sites, and low undetected error rate. The maximum message length may be short (some hundred octets).

(2) Text editing : The requirements are as above, but in addition, text files must be transferred between the editing sites (often intelligent terminals) and the document storage sites, which requires high transmission rates, low rates for errors and message loss, and long messages.

(3) Interactive graphics : As above; a high transmission rate is important.

(4) Remote submission of batch jobs : This application may be considered as a particular case of file transfer, characterized by high throughput, low rates for errors and message loss, and long messages.

(5) Distributed processing requires, in general, a mixture of long and short messages, good response time to shorten the time of resource utilization, and a low undetected error rate.

(6) Real-time control applications, in addition, usually need very good response-time characteristics for short messages.

5.2. DATA TRANSMISSION SERVICES

Different data transmission services are provided by private and public networks and communication channels. They may be classified as follows :

5.2.1. *Dedicated circuits*

A dedicated circuit provides a transmission path for bit sequences between two fixed points. It may be based on analogue or digital transmission techniques, such as telephone voice channels, broad band radio channels, possibly via satellites, digital circuits, or optical fibers. Except in the case of satellite links, the transmission delay is short (of the order of some milliseconds). The bit error rate of a circuit depends on the underlying transmission technology (order of 10^{-4} to 10^{-5} for telephone channels, 10^{-8} for digital circuits). Line protocols (see chapter 6) are usually implemented to adapt the transmission service to the communication requirements.

5.2.2. *Switching*

When a transmission network, or several interworking networks are used, the switching facility allows a user to dynamically chose different communication partners. Except for possible (fixed) multiplexing of several (logical) circuits over the same network access path, the dedicated circuit connecting the user equipment to the network (called "network access line") is either allocated to one connection at a time, or shared between several connections (statistically multiplexed). For dynamically established connections, the data transmission phase is preceded by a connection establishment phase and followed by a clearing phase, which involve the exchange of appropriate control information between the user and the network. In the cases of dedicated circuits, permanent packet-switched circuits and datagrams, these additional phases are not required.

5.2.3. *Circuit and packet switching*

Circuit switching provides, during the data transmission phase, the equivalent of a dedicated circuit. The network access line is dedicated to one connection at a time.

Packet switching networks provide the transmission of user packets between the different user equipments. Packet switching is characterized by a longer transmission delay (of the order of half a second) and a low error rate. The following packet-switched transmission services may be distinguished :

- Datagrams : Packets are self-contained and travel independently of one another. No connection establishment and clearing phase is needed. Out-of-sequence delivery and packet loss is not excluded. There is flow control at the user-network interface.

- Virtual circuits (permanent or switched) : The data transfer phase of these connections allows for flow control, error reporting and interrupt transmission. Several connections may be multiplexed through one network access line.

- Transparent packet circuits (permanent and switched) : The
  network access line is dedicated to one connection at a time,
  which during the data transfer phase, provides transparent
  transmission of packets from one end to the other.

The exact properties of the packet-switched services depend on the network providing the service. While the access protocol for virtual circuits to public data networks is internationally standardized (CCITT Recommendation X.25), there are certain variations in the service provided by different networks[1]. Local area networks often provide a datagram service, usually with broadcast facility.

Interworking between circuit and different packet-switched networks is possible if we assume that the purpose of the interworking is the provision of a connection-oriented message transport service with flow control, as defined in section 5.1, through the different networks. As shown in figures 4.14 and 4.16, it would even be possible that terminals or computers use the same protocol for obtaining the transport service, independently of the network to which they are connected. This requires, however, an agreement on such a standard access protocol.[2]

5.3. THE TRANSPORT PROTOCOL

As already mentioned in section 4.2.3, the role of the transport protocol layer is to provide the same message transport service, independently of the underlying transmission facilities used. In the case that a virtual-circuit transmission service is used, this service may be a sufficient transport service for certain applications therefore not requiring any additional transport protocol. For other applications the error performance, reliability or other parameters of the transmission service may not be sufficient, in which case on additional transport protocol would be used to provide the required service. An end-to-end transport protocol with an error detection and recovery function would also check the error performance of the underlying transmission service.

Figure 4.7 shows the system components that, together, provide the transport service. The local entity providing the service is usually called a "transport station". For each user, the transport station may select the most appropriate transmission service available and realize any additional end-to-end transport protocol in order to provide the required transport service.

Certain transport protocols are designed to operate over different kinds of transmission services, including datagrams, and interconnected transmission networks. These protocols are particularly robust, since they cannot rely on sequential packet delivery[3]. Other transport protocols, more specialized, are designed for use over virtual circuits[4]. They may provide additional error detection, reliability and end-to-end significance for message acknowledgements and flow control.

FOOTNOTES

1. The service provided by a particular network is well described in [Rybc 77].

2. The proposed "Frame Mode DTE" interface could be such a standard (see for example [Folt 78]).

3. See for example [Cerf 74] or class 4 of the ISO/CCITT Transport protocol [OSI TP].

4. See for example [Hert 78] or the classes 0 and 1 of the ISO/CCITT Transport protocol [OSI TP].

6. Link Protocols

This chapter deals with protocols used over a point-to-point physical communication channel. They provide a reliable data transmission service between the two stations connected via the channel, which is more or less unreliable. The different sections of this chapter deal with the transmission service provided by the physical channel and the different protocol sublayers into which a link protocol may be divided, as outlined in section 4.2.1. Similar considerations also apply to the lower protocol layers of local area networks with broadcast transmission[1].

Different kinds of data transmission services may be adopted for the communication between two stations, showing different characteristics such as the following :

(a) Transmission may be synchronous, asynchronous, or with flow control. In the synchronous case the transmission speed is fixed and usually determined by a clock; in the asynchronous case the speed is determined by the sender, though a maximum speed is imposed; whereas in the case of flow control the speed is determined by the sender and the receiver, within a maximum (the receiver indicates when he is ready to receive more data, and the sender indicates when new data is transmitted).

(b) The unit of transmission may be a bit, a block of bits of fixed size, or a block of varying size with a maximum size, or arbitrary long blocks. In the case of fixed size blocks, the information in a block may be presented to the receiver in parallel or sequentially, i.e. bit by bit. In the latter case, a clock is normally used to indicate when the next bit of a block is presented.

In this chapter we concentrate on protocols suitable for long distance communication, where the underlying physical channel provides bit sequential synchronous or asynchronous transmission[2]. The protocol layers discussed in this chapter build, on top of this service, a quasi error-free, variable block size, data transmission service with flow control.

6.1. TRANSMISSION OF BITS

The lowest level digital service is often called "physical level" and, for long distance communication, usually provides bit sequential, synchronous or asynchronous data transmission. The essential characteristics of such a service are listed in section 4.2.1.

6.1.1. *Interface procedures*

Different interface procedures (i.e. physical layer protocols, as shown in figure 4.9) may be used to access the bit transmission service. The simplest interfaces are those for sequential bit transmission in asynchronous and synchronous mode.

A typical interface for asynchronous transmission is the so-called "start-stop" interface[3] which consists of four interface circuits, two (signal and return) in each direction of transmission. Separately for each direction, a continuous *one* signal means that the sender is ready for data transmission. Data is usually transmitted in fixed-sized blocks of eight bits. To distinguish the data from the continuous *one* signal, a so-called "start bit" of value *zero* is inserted before each block; and to clearly identify the start bit of an immediatly following block, a so-called "stop bit" of value *one* is added after each block. If the next block does not immediatly follow, the *one* signal of the stop bit is extended up to the following start bit. A typical timing diagram is shown in figure 6.1. To correctly receive the transmitted data, the receiving station has to sample the received signal at appropriate times, as indicated in the figure. For this purpose it uses a clock which runs at approximately the same speed as that of the sender and is adjusted by every start bit.

A synchronous interface may be defined over the above interface circuits, but a typical interface standard[4] uses a common return for all signals, and provides two additional signal circuits for the exchange of control information between the transmission service and its user. The service provides bit timing signals, to be used for reception and sending of data, over an additional circuit. In this case the user equipment does not need a clock. Continuous synchronization between the timing signals at both ends of the connection is maintained by the transmission service (see also section 6.1.3).

6.1.2. *Physical transmission media*

The simplest means of transmitting electrical signals is a pair of wires. A large number of parallel wires are used for local (parallel) interfaces, whereas simple twisted-pair wires are used over distances of up to several kilometers. The electromagnetical properties of the installation impose a maximum useful speed (which may be measured in bits per second, or in frequency).

Optical fibers are a similar transmission means based on light, as opposed to electrical current. They are thin fibers of an optically transparent material which have the property of keeping the light, which enters at one end, within the fiber until it exits on the opposite end. Therefore they are also called "light guides". With the addition of suitable elements at the ends of the fiber for emitting and detecting the light, these fibers may be used for the transmission of electrical signals.

A different means are freely propagating electro-magnetic waves, such as radio or laser. Sometimes, radio waves are directionally focused, although less so than lasers, and are used to establish point-to-point connections which are functionally similar to the connections established by wires or optical fibers. Often, however, radio waves are broadcast, i.e. may be received at arbitrary places in a large geographical area. This is also true for transmission via satellite radio. The latter is characterized by a transmission delay of about half a second, which is several orders of magnitude larger than the delay through the other transmission media mentioned.

In practice, the characteristics of a transmission medium are strongly dependent on the equipment used to send and receive the signals, and for the intermediate reamplification of the signal. Depending on the techniques used in these equipments, one may distinguish between analogue and digital transmission channels[5].

An analogue channel transmits the continuous variations of the input signal to the output side. Usually only variations within a certain frequency range are transmitted. Typical examples are telephone channels, and so-called "broadband" channels used for television transmissions. For the transmission of digital signals over such channels, different modulation techniques may be used to code the digital signals in terms of continuously varying signals of certain frequencies[6]. For this purpose, modulation and demodulation equipments (called modems) are placed at the sending and receiving sides.

A digital channel distinguishes only two input or output states, namely *zero* and *one*. This restriction simplifies the reception and reamplification of the signal, and leads to lower transmission error rates. A digital channel may be used directly for the transmission of digital signals. Usually a digital channel is inherently either synchronous or asynchronous. With a suitable coding technique, a digital channel may also be used to transmit analogue signals. For example, pulse code modulation (PCM) is used to transmit telephone conversations over digital circuits in many telephone networks. In this case a synchronous channel of 56 K bits per second is sufficient to transmit a voice frequency spectrum of up to 4 KHz. Inversely, the synchronous digital speed that may be obtained over an analogue telephone channel lies typically between 2400 and 9600 K bits per second, depending on the modems and channel quality[7].

6.1.3. Bit synchronization

For the reception of a digital signal (or its reamplification, also called regeneration) it is necessary to know at which instants the signal must be sampled to obtain the information transmitted. One possibility is to transmit the sampling information separately, for instance in the form of "new data signals" (in the case of flow control), or in the form of the sender clock (in the case of a synchronous interface). Over long distances, this approach, however, is not practical. Instead, the receiver usually relies on its own clock which, of course, must run at the same speed as the sender's clock. If it is not properly adjusted transmission errors occur in the form of inserted or lost bits, as shown in figure 6.2.

In the case of synchronous transmission where the sender and receiver clocks must stay synchronized over long periods of time, the receiver cannot rely on a free-running clock alone, but the receiver's clock is continuously adjusted to the sender's clock by observing the transitions of the data signal. This adjustment is only possible as long as sufficient changes occur in the data signal; long strings of either *zeroes* or *ones* may lead to clock desynchronization and cause transmission errors. Therefore this method leads to non-transparency (i.e. certain bit sequences are not allowed as data) unless special precautions are taken (see section 6.2).

This synchronization introduces a kind of master-slave relationship between the clocks of the sender and receiver. This may lead to problems if additional synchronization constraints are imposed on the clocks. For example, in the case of two-way simultaneous (FDX) transmission as indicated in figure 6.3, the sender and receiver at a given station usually use the same clock, which leads to a circular timing dependence. In the case of a synchronous network, as shown in figure 6.4, where the clocks of all nodes must be synchronized, the problems of mutually dependent synchronization relations are usually solved by introducing a

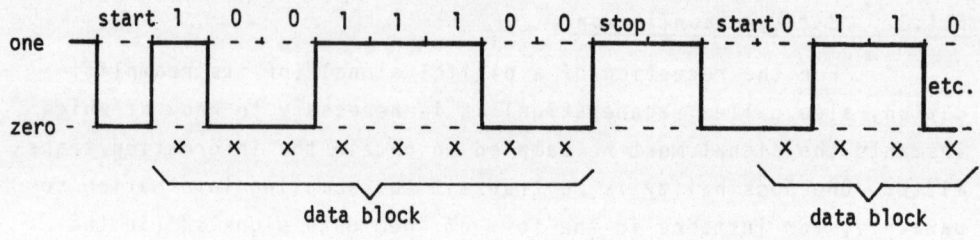

FIGURE 6.1: Timing diagram for asynchronous transmission

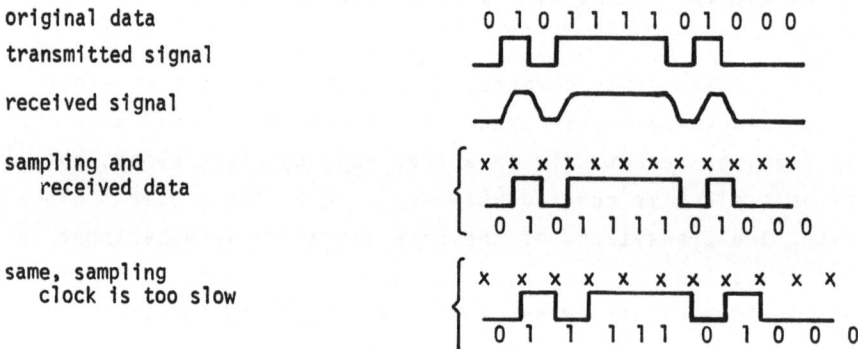

FIGURE 6.2: The importance of clock synchronization

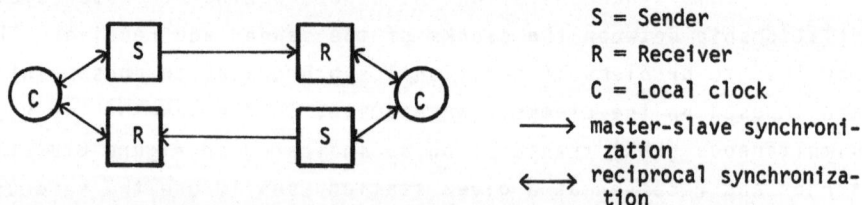

S = Sender
R = Receiver
C = Local clock
⟶ master-slave synchronization
⟷ reciprocal synchronization

FIGURE 6.3: Clock synchronization for two-way simultaneous transmission

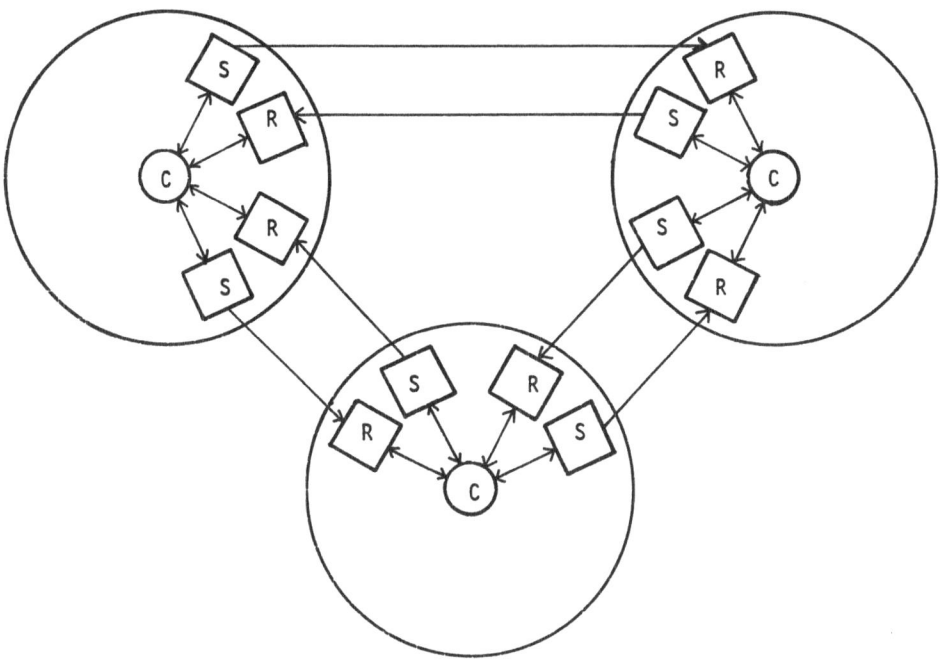

FIGURE 6.4: Clock synchronization in a network

data | 0 1 0 1 1 1 1 1 1 0 0 0 1

bit stuffed data | 0 1 0 1 1 1 1 1 0 1 1 0 0 0 1

transmitted signal | 0 | 1 1 0 0 0 0 0 0 1 1 1 0 1 0 0

FIGURE 6.5: Bit-stuffing

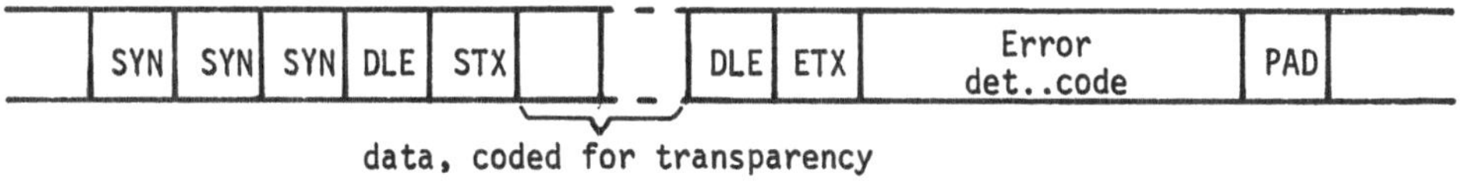

| SYN | SYN | SYN | DLE | STX | | | DLE | ETX | Error det..code | PAD |

data, coded for transparency

FIGURE 6.6: Character-oriented frame format

master clock on which all others depend either directly, or in
a linear chain. If the data processing related to the sender or
receiver is directly coupled (without intermediate buffering) to
the data transmission then the processing, too, must be synchronized to the transmission clock.

Most data processing applications, however, are not directly synchronized with the transmission speed. Instead, their
speed is synchronized through flow control which acts on information frames or packets, as explained below. Therefore the above-
mentioned synchronization problems do not exist in simple packet-
switched networks.

6.2. TRANSPARENCY AND FRAMING

As pointed out above, not all transmission services provide bit sequence transparency (i.e. all possible bit sequences
may be transmitted); though this is an important requirement for
data transmission. Also, the above mentioned services do not indicate where, within the continuous bit sequence of received information, a message starts[8]. For most data transmission applications, it is important to know the block structure of the received
data in order to be able to decode the received information.
Therefore the data is usually structured into "frames" such that

the receiver is able to detect the beginning and end of each
frame. This also has the advantage that a transmission network
may distinguish between the reception of framed data and inter-
frame idle traffic.

The protocols providing transparency and framing, respectively, are usually closely related. In the following, we discuss
three typical methods.

6.2.1. Bit-oriented method

The method described in the following is part of the
HDLC standard, and is sometimes refered to as "bitstuffing".

Bit sequence transparency over physical channels that
do not transmit continuous sequences of *zero* or *one*, is obtained
in two steps. The first step is the bitstuffing, which avoids
continuous bit sequences of *one*. It provides the insertion of an
additional bit of value *zero* into the bit stream after each sequence of five consecutive *ones*. This additional bit is removed at the
receiving side. The second step, avoiding continuous sequences of
zero, applies the so-called NRZI coding to the resulting data
stream. This coding converts a *zero* bit into a change of state of
the transmitted signal, and a *one* bit into a "no-change". An example of the operation of this protocol is shown in figure 6.5.

So-called "flags" are used for framing. A flag is a bit
pattern of 0111 1110 in the bitstuffed data stream, which cannot
be obtained by bitstuffing, since it contains six consecutive *ones*.
Flags mark the beginning and end of a frame, and continuous flags
indicate idle traffic.

This bit-oriented protocol allows for frames of arbitrary length (in bits). It is usually implemented in specialized
hardware, since software implementations would be inefficient.

6.2.2. *Character-oriented method*

The method described in the following exists in a variety of different versions[9]. The basic idea is to reserve one escape character (i.e. *data link escape*, DLE) to indicate that the following character is not part of the data stream, but has a control function. For instance the beginning and end of a frame are indicated by the character sequences DLE STX *(start of text)* and DLE ETX *(end of text)* respectively. Transparency is obtained by inserting, from time to time, a DLE SYN *(synchronization)* sequence into the data stream, which ensures the necessary transitions of the transmitted signal; and a character of the data stream with the value DLE is transmitted as a DLE DLE sequence. The receiver has to perform the corresponding decoding.

The character-oriented method requires not only bit synchronization, as discussed in section 6.1.3, but also character synchronization, i.e. the receiver must know which received bit starts a new character. The character synchronization is obtained by preceding each frame by a sequence of at least two SYN characters; and when the receiver waits for a frame it looks for a SYN bit pattern. Note that the bit pattern of a SYN character is such that, within a sequence of several SYN characters, the only SYN bit pattern that may be found coincides with the original characters.

The complete frame format is shown in figure 6.6. We note that this format foresees two octets outside the data field for the error detecting code (see section 6.3). This means that the format is not cleanly spread between the transparency and framing layer and the error detection layer. The final PAD character is added because some receivers loose the last character of a received block.

6.2.3. *Method based on envelope transmission*

We here assume that the underlying physical transmission service provides transmission of envelopes, i.e. mini-blocks typically of eight bits each. Examples are a start-stop transmission service, or a synchronous service with an additional circuit which provides an envelope alignment signal indicating the beginning of an envelope, or the bits of an envelope may be transmitted in parallel. If transparency is not provided by the physical transmission service, it may be obtained by a scheme such as the character oriented method; or one bit in each envelope may be reserved to introduce an alternating bit value.

Although the physical transmission service delimits the envelopes, it is usually necessary to indicate which envelope begins and ends a frame. Again, either a character-oriented approach may be used, reserving certain envelope values for control functions, or one bit of each envelope may be reserved to indicate the presence of a "flag". We note that for the protocols above the framing level, the method of reserving a certain bit or field within a frame or message is the usual way to transmit control information. This is not possible without an underlying framing structure. In this context, envelopes may be considered as mini-frames.

6.3. TRANSMISSION ERROR DETECTION AND CORRECTION

6.3.1. *Principles*

The origin of errors

Transmission errors are introduced in most physical transmission channels by the statistical fluctuations of the received signal, or by "noise" introduced by switching or other external influences. Statistical fluctuations give rise to an error pattern where the probability, for a given bit of a transmitted sequence, to be erroneous is independent of the other bits in the sequence. This property is called "bit independence"; it implies that for a bit error probability of p, the probability for two consecutive bits to be both in error is of the order of p^2, which is usually much smaller. On the contrary, externally introduced noise often gives rise to burst errors, which are strings of two to ten, or more, bits containing several bit errors. While single bit errors are relatively easy to detect and correct, this is much more difficult for burst errors (see below).

Typical error performances lie between 10^{-4} for analogue telephone channels and 10^{-8} for digital circuits. We note that telephone channels have a strong component of burst errors due to switching noise, while radio transmission channels usually exibit bit independent transmission errors.

Apart from the errors introduced by the physical transmission channel, errors may be introduced within the communication system layers above. For example, transmission errors may be introduced by a malfunction of the transparency and framing hardware discussed above, or by a central memory error in a switching computer.

Error_detection_and_correction

For a given system layer, any of the following approaches may be taken in respect to transmission errors :

(a) Errors are ignored as far as possible. We note, however, that errors in the control information of the layer may lead to apparent protocol errors and desynchronization between the communicating partners.

(b) Errors are detected as far as possible, and reported to the next higher system layer. The higher layer will usually perform an error recovery.

(c) Errors are detected and recovered as far as possible within the same layer.

For the approaches (b) and (c), the performance may be characterized by the overhead introduced on the one hand, and the probability that an error is not detected (for (b)), and that an error

is either not recoverable, or not detected or wrongly recovered
or introduced by the recovery mechanism(for (c)), on the other
hand. In the case of error detection, the probability p that
an undetected transmission error occurs within a given data block
may be calculated as

$$p = \sum_i p_i \cdot q_i$$

where the sum is taken over all types of errors that may occur,
p_i is the probability of an error of type i in the block, and
q_i is the probability that an error of type i is not detected.

Error detecting or correcting codes are used for approaches (b) or (c) respectively. In both cases, redundancy is introduced into the transmitted data which allows the detection or correction of transmission errors by the receiver. Neither types of code require any feedback from the receiver to the sender. However, error detecting codes are usually used in conjunction with a next-higher system layer which applies some kind of retransmission protocol to recover from the error; and this protocol relies on feedback in the form of acknowledgements (see section 6.4.1)[10].

Architectural consideration

The layered structure of a typical communication system architecture is explained in chapter 4. As pointed out, the recovery of transmission errors is typically performed by an error detecting code and a retransmission protocol operating over a dedicated or switched circuit. However, many variations exist.

If the error performance obtained by a standard system structure, characterized by an effective error probability p, as given above, is not sufficient for an application, an additional error recovering system layer may be introduced. The resulting error probability p' is then given by

$$p' = \sum_i p_i \cdot q_i \cdot q_i'$$

where the q_i and q_i' are the probabilities that an error of type i is not detected by the standard and additional layer respectively.

Error correcting codes may be used in situations where retransmission protocols are inefficient, for example in the case of high error probabilities, or long transmission delays, in particular over satellite channels. If introduced in an additional architectural layer below the framing layer, error correcting codes will reduce the probability that frames are lost due to transmission errors, and the number of errors detected in the layers above will be smaller, thus reducing the frequency of retransmissions.

In the case of communication through a network (see for example figure 1.3), many different transmission links are involved; for instance network access lines, links between the network nodes, and possibly front-end to host computer connections. In most cases, transmission errors are recovered separately on each link, as shown by the architecture of figure 6.7 (a). In the case of recovery by retransmission, such step-by-step error recovery is more efficient than end-to-end recovery as shown in figure 6.7 (b)[11]. However, in the case of step-to-step recovery, the effective end-to-end error probability is approximately

$$p = p^{(1)} + q^{(2)} + \ldots + p^{(n)}$$

where the $p^{(i)}$ are the effective error probabilities of the individual links with their respective error recovery mechanisms. It is clear that the end-to-end error performance can never be better than the worst link. In this case, an additional end-to-end error recovery mechanism could be interesting. Usually incorporated in the transport layer, it leads to a lower error probability p', as mentioned above, and also detects (and possibly recovers) eventual malfunctions in all the system layers below the transport layer.

6.3.2. *Error detecting codes*

Most error detecting codes used are block codes, which means that for each block of information a redundant error detecting code is calculated and sent together with the information. A typical frame format is shown in figure 6.8. The receiver calculates the code using the same algorithm, and if the calculated code is not the same as the received one a transmission error must have occured. The most important codes are the following :

(a) Simple parity : A parity bit is added to each information block. A transmission error is detected if and only if an uneven number of bits in the frame are in error. This is not sufficient for most applications.

(b) Longitudinal parity or checksum : In the case of an information block structured into bytes (i.e. octets or central memory words), as shown in figure 6.9, an additional byte is added containing the longitudinal parity (calculated byte-wise), or the higher-order truncated byte sum of the information block. For an arbitrarily erroneous frame, the probability of non-detection is 2^{-r}, where r is the number of bits in a byte. These error codes are particularly suited for software implementation.

(c) Cyclic codes : This is a large class of codes which are based on polynomial division modulo 2. Each cyclic code is characterized by a particular polynome P of order r, and coefficients 0 and 1 . The information block, in turn, is interpreted as a polynome and divided by P . The rest of the division is the code and contains r bits. As in the case above, the non-detection probability for arbitrary errors is 2^{-r}, but with a suitable choice of the polynome P it is possible to obtain codes which detect <u>all</u> errors involving two, or an uneven number of bits, or burst errors with a length smaller or equal to r^{12}. A simple implementation of these codes in specialized hardware is possible.

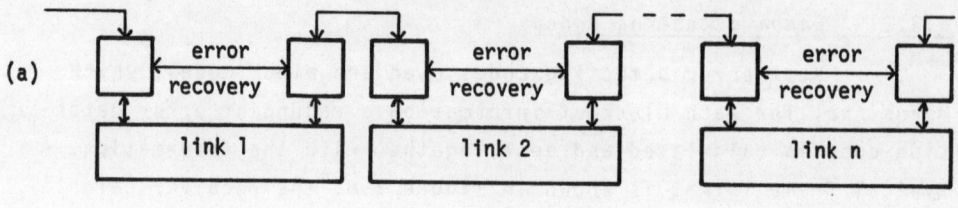

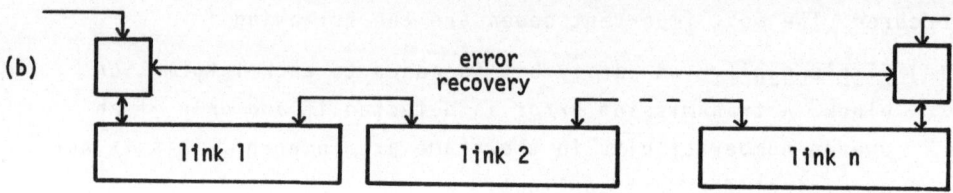

FIGURE 6.7: Step-by-step and end-to-end error recovery

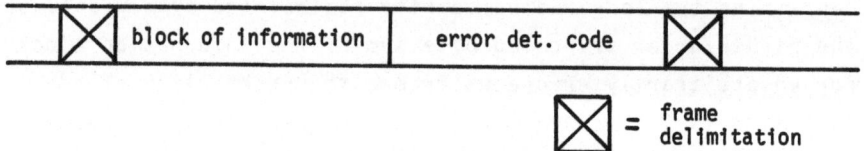

FIGURE 6.8: Typical frame format with error detecting code

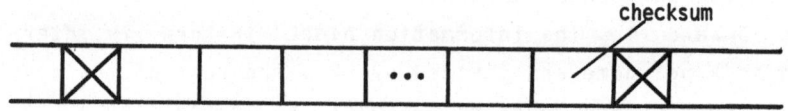

FIGURE 6.9: Frame format including checksum

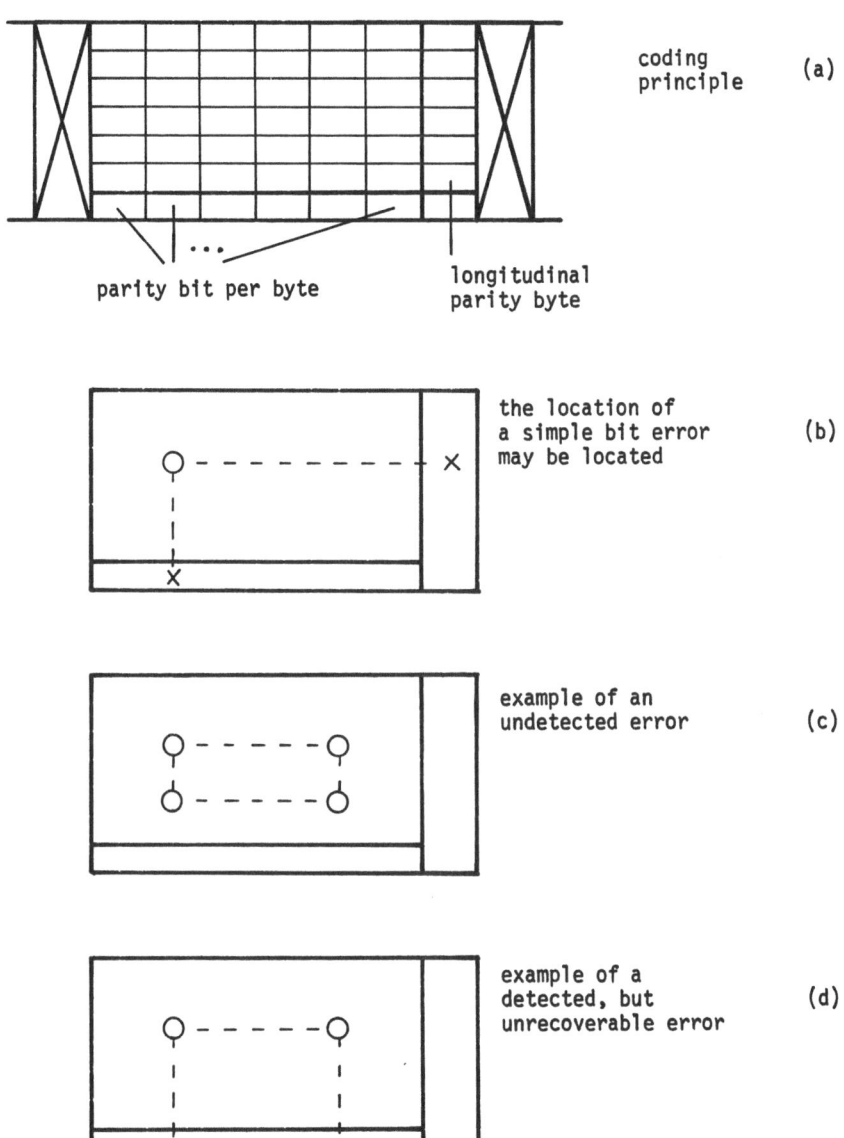

FIGURE 6.10: Error detection and recovery with parity

6.3.3. *Error correcting codes*

Error correcting codes may be block oriented, as the detecting codes discussed above, or evolutionary, which means that they apply to a continuous information bit stream, which is coded as a different bit stream containing redundancy. An example of a simple block oriented correcting code is longitudinal parity used together with simple parity for each byte, as indicated in figure 6.10. As shown in the figure, this code may be used to correct single bit errors, but more complex error configurations are either unrecoverable (but detected), or undetected or wrongly recovered.

For the correction of errors involving more than one erroneous bit, codes have been developed based on large Hamming distances between the different allowed code words, including the redundancy[13]. Evolutionary codes, too, correct any number of bit errors provided they are not too close together[14]. For burst errors involving more than two bits, correcting codes become very complicated. This is the main reason why, in most applications, simple error detecting codes with retransmission protocols are used instead of error correcting codes.

6.4. RETRANSMISSION PROTOCOLS

6.4.1. *Principles*

Retransmission protocols are typically used as line protocols or, as part of a transport layer, over an end-to-end transmission service. They recover transmission errors, as well as loss and out-of-sequence delivery of data blocks by the underlying transmission service. The principle of operation is as follows. Data to be transmitted is partitioned into packets of suitable size, if it is not presented already in this form. The packets are sequentially numbered by the sender and kept in a data buffer until their correct reception at the other side is known to the sender. The packets are transmitted sequentially, together with their number and a transmission error detecting code. The receiver checks the error code

and the sequence number to ensure that the packets are accepted
in the right order and without errors. Via a feedback channel, the
receiver returns acknowledgements, or sends retransmission requests
to the sender if packets are missing or errors are detected. In the
case of data transmission in both directions, this process is duplicated for each direction. Then the feedback information, for transmission, may be associated with the data packets transmitted in the
opposite direction (this is called "piggy-backing").

The procedures described rely on an initialization procedure which establishes agreement, between the sender and receiver,
on the sequence number of the first data packet to be transmitted.
This procedure is also important for restarting data transmission
after a failure. For example, a long term failure of the underlying
transmission service leads to repeated packet loss or transmission
errors. If a given data packet is retransmitted a certain number of
times without success, the situation is usually considered a failure
unrecoverable by the retransmission protocol. This is indicated to
the next higher system layer, and may be followed by a reinitialization of the retransmission protocol.

Many different factors influence the efficiency of a retransmission protocol. The most important aspect is the maximum data
throughput. In the case that data packets are handled one by one
(i.e. protocol of type "alternating bit") the optimal packet size
may be determined from the error probability and transmission overhead (size of framing, error detection and retransmission control
information)[15]. In the case of several outstanding, i.e. non-acknowledged, packets and data transmission in both direction, the
situation is quite complex[16]. The buffer size of the sender is also
an important design consideration. It must be equal to the packet
size times the maximum number of outstanding packets. This, in turn,
is related to the transmission speed and the delay in obtaining
acknowledgements[17]. We note that the number of outstanding packets
is also limited by the number of bits reserved for representing
the sequence numbers in the transmitted frames, because a cyclic
numbering scheme is used. Another design consideration is the

choice between a sequential or selective retransmission strategy. Selective retransmission means that the sender retransmits only those packets for which the receiver detected loss or an error. A simpler strategy, but less efficient when many packets may be outstanding, is sequential retransmission, which implies retransmission of all packets starting from a lost or erroneous packet, and possibly retransmission of some packets that were already successfully transmitted.

Usually, retransmission protocols also provide flow control, i.e. producer-consumer synchronization, for the next-higher system layer. The mechanisms used to provide flow control may be classified as either stop-and-go or credit schemes. In the case of stop-and-go, the sender may send a packet anytime, and may be told by the receiver that it is "not ready", in which case the packet must be retransmitted when the receiver is "ready". This is a very simple scheme, but generates unnecessary traffic. If the protocol operates over a dedicated circuit this extra traffic is not harmful, since the circuit could not be used for any other purpose anyhow. However, if the protocol uses a shared transmission service, such as in the case of several logical links being multiplexed over one circuit, or in the case of end-to-end protocols, this extra traffic decreases the overall system efficiency. In these situations, a credit scheme is preferable, since it generates no extra traffic. The sender may send a data packet only after it has received the necessary credit from the receiver. The receiver would usually allocate the necessary buffer space for the reception when it sends the credits to the sender[18].

The concept of a "window" may be used to describe the packet sequencing and flow control mechanisms[19]. The window of the sender includes the sequence numbers of the outstanding packets, possibly to be retransmitted, and the numbers of additional packets that may be sent according to the flow control rules. The window of the receiver contains those sequence numbers which guarantee, when received, that the accompanying data packet is an expected one and not an outdated version. Both windows must be small enough as to avoid sequencing ambiguities due to the cyclic numbering scheme. A typical situation is shown in figure 6.11.

6.4.2. The "alternating bit" protocol

We call the protocol described below the alternating bit protocol because it uses a single bit to represent the sequence number of a data packet. Although very simple, it shows a robust behaviour in respect to errors of the underlying transmission service, and is one of the earliest protocols described in the literature[20]. It has been used in several networks, and many retransmission protocols in commercial operating systems operate in a similar manner[21].

The protocol uses the underlying transmission service in a two-way alternate mode, and provides reliable data transmission simultaneously in both directions. Each communication station has a *send buffer* containing the next data packet to be transmitted, and a buffer to receive the next data packet from the opposite station. It has in addition an *alternating bit* variable, which indicates the sequence number of the next data packet to be sent. The operation of a single station is shown in figure 6.12. Each frame transmitted contains the alternating bit of the sending station and the contents of the *send buffer*, unless it is empty.

No initialization procedure is given for this protocol. It is assumed that station A starts out in state 1, and the other in state 3 with an empty send buffer, while the initial value of the *alternating bit* variable is *one* in both cases. In the absence of transmission errors, only the fat transitions of figure 6.12 will be executed. A transmission error, detected by some error detecting code in the system layer below, will lead to a retransmission of the last frames in both directions. The loss of a transmitted frame will lead to a deadlock, unless time-out transitions are introduced, as indicated in the figure. It is assumed that these transitions may only be activated in one of the stations, and only after a certain time-out period has elapsed since the transmission of the last frame.

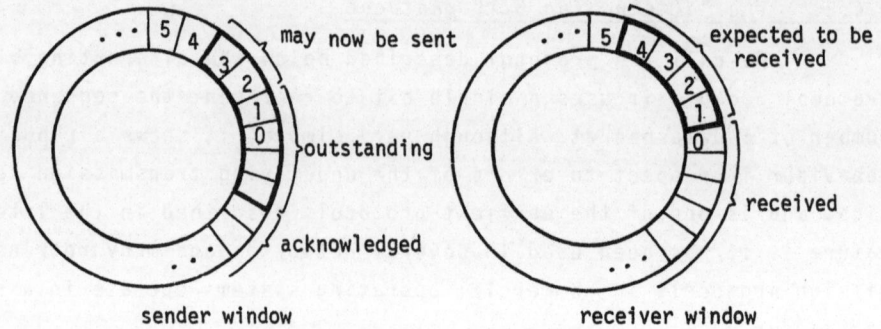

FIGURE 6.11: The "window" concept

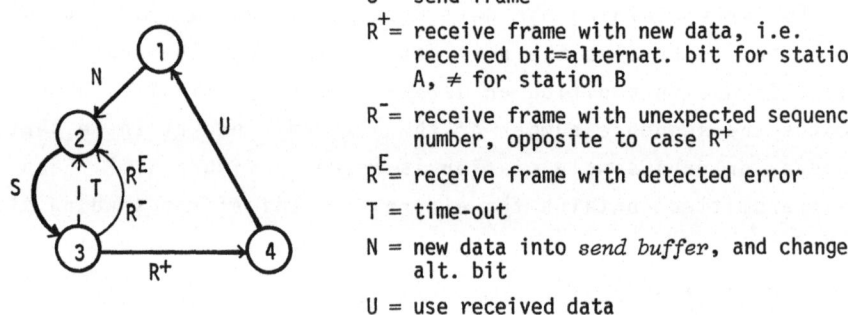

S = send frame

R^+ = receive frame with new data, i.e. received bit=alternat. bit for station A, ≠ for station B

R^- = receive frame with unexpected sequence number, opposite to case R^+

R^E = receive frame with detected error

T = time-out

N = new data into *send buffer*, and change alt. bit

U = use received data

FIGURE 6.12: Transition diagram for an alternating bit protocol station

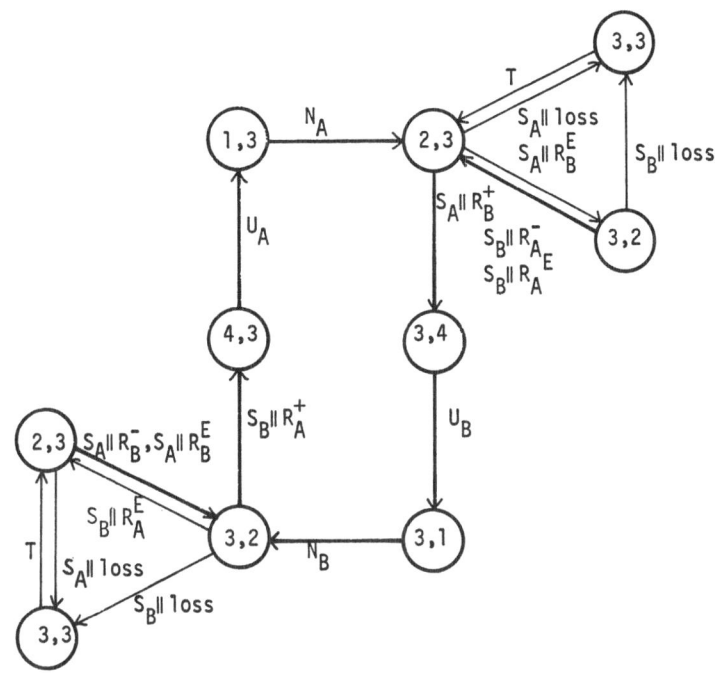

FIGURE 6.13: Overall system states reachable in the alternating bit protocol
(Notation: $S_A \| R_B^+$, for instance, means that station A does the transition S, which is followed by the transition R^+ of station B).

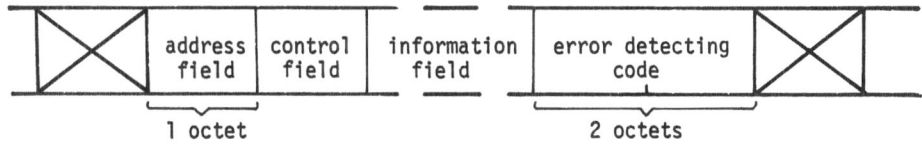

FIGURE 6.14(a): HDLC frame format

	bits	0	1	2	3	4	5	6	7
information (I) frame			N(R)		P/F	N(S)			0
supervisory frame			N(R)		P/F	X	X	0	1
unnumbered frame		X	X	X	P/F	X	X.	1	1

FIGURE 6.14(b): Coding of the HDLC control field

An analysis[22] of the operation of two communicating stations leads to the diagram of figure 6.13. It shows the possible states and transitions of the overall system which are reachable from the initial state. Each state in the diagram is characterized by the states of both stations, and only those states of the overall system for which all transmitted frames have been received (or lost) are considered. The time-out period is assumed to be chosen such that a time-out transition occurs only after a message has actually been lost, i.e. it must be longer than the maximum response time of the other station, including the transmission delays.

The diagram of figure 6.13 demonstrates the correct operation of the protocol. One may see, by inspection, that each state of the overall system has a successor, i.e. there is no deadlock, and except in the case of permanent transmission errors or losses, the operation always leads back to the normal cycle of operation, which is indicated by the fat transitions. The diagram also shows that the order in which the data packets are exchanged with the next-higher system layer are always such that only correctly transmitted packets are delivered, and no duplication or losses may occur.

6.4.3. *The HDLC classes of procedures*

The alternating bit protocol, explained above, provides adequate recovery from transmission errors and losses, but presents several shortcomings. It cannot take advantage of a simultaneous two-way transmission service; it is inefficient when the transmission delay is longer than the time required to transmit a data packet; and there are no proper reinitialization and flow control mechanisms. The HDLC classes of procedures, for example, overcome these problems. The following description is based on the HDLC standard[23], but the same principles of operation may also be found in many other related protocols designed for simultaneous two-way transmission and possible transmission delays.

Basic properties

The following basic properties of the HDLC classes of procedures make them suitable for application in a variety of different situations. The standard specification concentrates on the protocol aspects which are essential for compatibility between different stations, and leaves unspecified many other aspects, which may be chosen for each protocol implementation according to the specific requirements.

In order to cater for a delay between the transmission of a data packet and its acknowledgement, HDLC uses cyclic (modulo 8) sequence numbering. Up to seven data packets may be transmitted without being acknowledged[24]. The acknowledgements are returned in the form of a *receive sequence number* NR which acknowledges all packets up to the number (NR-1). Acknowledging NR numbers may be piggy-backed in the information (I) frames, which transport a data packet in the opposite direction, and are also contained in supervisory frames which are used for retransmission and flow control. The format of the transmitted frames is shown in figure 6.14.

A cyclic error detecting code is included in each frame. A received frame with a detected error is ignored, which is equivalent to being lost. The loss of I frames is recovered as follows. The receiving station keeps a *receive variable* VR which always contains the sequence number of the next data packet to be received; and out-of-sequence received packets are not accepted. If a packet is lost the following packets will not be accepted, and therefore not be acknowledged. After a time-out period, the sending station will sequentially retransmit the packets that have not been acknowledged. As an option, the receiving station may also send a *reject* (REJ) supervisory frame as soon as the reception of an out-of-sequence packet indicates that the previous packet was lost. This accelerates the recovery process, since the sending station may start the retransmission as soon as the REJ is received.

A kind of stop-and-go flow control mechanism is provided by the supervisory frames *receive ready* (RR) and *receive not ready* (RNR), which may be sent by the receiving station.

The three different classes of HDLC procedures, described below, may be distinguished. They are not compatible with one another, but it is possible that a given station be capable of communicating according to several classes.

Unbalanced class with normal response mode (NRM)

This is the simplest HDLC class of procedure. It is called "unbalanced" because one of the communicating stations is considered to be "primary" and has the overall control of the communication link, while the other station is a "secondary" which only "responds" to the "commands" received from the primary.

In normal response mode, the secondary station may only send frames when it is polled by the primary. For this purpose, the primary sets the P-bit of a transmitted frame to *one* (see figure 6.14). When this P-bit is received by the secondary, it may transmit a sequence of frames, where the last frame of the sequence is indicated by a F-bit of value *one*. State diagrams controlling the normal response mode of the primary and secondary stations are shown in figure 6.15, and a typical sequence of exchanged frames is shown in figure 6.16, where it is assumed that the transmission service supports two-way simultaneous transmission, and data transfer takes place in both directions.

Unbalanced class with asynchronous response mode (ARM)

This class is similar to the one described above. However, in asynchronous response mode the secondary, as well as the primary, may send frames at any time.

In this response mode, the P/F-bit may be used by the primary station for "checkpointing", which is a mechanism by which the primary may recognize a particular received frame as being the

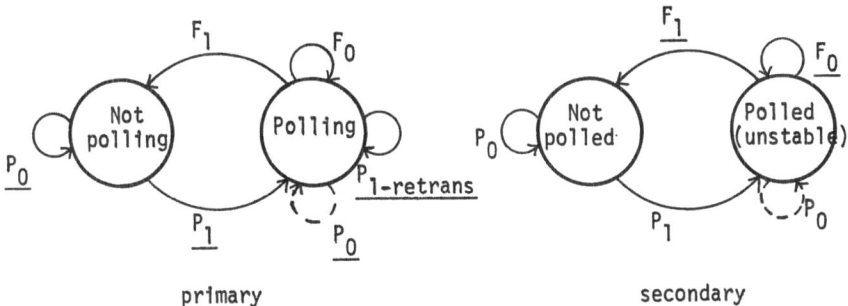

FIGURE 6.15: HDLC normal response mode (Note: Dotted transitions in full duplex transmission only. An unstable state must make a sending transition at the earliest opportunity.

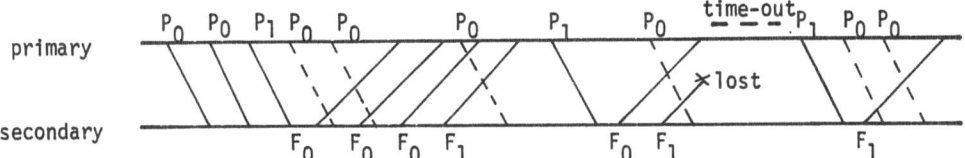

FIGURE 6.16: Example of exchanged HDLC frames in FDX normal response mode

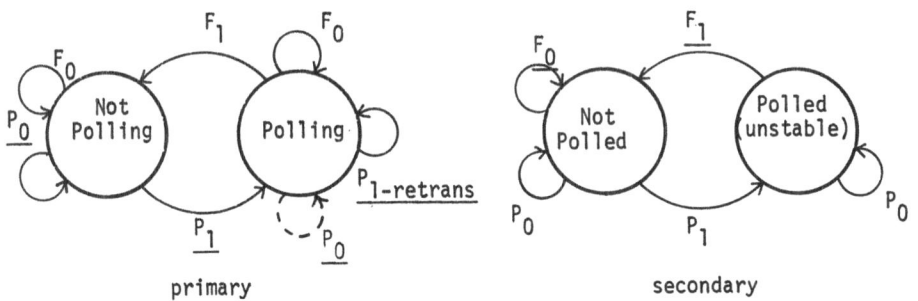

FIGURE 6.17: HDLC asynchronous response mode

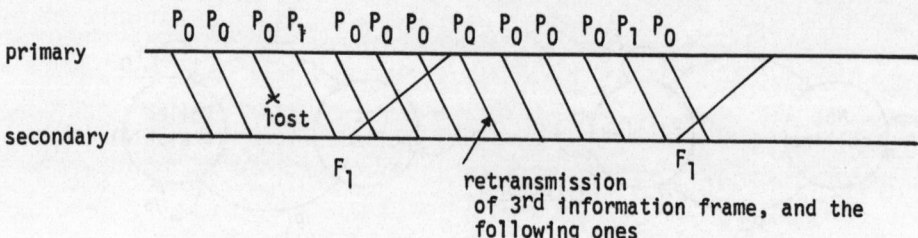

FIGURE 6.18: Example of exchanged HDLC frames in asynchronous response mode.

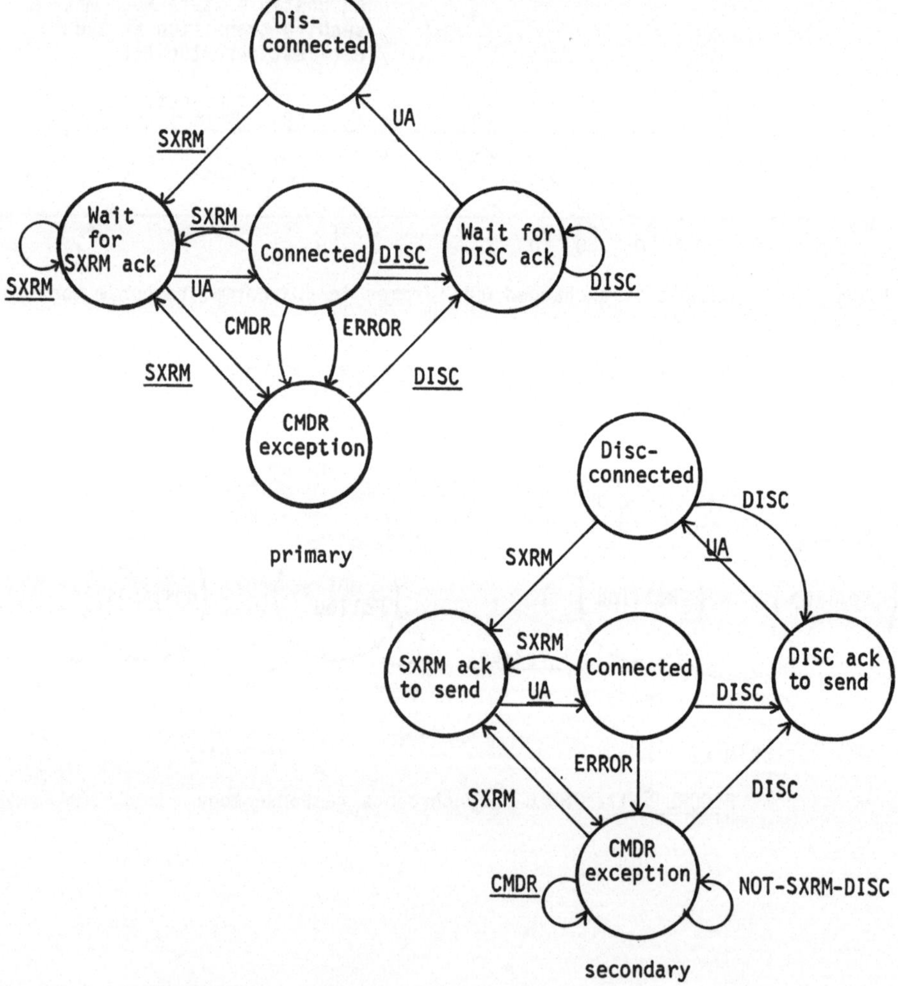

FIGURE 6.19: Unbalanced link set-up procedure (HDLC)

response of the secondary to a particular, previously sent, command
frame. The mechanism is specified by the transition diagrams of
figure 6.17, which require that the secondary, in response to the
reception of a command with the P-bit equal to *one*, immediately
sends a frame with the F-bit equal to *one*. This mechanism may be
used to determine whether, and from which sequence number, retransmission is required, as shown in the example of figure 6.18.

Balanced_class

Two stations communicating according to the balanced class
of procedures have equal responsability for the link. They use the
asynchronous response mode, described above, and each contains some
primary and some secondary functions. The primary function of one
station is responsible for the data transfer to the opposite station,
and for this purpose, communicates with the secondary function on
the other side. To provide the checkpointing function independently
in both directions, it is necessary to distinguish between commands
(sent by a primary) and responses (sent by a secondary). This is
accomplished by using two different station address values (see
figure 6.14).

Procedures_for_link_(re-)initialization_and_disconnection

So far we have considered the data transfer phase. It must
be preceded by the so-called "link set-up" phase, which initializes
the data transfer protocol. The same initialization procedure may
be executed after a procedure error or major transmission failure,
in which case it is called a "link reset". To return to the
"disconnected" link state, a disconnection procedure may be executed.

In the case of the unbalanced classes, these procedures
are initiated by the primary station (for details see figure 6.19),
whereas in the balanced case, both stations may initiate them. The
initiating station may choose the class of procedure to be used
over the link, provided that the chosen class is implemented in
both stations involved.

Additional facilities

Without pretending to give a complete description of the HDLC procedures, we mention below some of the additional functions foreseen :

(a) Error reporting : An exceptional situation that cannot be handled by a station may be reported to the station responsible by a *command* or *frame reject* frame (CMDR or FRMR).

(b) Selective retransmission is foreseen as an optional facility.

(c) A secondary station may deny the link set-up by responding with a DM *(disconnected mode)* frame.

(d) Unnumbered information (UI) frames may be exchanged as an optional facility.

6.4.4. *Multiplexing*

In the context of retransmission protocols, multiplexing means that several logical links, each executing an independent protocol, share the same underlying transmission service. Each frame transmitted belongs to one of these links, which is usually identified by an address field. In the case of HDLC, the first octet of each frame is reserved for the address.

The sharing of the transmission service is managed by multiplexing and demultiplexing units, as indicated in figure 6.20. The multiplexing unit selects the logical link which obtains the right to transmit the next frame to the other side and transmits the frame after adding the correct address. It may take into account the states of the different links and distinguish different priorities for deciding the order of transmission. The demultiplexing unit simply reads the address field, and forwards the frame to the corresponding protocol handler.

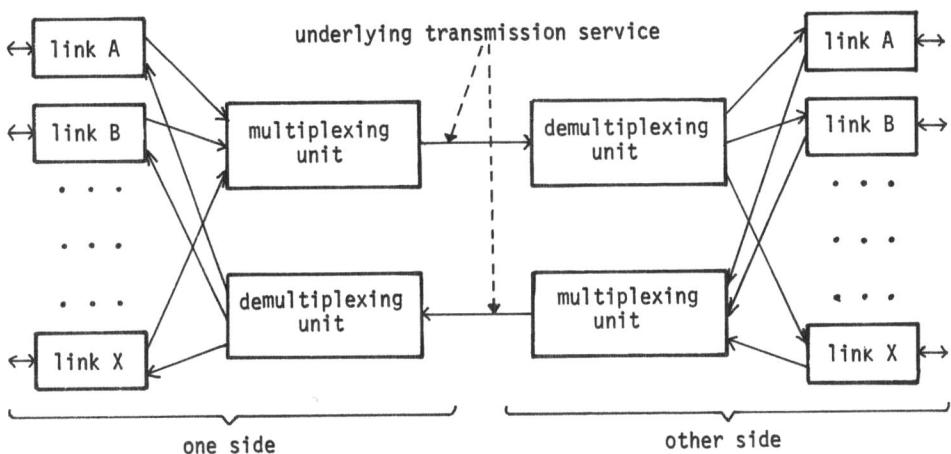

FIGURE 6.20: Multiplexing of several logical links over one transmission service

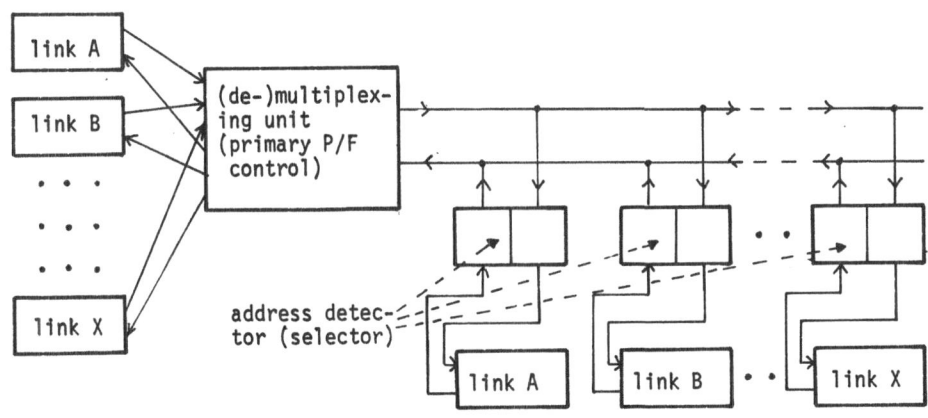

FIGURE 6.21: Multi-point configuration

So far we have assumed that a multiplexing unit on each side of the underlying transmission service determines the order in which the different logical links may transmit frames. Apart from this possible restriction in the speed of execution, the protocols involved operate independently of one another.

In the case of multi-point configurations, as shown in figure 6.21, this assumption is not true. Usually, there is one central station to which all logical links connect. At this station is not only a multiplexing unit which determines the order in which frames may be sent _from_ that station, but this station also centrally determines the order in which frames may be sent _to_ that station by the other connected stations. In HDLC, for this purpose, the normal response mode is used over all links involved such that the central station contains the primaries. Then the transmission of frames _to_ the central station is coordinated by polling the other stations in an appropriate order. To avoid collision conflicts, only one secondary station of a single link may be polled at any given time.

FOOTNOTES

1. See for example [Metc 76] or [IEEE 82].

2. In a local context, small data blocks (for instance octets or memory words) are often presented in parallel, and separate circuits are used for signalling flow control or clock pulses. A standard interface of this kind is described in [Knob 75]. Other examples are the bus interfaces used within a computer system.

3. The following description is based on the X.20 interface standard for based circuits; also RS-232-C, including the new electrical characteristics of RS-423 or RS-422.

4. The following is a description of the X.21 standard interface circuits; also RS-232-C.

5. For more information about different transmission media and communication techniques see for example [Mart 69].

6. The principal techniqués use an analogue carrier with phase-shift, frequency or amplitude modulation. More about modulation techniques for data transmission over analogue channels may be found in [Mart 69] or [Mart 72].

7. The technology of digital channels is relatively young, compared to analogue communication technology. At present, digital channels have many advantages over analogue ones, especially in relation to data communications and switching (electro-mecanical switching centers in telephone networks are being replaced by electronic ones).

8. This is also the case for character stream interfaces to virtual circuits, as provided by a packet assembly and disassembly (PAD) service for asynchronous terminals (see for example [Davi 79], chapter 8, or CCITT Recommendations X.3 and X.28).

9. The version used in IBM's BSC protocol has become a kind of de-facto standard. The following description is based on the character-oriented frame format used in [DATAPAC].

10. Error correcting codes are particularly useful over satellite links where retransmission is inefficient because of the large transmission delay. A comparison of error correcting codes and error correction by retransmission is, for example, given in [Burt 72].

11. In the case of end-to-end recovery the delay for obtaining acknowledgements or retransmission requests are higher. The effect on the average transmission delay for frames is negligeable if retransmissions are rare. However, there is also an effect on the buffer space required (see footnote 17).

12. For more details, see for example [Mart 70].

13. A similar code is used in certain LSI memories to correct more frequent storage errors.

14. For more details see for example [Gall 68].

15. See for example [Mart 72].

16. Many analysis of protocol efficiency involve simulation studies. (See for example [Dant 75], or [Lela 78]). But analytical techniques based on Markov models and queuing analysis give also some useful results. (See for example [Masu 78], or [Wang 82].

17. The average number of outstanding frames is equal to 2 x D x N, where D is the average transmission delay for packets between the two subsystems, and N is the average number of packets sent per unit time, if we assume that the acknowledgements are returned in packets which are sent immediately.

18. We note that the credit scheme has another advantage over the stop-and-go scheme, namely that it operates over a transmission service which does not guarantee frame sequencing. This is important for end-to-end protocols using a datagram transmission service (see chapter 5),

and for multi-circuit link protocols which use several alternative circuits as transmission service in order to increase the reliability and availability of the logical link [Chun 79], [Jame 78].

19. See for example [Cerf 74].

20. See [Bart 69].

21. The best known example is IBM's BSC protocol used for remote job entry.

22. For more details see [Boch 77] or [Boch 78].

23. See for example [Carl 80]. A more algorithmic, formalized specification is given in [Boch 77 b].

24. Over transmission services with especially long delays, an extended numbering cycle (modulo 128) may be used.

7. Technological Developments and Standards

Due to the advances in the micro-electronic technology, the cost of hardware is drastically decreasing for data processing and communication devices. It is interesting to note that the hardware cost goes down appreciably faster for data processing components, such as memories and processors, than for data communications equipment. This development, therefore, favors future systems which perform data processing at the locations where the data is collected, stored or needed, thus reducing the amount of data transmitted. In most cases these systems will be distributed.

As the hardware costs decrease, more and more system functions will be "realized in hardware" instead of being "programmed in software". The development of specialized hardware may become a discipline similar to the development of system software. The distinction between hardware and software will be become of less importance.

It is important to note that the overall cost of data processing systems will be determined mainly by the cost for designing the hardware and software, which remains essentially constant in time, while the cost for hardware will become relatively small. Therefore it will be very important, and it is already so now, to reduce the amount of design work to be done for any new data processing system.

Modular design, advocated by software engineering approaches such as structured programming, top-down design etc., seems to be necessary for building larger systems in order to avoid a kind of exponential increase of the required design effort. However, it does not reduce the effort needed for designing a given simple module. The only way to reduce this effort seems to be the use of a module which is already built and satisfies the design requirements.

In order to avoid "inventing the wheel" again and again, it is necessary to build software libraries which contain programs of modules which provide frequently-needed functions. To make these modules usable the service provided by each module must be precisely defined, as well as their interface with other modules. It would be useful to develop standards for the most widely used service modules.

The possible reduction of the design effort for new systems is not the only reason for developing standards. The need for interworking between different systems is another important reason. The development of standards for data communication has the main objective of providing a meaningful exchange of data between different systems without requiring ad hoc adaptations between each pair of systems.

The present situation of communication standards is such that reasonable international standards exist for physical interfaces, line protocols and certain network access protocols[1], while higher level protocol standards are still being developed. A "Reference Model for Open Systems Interconnection" has been established[2] and provides a framework in which these existing and new protocol standards can be developed. We believe firmly that the adoption of reasonable standards for all functions commonly found in distributed computer system is very important for the present and future applications of these systems[3].

FOOTNOTES

1. A progress report on data communication standard developments may be found in [Gree 82] and [OSI 83].

2. See section 4.2.4.

3. Some arguments may be found in [Sand 76] and [Boch 77 c].

Part III
Formal Description Techniques

The chapters VIII through X deal with specification issues. Chapter VIII explains the different usages for protocol and service specifications during the design and implementation of a distributed system. No particular specification technique is assumed. In chapter IX, a formal model for system description, based on the concepts of system states and transitions is explained from a more theoretical point of view, and applications to many different simple examples are described. This model captures the parallel processing which is possible in a distributed system. Chapter X deals with a formal description technique based on an extended state transition model similar to one being developed for the formal specification of OSI protocols. The basic concepts of the description technique are explained, and it is applied to the specification of a simplified transport service and protocol.

8. Role of Specifications in the Design of Distributed Systems

The design and implementation of communication software has much the same problems as any software development project. However, certain points make communication software a special case:

(a) Compatibility between different, sometimes heterogeneous system components must be ensured.

(b) Often the different components of the system are implemented by different groups of people in different organizations.

(c) The overall behavior of the system is difficult to understand due to the parallel operations in the different system components.

These points show the importance of precise specifications for the different components of the system, and the verification of their correct behavior. While for non-distributed software each system layer or component is usually first defined by a specification and then implemented, the situation is more complex in the case of distributed software or protocols. This is shown in figure 8.1, and explained in more detail in section 8.1. Essentially, there are two levels of specification for a protocol layer, namely the "service specification" which specifies the overall behavior of the subsystem of level n shown in the figure, and the "protocol specification", which defines the behavior of the component of a local subsystem corresponding to the given layer, also called "entity". The entities within the same layer (usually at different locations) cooperate with one another for providing the specified service.

During the life cycle of a protocol, a precise specification must be given for many purposes. Early descriptions provide a reference for cooperation among designers of different parts of a distributed system. The design must be checked for

logical consistency. Then the protocol is implemented. If the
protocol is in wide use, as in the case of a protocol standard,
many different implementations may have to be checked for
compliance with the protocol specification. Although narrative
descriptions and informal walk-throughs are invaluable elements of
this process, painful experience has shown that by themselves they
are inadequate.

As in the case of general software development, the sole
use of natural language for system specification presents many
problems. While it gives the illusion of being easily understood,
it leads to lengthy informal descriptions which often contain
ambiguities and are difficult to check for completeness and
consistency. Therefore, it is generally believed that formalized
specification techniques should be used during the design of
protocols to aid in the validation and implementation efforts.

In summary, a protocol specification serves as a
reference for many different activities, including

(a) the validation of the design,
(b) the development of an implementation, and
(c) the assessment of an implementation for compliance with the
specification.

These different usages of specifications are discussed in more
detail below.

8.1 *SPECIFICATION OF DIFFERENT SCOPE AND DETAIL*

The broad meaning of the term specification is any
information that helps describe the object being specified.
However, its proper usage in engineering is much narrower,
involving the key concept "abstraction". A specification should
state all the requirements that an object must satisfy, <u>and no
more</u>. To be abstract, it must separate the essential from the
unessential, covering the former, and omitting the latter.

As explained in section 2.3, system descriptions at different levels of abstraction may exist. In the engineering sense, the "specification" of a system or subsystem is the most abstract description defining the requirements. In the context of a layered protocol architecture, as explained in chapter 4, the following classes of specifications must be considered. Some examples are given in chapter 10 and the annexes 1 and 2.

8.1.1 *The "Reference Model"*

At this level of detail a distinction is made between different components within the system. The general role of each component is (informally) stated. The interactions between the components are defined as far as the interconnection structure is concerned, that is which component interacts with which other component. This level of description is rather incomplete; however, it defines the internal structure of the overall system in terms of components (i.e. layers, entities, etc.) as for example shown in figures 4.2 and 4.3. These components, in term, are the object of specifications at more detailed levels.

8.1.2 *Service specifications*

The service specification for the (N)-layer of a system defines the behavior of the system component, called "subsystem level n" in figure 8.1, which consists of the entities in the (N)-layer and the layers below. It specifies (a) the possible types of interactions (also called "service primitives") of the component and (b) the possible execution orders for these interactions. The specification defines the communication service provided to the "users".

In the case of a transport service, for example, some basic service primitives are *connect, disconnect, send,* and *receive*. The execution of a service primitive involves two system components, the service providing and the service using entities in layers N and N+1, respectively. Such an execution is associated with the exchange of parameter values between these two

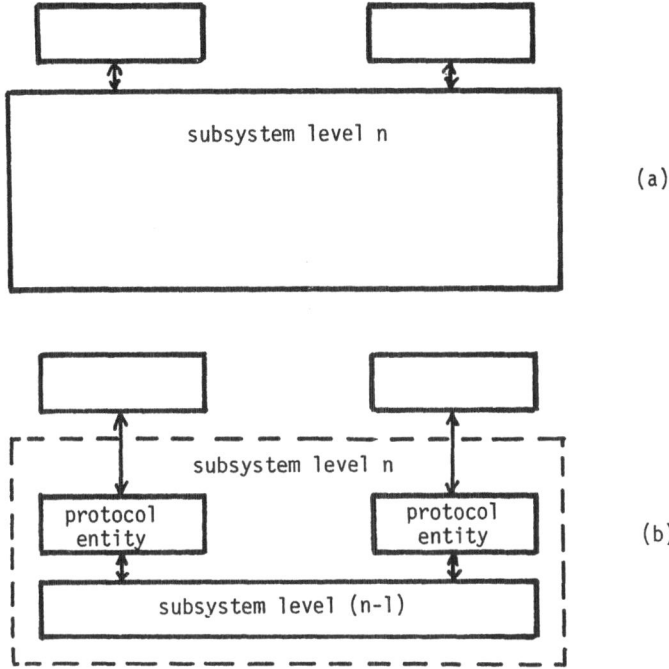

FIGURE 8.1: Component structure of a communication subsystem at different levels of detail:
(a) Service specification
(b) Protocol specification

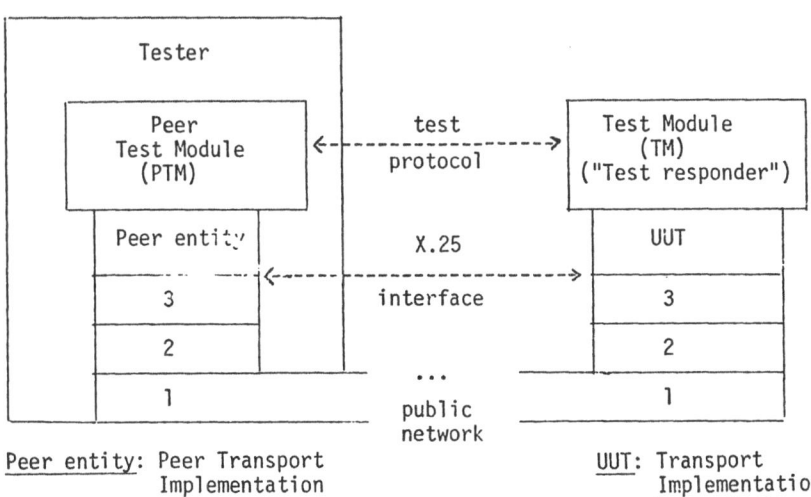

FIGURE 8.2: Test architecture for remote protocol implementation assessment: testing a transport protocol implementation

entities. The possible parameter values and the direction of transfer must be defined for each parameter. Clearly, the service primitives should not be executed in an arbitrary order and with arbitrary parameter values (within the range of possible values). At any given moment, the allowed primitives and parameter values depend on the preceding history of interactions. The service specification must reflect these rules by defining the allowed sequences of interactions directly, or by refering to a "state" of the service which, in turn, may be changed as a result of an interaction.

Usually, a service primitive is associated with a "service access point" which is the interface where it can be invoked. It is important to note that a given service specification includes certain rules about the execution order of service primitives at each given service access point, independently of the execution of primitives at other access points. These rules, including the definition of the possible interactions at the access point, can be considered a specification of an "abstract interface", since it defines those interaction possibilities that must be realized by any interface that implements the access point. These rules are sometimes called "local rules" since they refer to a single local access point.

In addition, a service specification also includes so-called "global rules", which relate interactions at different access points, and define the end-to-end properties of the communication service. Considering again the example of a transport service, a local rule is the fact that *send* and *receive* interactions may only be executed at a given access point after a successful *connect*. An example of a global rule is the fact that the message parameter of the i-th *receive* on one side is equal to the message parameter of the i-th *send* on the other side.

Last but not least, the required or expected quantitative properties of the service must be specified. This aspect includes information on throughput, delay, as well as probabilities for certain malfunctions, such as undetected errors, failures to establish a connection, or disconnections initiated by the service[1].

8.1.3 *Protocol Specifications*

Although irrelevant to the user, the protocol designer must be concerned with the internal structure of a protocol layer. In a distributed environment with physically separated users, a protocol layer must be implemented in a distributed fashion, with entities local to each user. These entities communicate with one another via the service of the lower layer, as shown in figure 8.1. A specification of the entities defines the rules for the interactions between the entities, and the way the entities provide the communication service to the users. Such a specification is called a "protocol specification"[2]. Hence a protocol specification must describe the operation of each entity within a layer in response to commands from its users, messages from the other entities (also called "protocol data units" (PDU), received via the lower layer service), control interactions from the layer below, and internally initiated actions (e.g. time-outs).

As in the case of a service specification, this involves the specification of (a) the possible interactions of each entity and (b) the possible orders of execution of these interactions. The protocol specification may leave certain details of the behavior unspecified if these details are not relevant for the compatibility of the communicating entities. It is, however, often not easy to decide how much detail is needed.

8.1.4 *Implementation specifications*

These are descriptions similar to protocol specifications, but they give more details about the specified entity. Additional details may include:

(a) certain aspects of the behavior of an entity left unspecified in the protocol specification,

(b) certain aspects of the internal structure of an entity (a protocol specification, ideally, does not define the internal structure of the entity),

(c) certain details about the interface to be used for the implementation of the service access points for the layer in question or the layer below (i.e. details not defined by the "abstract interface" implied by the service specification), and sometimes

(d) an algorithm or program implementing the rules of the protocol.

As indicated by the last point, such a specification may in fact come close to the definition of a complete implementation.

8.2 *SYSTEM DESIGN VALIDATION*

In its broadest interpretation, system validation aims to assure that a system satisfies its design specifications and (hopefully) operates to the satisfaction of its users. Validation activity is important during all design phases, and may include checking the logical consistency of the design (often called "verification"), simulation studies, analytical performance predictions, and testing of the final system implementation. Many of these activities, such as performance predictions are based on the system specifications, and may be done during the design phase before any system implementation exists, in order to avoid possible design errors. While testing and simulation techniques only validate the system for certain test situations, verification techniques allow, in principle, the consideration of all possibly situations that the system may encounter during actual operation.

Considering a given protocol layer as shown in figure 8.1 and recalling that specifications are given for the communication services of layers N and (N-1), and for protocol entities of layer N, one may conclude that consistency checking can be applied to the following two problems:

a) *Protocol validation* is the analysis of the behavior of the commuticating entities of the (N)-layer, based on their specification (i.e. the protocol specification) and the specification of the service provided by the (N-1)-layer, in order to determine that the service provided by the entities satisfies the (N)-layer service specification. If this is not the case, the problem may rest either in the protocol, or in the service provided by the layer below.

b) *Protocol implementation assessment* is the analysis of the implementation of an entity in order to assure that it satisfies the protocol specification.

Protocol validation, sometimes called "protocol design validation", is discussed shortly below. It involves the analysis of a distributed system of concurrent processes (entities). Implementation assessment on the other hand, involves only one entity at a time and is similar to the problem of "ordinary" software validation, where an implementation is compared with its specification. This problem is considered in section 8.3. Note that, for a given protocol, the design validation is only made once, while each implementation of the protocol must be validated against its specification.

The service specification itself cannot be validated, but rather forms the standards against which the protocol is compared. However, it may be checked for internal consistency. The designer must make sure that it reflects the user's desires, and provides an adequate basis for the higher system layers which use it. Unfortunately, techniques to achieve these goals are not well understood.

Protocol validation is a case of checking the consistency of a more refined system specification (of the N-entities and (N-1)-service) with a more abstract specification (of the N-service). It includes showing that (a) all actually occuring interactions satisfy the constraints of the (N)-layer service specification (also called "partial correctness" or "safeness"), and (b) the system is live (in particular, there are no deadlocks). Different validation techniques may be used, such as executing the protocol specification or an implementation and testing its behavior, making simulations, or applying various verification techniques[3]. Performance issues must also be considered for protocol validation. Typical techniques used for this purpose are analytic performance predictions, simulations, and measurements on protocol implementations.

It is important to note that certain general properties of a protocol, such as absence of deadlocks or the completeness of the specification with respect to the possible PDU's received from the peer entity, can be checked without reference to the N-service specification. Such an analysis may be based on a partial protocol specification considering only the interactions with the peer entity through the (N-1)-service of the layer below[2]. However, such a partial protocol is not sufficient for checking the consistency between the different layers of a protocol hierarchy. This consistency requires a complete protocol validation which relates the N-layer service to the N-layer protocol and the service of the layer below.

8.3 *PROTOCOL IMPLEMENTATION ASSESSMENT*

As mentioned above, the purpose of protocol implementation assessment is to show that a given system component, which implements a particular protocol, satisfies the requirements of the protocol specification. Then, the assessment of two system components implementing a (N)-layer protocol, together with the validation of the protocol itself, ensure that the components provide the (N)-layer communication service (assuming that the (N-1)-layer communication service used by the protocol is correctly implemented). Protocol implementation assessment is applied in a variety of situations ranging from debugging newly developed communication software to certification of a finished product. The term "certification" is used in cases where some official organization certifies that a given protocol implementation has been validated against the protocol standard.

The main method for implementation assessment seems to be testing, where the behavior of the component under test is observed at the lower and upper layer interfaces. A typical test configuration is shown in figure 8.2, where the Tester may communicate over distance with the component under test through a network. The situation is related to the traditional testing of software modules[4]. Assessment methods related to simulation and program verification may also be used.

In the case of lower-level protocols, including X.25, the interactions of the protocol have mainly a "local" significance since they are usually used to access some data transmission network. The validation of a new implementation is usually made in respect to a given network, and the objective is that the implementation be able to access the network in a satisfactory manner. Therefore slightly different interpretation of an international standard (as defined by different networks) can be tolerated as long as all parties concerned, within the range of the given network, are willing to adapt to the particular interpretation.

In the case of the higher-level OSI protocols, the interactions take place between arbitrary Open Systems. Therefore particular interpretations are only permitted as long as all interpretations (in the entire "universe") of a given protocol standard are compatible. It must be assumed (and demonstrated by the protocol design validation) that any protocol implementation satisfying the requirements of the protocol specification is compatible with any other such implementation. Therefore the validation of protocol implementations for higher-level protocols must be done in respect to the protocol specification.

Plans for instituting "certification centers" for OSI protocols exists in several countries[5]. Different approaches may be considered for the certification of an Open System for its conformance with OSI protocol standards. The validation can be made most complete when the system provides access to the interfaces between the different protocol layers, such that effectively, each layer of the system to be validated may be tested separately. It is also possible to make some overall tests involving many layers at once, for example from the Transport layer up through the Presentation layer using the lower-level network access protocols and the application interface provided by the Presentation service as "access points" to the component under test.

8.4 PROTOCOL IMPLEMENTATION

As mentioned in section 8.1.4, a protocol implementation is a refinement of the protocol specification. The main aspects that must be defined during this refinement step relate to (a) the upper and lower layer interfaces through which the implemented component interacts with the user, and the underlying transmission service, respectively, (b) the buffer management, and (c) the relative priority of different actions that are allowed according to the protocol specification, such as flow control, acknowledgments, multiplexing priorities, etc.

Particular interface problems arise in the following two cases:

a) The incorporation of new communication protocols into an existing operating system is a very delicate problem. These problems must be solved for the host computers that participate in a heterogeneous computer network. In most cases, the user cannot count on much help from the computer manufacturer. Different solutions to the interworking of host operating systems with standard network protocols (network access, as well as higher level protocols) are described in the literature[6].

b) The different protocol layers in one local subsystem may be implemented on separate micro-processors with their own memory[7].

The implementation process can be simplified by using tools that derive more or less automatically an implementation, or parts thereof, from a formal specification of the protocol or an implementation specification. Many formal description techniques either support direct execution, usually in an inefficient emulation mode, or allow semi-automatic implementation by relatively straight-forward transformation from the formal description into an implementation in terms of a high-level programming language. Such a transformation is usually simplified if the programming language supports the definition of data structures (as in Pascal, for example), abstract data types, parallel processes, and the specification of the physical representation of data structures in memory[8]. As an example, the development of an X.25 implementation from a formal specification is described in Annex 2.

FOOTNOTES

1. A more detailed discussion of the performance parameters for the Transport service and their relation to the protocol is given in [Ragu 82].

2. Sometimes the term "protocol specification" is used in a different sense, including only the definition of the rules for the interactions between the entities, independent of the provided service.

3. A review of protocol specification and verification techniques may be found in [Boch 80b]; see also [Suns 81], [INWG 82]. Some examples of different specification and verification techniques for protocols may be found in [Boch 78], [Rudi 78], [Sten 76], [Boch 77], [Bert 82], [Hail 80], and [Schw 82]. Testing approaches based on the execution of protocol specifications are reported in [Lela 78] and [Jard 81,82]. Similar approaches have been used for performance simulation [Lela 78], [Didi 82]. Certain general techniques for software specification, verification and testing are also relevant for protocols.

4. Typical approaches to protocol implementation assessment are discussed in [Rayn 82]. Issues of test sequence selection are discussed in [Boch 82] and [Sari 82].

5. See for example [Rayn 82].

6. See for example [Davi 77] or [Depa 76].

7. Experiences with this approach are described in [Barb 78] and [Cave 78].

8. Hand translation from a formal specification into a Concurrent Pascal implementation is discussed in [Boch 79b] (see also Annex 2). Semi-automatic translations of formal protocol specifications are reported in [Blum 82] and [Gagn 82].

9. A State Transition Formalism for the Description of Systems

This chapter presents a general formalism for the description of systems with parallelism[1]. The basic notions of parallel systems are defined in terms of this general model. A number of different system description methods are related to this general model, as discussed in section 9.9. This chapter makes abstraction of any physical fragmentation of the system into several components. For the major part of the chapter, the notion of parallel processes is irrelevant, only quasi-parallel state transitions are considered.

9.1. THE BASIC MODEL

9.1.1. *Transition systems*

The system to be described is characterized by a (usually infinite) set of possible states Q. At any given time, the system is in a particular state $q \in Q$. The system may effect a transition. We write $q \longrightarrow q'$ to indicate that the system may make a transition from state q to state q', and say that q' is "directly accessible" from q. A transition is considered instantaneous and atomic (however see section 9.1.3). Being in a state q, the system may select, after some finite time, any transition that is possible from q, for execution. Generally this freedom introduces non-determinism into the system behavior.

Definition : A system is "deterministic" iff for each $q \in Q$, there is at most one q' such that $q \longrightarrow q'$. Otherwise the system is "non-deterministic".

An example of a non-deterministic system is shown in figure 9.1.

9.1.2. *Operations*

There is a set O of operation symbols. A transition $q \longrightarrow q'$ may be labelled with an operation symbol $o \in O$, which is written $q \overset{o}{\longrightarrow} q'$. The unlabelled transitions of the system may be written as $q \overset{\lambda}{\longrightarrow} q'$.

Definition : An operation $o \in O$ is "enabled" in state $q \in Q$ iff there is a state q' such that $q \overset{o}{\longrightarrow} p'$.

Definition : An operation is "functional" iff for each $q \in Q$ there exists <u>at most one</u> q' such that $q \overset{o}{\longrightarrow} q'$. For a functional operation $o \in O$, the following entities are defined :

- The "enabling predicate" $P_o : Q \longrightarrow boolean$ is a boolean predicate on the states of the system, which indicates whether the operation is enabled in a given state or not.
- The "transition function" $F_o : Q \longrightarrow Q$ is a partial function on Q which is defined for those states where P_o is *true* (the operation is enabled) and indicates the new state of the system.

An example of a non-deterministic system with two functional operations is shown in figure 9.2.

9.1.3. *Transitions and relations between states*

The set of all transitions of the system can be considered a relation on $Q \times Q$, which we write $\longrightarrow$. Clearly, any pair (q,q') is an element of this relation, $(q,q') \in \longrightarrow$, iff $q \longrightarrow q'$. Similarly, each operation $o \in O$ is associated with a relation, written $\overset{o}{\longrightarrow}$ or simply o, which is defined by

$$(q,q') \in \overset{o}{\longrightarrow} \text{ iff } q \overset{o}{\longrightarrow} q'.$$

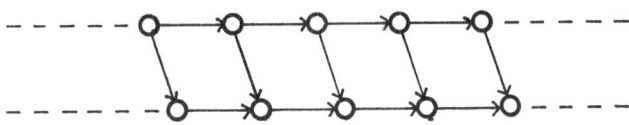

FIGURE 9.1

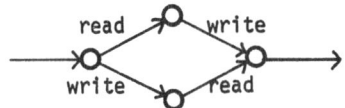

procedure outin;
    cobegin
        write (output,Y);
        read (input, X);
    coend;

FIGURE 9.2

FIGURE 9.3

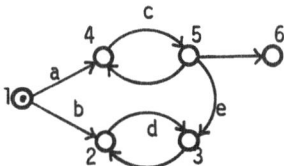

FIGURE 9.4

We write $o_1 \cdot o_2$ for the relation corresponding to the sequential execution of the operations o_1 and o_2, i.e. $q \xrightarrow{o_1 \cdot o_2} q'$ iff there is a q'' such that $(q,q'') \in \xrightarrow{o_1}$ and $(q'',q') \in \xrightarrow{o_2}$, i.e. $q \xrightarrow{o_1} q'' \xrightarrow{o_2} q'$. Similarly, we write $o_1 \cdot o_2 \ldots o_n$ for the relation corresponding to the sequential execution of n operations $o_1, \ldots, o_n$.

Figure 9.3 shows a particular labelling of the transition diagram of figure 9.1 with the operations o_1 and o_2, and indicates the pairs of the relation $o_1 \cdot o_2$. We note that a composite relation may be completely empty, although the components are not. An example is the following transition system:

$$Q = integer \times integer \ ;$$

the operations are o_1 and o_2, both functional:

$$P_{o_1} \equiv true \ ; \ F_{o_1}(x,y) = (0,y) \ ;$$
$$P_{o_2}(x,y) \equiv (x \neq 0) \ ; \ F_{o_2}(x,y) = (x, y \ div \ x) \ .$$

The relation $o_1 \cdot o_2$ is empty. A more familiar notation is the following: We consider a state space characterized by two integer variables X and Y, and two statements "X:=0" and "Y:=Y/X". Their sequential execution results in an undefined result (division by zero results in an exception condition). In the following sections, a notation such as

$$o_1 : x:=0 \ ,$$
$$o_2 : y:=y \ div \ x$$

will sometimes be used.

In the presence of unlabelled transitions in the system, it is sometimes useful to consider the relations generated by operations preceded or followed by unlabelled transitions. We call these relations generalized operations, and write $\hat{o}$ for the relation corresponding to the execution of an operation $o \in O$ preceded and followed by zero, one or more unlabelled transitions, i.e.

$(q,q') \in \delta$ iff $q \xrightarrow{o} q'$

or $q \xrightarrow{o} q_1 \xrightarrow{\lambda} \ldots \xrightarrow{\lambda} q'$

or $q \xrightarrow{\lambda} \ldots \xrightarrow{\lambda} q_1 \xrightarrow{o} q'$

or $q \xrightarrow{\lambda} \ldots \xrightarrow{\lambda} q_1 \xrightarrow{o} q_2 \xrightarrow{\lambda} \ldots \xrightarrow{\lambda} q'$.

9.1.4. Abstraction

We consider the possibility that a system be described at different levels of abstraction, a higher description level showing less detail of the system's operations than a lower level. In the following, we discuss the relationship between two descriptions of a system at different levels of abstraction, within the framework of transition systems (see also Annex 3).

The lower level transition system, corresponding to a system description giving more detail, is characterized by a state space Q and a relation of transitions $\longrightarrow$ labelled by the operations $o \in O$. The higher level transition system, corresponding to an abstracted description of the same system, is characterized by a state space Q', transitions, and operations $o' \in O'$. Q' corresponds to a partition of Q, such that each $q' \in Q'$ corresponds to a subset of Q within this partition. In general, not all subsets in the partition of Q are represented by a state $q' \in Q'$. Therefore the system, according to the detailed description, may be in a state for which there is no corresponding state in the abstracted description. This means that from the point of view of the latter, the system is in the process of making a transition (which is, however, considered an undivisible operation). In the particular case that each subset of Q, corresponding to a $q' \in Q'$, consists of a single element, the state space Q' of the abstracted system may be identified with a subset of the states of the detailed system, i.e. $Q' \subset Q$.

The transitions of the abstracted system description correspond to the transitions of the detailed description, such that there is a transition $q_1' \rightarrow q_2'$ iff there are two states q_1 and q_2 corresponding to q_1' and q_2', respectively, and a finite sequence of transitions $q_1 \rightarrow \ldots \rightarrow q_2$.

The labelling of transitions in the abstracted system description is related to the labelling of the detailed description according to the "implementations" of the operations $o' \in O'$. An implementation of an operation $o' \in O'$ is the specification of the relation corresponding to o' in terms of the operations and generalized operations of the detailed system description. An implementation may be of the form

$$\xrightarrow{o'} = \bigcup_k s^{(k)}$$

where the $s^{(k)}$ are operation sequences of the form $s = \tilde{o}_{i_1} \cdot \tilde{o}_{i_2} \ldots \tilde{o}_{i_n}$ and $\tilde{o}_{i_j}$ is either o_{i_j} or $\hat{o}_{i_j}$.

For example, we may define the operation *outin* of figure 9.2 by

$$\xrightarrow{outin} = read.write \cup write.read .$$

Another example is the definition of the operation of exchanging the values of two variables x and y using a variable z for intermediate storage as

$$\xrightarrow{exchange} = o_1 \cdot o_2 \cdot o_3 \cup o_4 \cdot o_5 \cdot o_6$$

where
$o_1 : z := x$ and $o_4 : z := y$
$o_2 : x := y$ $o_5 : y := x$
$o_3 : y := z$ $o_6 : x := z$.

9.1.5. *Parallelism and functionality*[2]

Definition : Two operations o_1 and o_2 "commute" iff $o_1.o_2 = o_2.o_1$, i.e. the result of their execution is independent of the order of execution.

For example, the operations (x:=x+1) and (x:=x-2) commute with one another, but do not commute with the operation (x:=x*2). If the state space of the system is characterized by the values of the variables, a sufficient condition for two operations o_1 and o_2 to commute is

$$R_{o_1} \cap R_{o_2} = R_{o_1} \cap D_{o_2} = D_{o_1} \cap R_{o_2} = \emptyset$$

where R_{o_i} is the range of operation o_i (i=1,2), i.e. the subset of those variables the values of which may be changed by the operation, and D_{o_i} is the domain of the operation, i.e. the subset of variables on which the new values may depend.

In the framework of transition systems, the consideration of parallelism is a form of abstraction. We consider first sequential execution to make the point. As above, we consider two descriptions of a system, one at a more detailed and one at a more abstracted level. Clearly, the sequential execution of two operations o_1' and o_2' in the abstracted description is implemented in the detailed description as

$$o_1'.o_2' = \bigcup_{k,k'} s_1^{(k)}.s_2^{(k')}$$

where we have assumed that the individual operations are implemented as

$$o_1' = \bigcup_k s_1^{(k)} \text{ with the } s_1 \text{ of the form } \tilde{o}_{i_1}.\tilde{o}_{i_2}...\tilde{o}_{i_n},$$

$$o_2' = \bigcup_{k'} s_2^{(k')} \text{ with the } s_2 \text{ of the form } \tilde{o}_{j_1}.\tilde{o}_{j_2}...\tilde{o}_{j_m};$$

i.e. an execution sequence of $o_1'.o_2'$ is a possible execution sequence of o_1' followed by one of o_2'.

The parallel execution of two operations o'_1 and o'_2, written $o'_1 \| o'_2$, is defined by considering the detailed description of the operations. A possible detailed execution sequence of $o'_1 \| o'_2$ is obtained by merging two possible sequences of o'_1 and o'_2, respectively. More exactly, if $s_\|$, of the form $\tilde{o}_{\ell_1} \cdot \tilde{o}_{\ell_2} \ldots \tilde{o}_{\ell_k}$, is a possible execution sequence of $o'_1 \| o'_2$, then there exist sequences $\tilde{o}_{i_1} \cdot \tilde{o}_{i_2} \ldots \tilde{o}_{i_n}$ and $\tilde{o}_{j_1} \cdot \tilde{o}_{j_2} \ldots \tilde{o}_{j_m}$ of o'_1 and o'_2, respectively, such that

- $\tilde{o}_{\ell_1}$ is either $\tilde{o}_{i_1}$ or $\tilde{o}_{j_1}$,
- $k = n+m$ and
- if $\tilde{o}_{i_1}, \tilde{o}_{i_2}, \ldots, \tilde{o}_{i_{n'}}$ and $\tilde{o}_{j_1}, \tilde{o}_{j_2}, \ldots, \tilde{o}_{j_{m'}}$ are elements of $\tilde{o}_{\ell_1} \cdot \tilde{o}_{\ell_2} \ldots \tilde{o}_{\ell_k}$ (n'+m'<k), then $\tilde{o}_{\ell_{n'+m'+1}}$ is either $\tilde{o}_{i_{n'+1}}$ or $\tilde{o}_{j_{m'+1}}$.

The relation corresponding to $o'_1 \| o'_2$ is the union over all such sequences.

An example is the operation *outin* of figure 9.2, which may be defined as *outin* = *read* $\|$ *write*.

If o'_1 and o'_2 are functional operations, their sequential execution clearly is functional. This is not generally the case for parallel execution. The possible sequences for parallel execution include, as a particular case, the sequential execution sequences $o'_1 . o'_2$ and $o'_2 . o'_1$. Therefore the parallel execution of (x:=x+1) and (x:=x*2), for example, leads to a non-functional operation. A more interesting example are the operations $o'_1 = o_1.o_2.o_3.o_7$ and $o'_2 = o_4.o_5.o_6.o_7$, where $o_7 : x:=0$ and $o_1,\ldots,o_6$ are as defined above. We have $o'_1 = o'_2$, and $o'_1.o'_2 = o'_2.o'_1 = o_7$, all functional. However, $o'_1 \| o'_2$ is not functional (consider for instance the possible execution sequence $o_1.o_4.o_2.o_3.o_7.o_5.o_6.o_7$ which is not equivalent to o_7).

Lemma : A sufficient condition for $o_1^i \| o_2^i$ to be functional is that each operation used for the implementation of o_1^i commutes with each operation used for o_2^i.

9.2. REACHABILITY AND EXECUTION SEQUENCES

In this section, we consider a system which is initially in a given state and then evolves according to the possible state transitions. We do not consider a particular sequence of transition, but instead consider all possible transition sequences. We discuss some concepts and properties of systems which are of interest for system validation and analysis.

9.2.1. *Possible operation sequences*

Definition : The "transitive closure" of a relation R is written R^* and defined as follows :
- (i) $(x,x) \in R^*$;
- (ii) $(x,y) \in R^*$ and $(y,z) \in R$ implies $(x,z) \in R^*$;
- (iii) all pairs of R^* are obtained by a finite number of applications of (i) and (ii).

Definition : A state q' is "reachable" from a state q iff $q \xrightarrow{*} q'$.

Definition : A state q is "final" iff it belongs to the set of final states, i.e. $q \in Q_F \subset Q$, which is an (arbitrarily) chosen subset of Q. A final state is characterized by the fact that the system may stay in such a state forever, even if further transitions are possible. In a non-final state from which further transitions are possible, the system <u>must</u> execute a transition after a finite time period[3].

Definition : An "operation sequence for state q" is a finite (possibly empty) or infinite sequence of operations corresponding to a possible sequence of transitions starting in the state $q \in Q$. We write $\sum_q$ for the set of all such operation sequences.

Starting in an initial state q , there are three reasons for obtaining a finite operation sequence :

(1) The corresponding transition sequence is finite and terminates in a final state.

(2) The corresponding transition sequence is finite and terminates in a state which allows no further transition.

(3) The corresponding transition sequence is infinite, but consists almost uniquely of unlabelled transitions, i.e. after an initial (finite) sequence of transitions, all following transitions are unlabelled.

A situation where the system arrives in a non-final state which allows no further transition is called a "deadlock".

Definitions : A state $q \in Q$ is "active" iff there exists a state q' such that $q \longrightarrow q'$. A system is "deadlock-free" iff all states accessible from the initial state are active.

For example, the system of figure 9.4 with $Q = \{1,2,3,4,5,6\}$, $O = \{a,b,c,d,e\}$, no final state ($Q_F = \emptyset$) and initial state 1 , allows operation sequences of the following forms :

$$a.c.c^* \quad , \quad a.c.c^*.e.d^\infty \quad , \quad a.c^\infty \quad , \text{ and } b.d^\infty ,$$

where we write "*" and "∞" to indicate a finite (possibly empty) and infinite repetition[4], respectively. The system has a deadlock in state 6, which accounts for the finite operation sequences of the form $a.c.c^*$.

9.2.2. Liveness

For most systems it is important to make sure that it never stops (absense of deadlocks) and that certain states or operations can always be reached or executed again. Considering only the case of transitions, we call these transitions the "key transitions" of the system. Similar to the choice of the final states, the choice of the key transitions depends on the system design and purpose (and is arbitrary, otherwise).

Definition : An "operation o is live" in a state q, written $\text{live}_o(q)$, iff there exist $q',q'' \in Q$ such that $q \xrightarrow{*} q'$ and $q' \xrightarrow{o} q''$.

Definition : A "system is live" iff all key transitions are live in all states accessible from the initial state of the system.

Definition : A state q is a "home state" of the system iff q is accessible from all states accessible from the initial state.

Lemma : If a system has a home state q_H and all key transitions are live in q_H, then the system is live.

Lemma : A system with a deadlock is not live.

Considering, for example, the system of figure 9.4, we see that the states 2 and 3 are accessible from all states, except the deadlock state 6. If we introduce an additional transition from state 6 to state 1, then states 2 and 3 are home states. If d is the only key transition, the system is live.

9.2.3. Equivalence between systems

Based on a comparison of the operation sequences that may be generated by different systems, we define the notion of "operational equivalence" as follows[5].

Definition: A system S' "simulates" a system S iff for each state $q \in Q$ of S, there exists a state $q' \in Q'$ of S' such that the set $\Sigma'_{q'}$ of operation sequences of system S' is equal to the set Σ_q of system S.

Definition : Two systems S and S' are "operationally equivalent" iff S' simulates S, and S simulates S'.

The operational equivalence between two systems depends on the level of details that are considered. Two systems may be equivalent when considered at a high level of abstraction, while the equivalence disappears when more details are considered. Sometimes it is sufficient to make abstraction from certain operations in order to obtain an equivalence between two systems. For example, the systems of figures 9.4 and 9.5 are equivalent when abstraction is made from the operation c.

9.3. SYNCHRONIZATION MECHANISMS

In the last section, we have considered all possible operation sequences that may be generated by a system starting in some initial state. In this section we consider decision algorithms to determine whether, after a given sequence of transitions, a given operation may be executed or not. Such algorithms are necessary for the system implementation. They may also be taken as a system description, because they determine which labelled transitions are possible in each state of the system. Since they are effective and determine the order in which the operations of the systems may be executed, we call such an algorithm a synchronization mechanism.

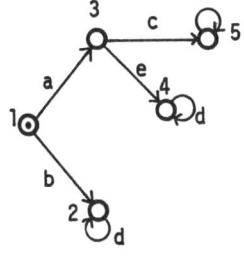

FIGURE 9.5

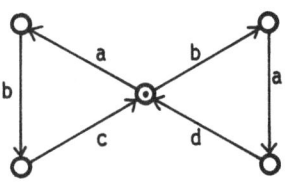

FIGURE 9.6

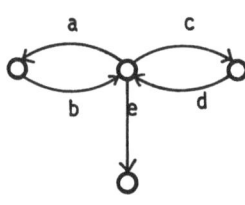

FIGURE 9.7

```
process p;
   begin  O_1; O_2; ...; O_n  end;
```

FIGURE 9.8

```
process p
   begin
      cycle O_1; O_2; ...; O_n  end-cycle
   end;
```

FIGURE 9.9

We call "activation condition" of an operation o, written AC_o, a necessary condition for executing a transition labelled o. It may be expressed in terms of the system state, or in terms of the partial operation sequence σ_p so far executed by the system. For the example of figure 9.5, it is necessary for the execution of the operation d that the system is in state 2 or 4, or equivalently that the executed partial operation sequence is of the form $b.d^*$ or $a.e.d^*$.

In the following, we use very often synchronization mechanisms of a particularly simple kind which are only based on execution counts for the different operations. A counter N_o is associated with each operation o, and counts the number of times a transition labelled o is executed since system initialization; and an activation condition for a given operation may only depend on the counters of (all) the operations. For example, the synchronization mecanism of the system of figure 9.5 is of this kind, but the one for figure 9.6 is not of this kind, since the possibility of executing the operation c depends on the order in which the operations a and b were executed, and not only on the number of times.

The semaphore is a popular synchronization tool[6]. A semaphore is an integer variable of special type on which only two functional operations P and V exist. The P-operation on a semaphore sem is characterized by the enabling predicate
$P_{P(sem)} \equiv (sem > 0)$, and the transition function
$F_{P(sem)}(sem) = sem-1$. Similarly, the V-operation is characterized by $P_{V(sem)} = true$ and $F_{V(sem)}(sem) = sem+1$.

Equivalently, a semaphore sem may be described by two dummy operations P(sem) and V(sem) with activation conditions depending on execution counters as follows:

$$AC_{P(sem)} \equiv N_{P(sem)} < N_{V(sem)} + K_{sem},$$
$$AC_{V(sem)} \equiv true,$$

where K_{sem} is a constant (the initial value of the semaphore).

As additional examples for the specification of synchronization with execution counters, we consider a system with two operations a and b. If the activation conditions (considered as necessary and sufficient conditions) are

$$AC_a \equiv (N_a = 0) \vee (N_b = 1)$$
$$AC_b \equiv (N_a = 1)$$

the operation sequence of the system is a.b.a ; for the activation conditions

$$AC_a \equiv AC_b \equiv (N_b = 0)$$

one obtains operation sequences of the form $a^*.b$. However, for obtaining operation sequences of the form $(a.b.c \cup b.a.d)^*$, it seems that counters are not sufficient for specifying the synchronization. However, activation conditions depending on the current system state (see for example figure 9.7) are clearly sufficient.

We note that in practice, several synchronization constraints are imposed on the operations of a system, each having a different origin. For example, a shared resource, the sharing processes, the system scheduling policy, etc., each may impose certain constraints on the order in which the operations of the system may be executed. Therefore the necessary <u>and</u> sufficient condition for the possibility of executing an operation is usually given by the conjunction of several necessary activation conditions. In the case of a functional operation o, one has

$$P_o \equiv AC_o^{(1)} \wedge AC_o^{(2)} \wedge \ldots \wedge AC_o^{(n)}$$

9.4. NON-INSTANTANEOUS OPERATIONS

Each transition of a system is considered an undivisible and instantaneous event. But for certain considerations, it is important to consider operations with a finite, non-negligeable execution time. Non-instantaneous operations may be described within the framework discussed so far, using an approach of abstraction as follows.

A non-instantaneous operation o' is considered at a more detailed level of description as the sequence $\bar{o}.o.\underline{o}$ (or simply $\bar{o}.\underline{o}$) of undivisible operations, where $\bar{o}$ is the beginning of the operation o', $\underline{o}$ its end, and o is the operation proper (which may be of no interest for certain considerations). The sequential order of execution of the operations $\bar{o}$, o, and $\underline{o}$ implies the following activation conditions :

$AC_o \equiv N_{\bar{o}} > N_o$,

$AC_{\underline{o}} \equiv N_o > N_{\underline{o}}$ (or $N_{\bar{o}} > N_{\underline{o}}$, respectively) .

Definition : For a non-instantaneous operation o', the "activity count", written *active(o')*, is equal to $(N_{\bar{o}} - N_{\underline{o}})$, and represents the number of operations o' in progress.

Lemma : The activity count of a non-instantaneous operation is always equal or greater than zero.

9.4.1. Mutual exclusion

Definition : Two non-instantaneous operations o'_1 and o'_2 are "mutually exclusive" iff the execution of one excludes, at the same time, the execution of the other, i.e. the predicate

$$\text{active}(o'_1) = 0 \quad \vee \quad \text{active}(o'_2) = 0$$

is always true.

Definition : A non-instantaneous operation o' is a "critical section" iff its activity count is never larger than one, i.e.

$$\text{active}(o') \leq 1 .$$

It is easy to see that the activation conditions

$$AC_{\overline{o_1}} \equiv \text{active}(o_2') = 0 ,$$
$$AC_{\overline{o_2}} \equiv \text{active}(o_1') = 0$$

impose mutual exclusion on the operations o_1' and o_2', and that the activation condition

$$AC_{\overline{o}} \equiv \text{active}(o') = 0$$

make o' a critical section.

An example for mutual exclusion is the readers-writers problem[7]. A simple version of the problem is presented by a memory resource which supports *read* and *write* operations to be executed by different processes. In order to keep the data in the memory logically consistant, it is necessary that at most one *write* operation is executed at any given time (the *write* operation is a critical section), and in order to read consistant data the *read* operations must be mutually excluded from the *write* operations. Therefore the synchronization problem is solved by the following activation conditions[8] :

$$AC_{\overline{read}}^{(1)} \equiv \text{active}(write) = 0$$

$$AC_{\overline{write}}^{(1)} \equiv (\text{active}(read)=0) \wedge (\text{active}(write)=0) .$$

9.4.2. *Queuing considerations and scheduling*

In the above solution of the readers-writers problem, a large number of readers may prevent a writer from executing a *write* operation. In order to give priority to the writers, an additional activation condition may be established for the *read* operation which prevents reading when a writer is waiting. In this section, we consider this and similar problems which are related to queuing, priorities and scheduling.

A simple approach for including the aspect of queuing for the execution of a non-instantaneous operation, is to consider an additional step, i.e. the request step, in the sequence of primitive operations that make up the execution of the non-instantaneous operation. Explicitely, the execution of a non-instantaneous operation o' is described in more detail by the sequence $\dot{o}.\bar{o}.o.\underline{o}$, where $\dot{o}$ is the request of the operation o', with the additional activation condition (to account for the sequential execution order)

$$AC_{\bar{o}} \equiv N_{\dot{o}} > N_{\bar{o}} .$$

Now we can define the "waiting count" for an operation o', written *waiting(o')*, as

$$\text{waiting}(o') = N_{\dot{o}} - N_{\bar{o}} .$$

The usefulness of this approach for the description of synchronization problems is demonstrated by the following examples. For its implementation, it is sufficient to keep two counters for each operation, one for *active* and one for *waiting*[9].

The readers-writers problems with priority for the writers is solved by adding to the system description the following activation condition which expresses the absolute priority of the writers over the readers :

$$AC_{\overline{read}}^{(2)} \equiv \text{waiting}(write) = 0 .$$

This is an example of several synchronization constraints being imposed for different reasons. $AC^{(1)}_{\overline{read}}$ is imposed for the logical consistancy of the system, and $AC^{(2)}_{\overline{read}}$ is imposed for priority considerations. The fact that these different aspect remain separate in the system description is an advantage of the method of using activation conditions for the specification of synchronization.

For giving equal chances, for accessing the resource, to readers and writers it seems to be necessary to have them wait on the same condition. This may be arranged by introducing a common primitive operation *enter* which is executed before the non-instantaneous *read* and *write* operations. If we adopt

$$AC_{enter} \equiv \text{active(write)} = \text{waiting(write)} = 0$$

as condition for "entering" the resource, $\text{active(write)} = 0$ is automatically satisfied at the beginning of *read* or *write* operations ; therefore this condition may be eliminated from the activation conditions $AC^{(1)}_{\overline{read}}$ and $AC^{(1)}_{\overline{write}}$.

9.5. PROCESSES

As the discussions of the preceding sections show, many important concepts of parallel systems may be described by the model of transition systems without using the concept of processes. We show in this section how this concept may be introduced into transition systems.

9.5.1. The concept

In addition to the set of states Q, the transitions, and the set of operation symbols O, we introduce a set P of distinct processes $p \in P$. A transition of the system may not only be labelled by an operation symbol $o \in O$, but also by one or more processes $p \in P$ which are those processes involved in the transition. Usually only one process is involved in a given transition; transitions involving several processes realize some kind of interprocess communication. For example, a *read* operation of the readers-writers system would involve (i) the resource (considered a process) and (ii) the "process" on behalf of which the reading is performed.

Since each activation condition of an operation in the system is usually related to a particular process, we consider sometimes independent sets of execution counters for each process. They are distinguished by superscripts indicating the involved process. Such a process specific execution counter for an operation is only incremented when a transition labelled with the particular operation and the particular process is executed. For example, the activation conditions for the readers-writers problem considered above depend on the execution counters associated with the resource, not on those associated with the processes that call on the resource. The following examples often involve the following kinds of simple processes.

Definition : A "simple sequential process" p is a process executing one given (finite) sequence of operations $o_1.o_2...o_n$, as shown in figure 9.8. It implies the activation conditions

$$CA_{o_1}^{(p)} \equiv (N_{o_1}^{(p)} = 0) \quad \text{and}$$

$$CA_{o_i}^{(p)} \equiv (N_{o_i}^{(p)} < N_{o_{i-1}}^{(p)}) \quad \text{for } i=2,\ldots,n \quad .$$

Definition : A "simple cyclic process" p is a process executing a given (finite) sequence of operations repeatedly, as shown in figure 9.9, giving rise to an operation sequence of the form $(o_1.o_2...o_n)^\infty$. It implies the activation conditions

$$CA_{o_1}^{(p)} \equiv (N_{o_1}^{(p)} = N_{o_n}^{(p)}) \quad \text{and}$$

$$CA_{o_i}^{(p)} \equiv (N_{o_i}^{(p)} < N_{o_{i-1}}^{(p)}) \quad \text{for} \quad i=2,\ldots,n \ .$$

9.5.2. Cooperation

We consider as an example the cooperation between a producer and a consumer process, as shown in figure 9.10. The producer process generates messages and sends them to the consumer process which, in turn, consumes them. We discuss in the following first a system with direct coupling between the two processes, and then a system where the processes communicate through a message queue.

If we consider the sending and receiving as one undivisible operation, which we call *transfer* (at a more detailed level of description the *send* and *receive* operations may be both implemented by the *transfer* operation) we obtain the following assignment of processes to the operations :

- *make* implies the process *producer*,
- *transfer* implies both processes *producer* and *consumer*, and
- *use* implies the process *consumer*.

The activation conditions are (conditions for simple cyclic processes, as explained above)

$$CA_{make}^{(producer)} \equiv N_{make} = N_{transfer}$$

$$CA_{transfer}^{(producer)} \equiv N_{transfer} < N_{make}$$

$$CA\binom{consumer}{transfer} \equiv N_{transfer} = N_{use}$$

$$CA\binom{consumer}{use} \equiv N_{use} < N_{transfer}$$

A simple analysis shows that these conditions imply a synchronization between the operations of the system which may be represented by the state transition diagram of figure 9.11.

We call this approach to the communication of the producer and consumer processes "direct coupling", since the processes communicate directly with one another through the execution of a common transition[10]. This implies close synchronization for the execution of this transition. Another possibility is to insert a *buffer* process between the *producer* and *consumer* processes[11]. In this case, there is direct coupling of the *buffer* process with the *producer* and the *consumer*, but the synchronization between the *producer* and *consumer* is weaker, depending on the buffer size.

A finite *buffer* process, operating as a finite queue of maximum length K, is characterized by the fact that it executes the operations *send* and *receive* in such an order that the activation conditions

$$AC\binom{buffer}{receive} \equiv N_{receive} < N_{send} \text{ and}$$

$$AC\binom{buffer}{send} \equiv N_{send} < N_{receive} + K$$

are satisfied.

In the case of a *producer* and *consumer* communicating through a *buffer*, we obtain the following assignment of processes to the operations :

- *make* implies the process *producer*,
- *send* implies the processes *producer* and *buffer*,
- *receive* implies the processes *consumer* and *buffer*, and
- *use* implies the process *consumer*.

```
process producer;
   var m: message;
   begin
      cycle make(m); send (m) cycle-end
   end;

process consumer;
   var m: message ;
   begin
      cycle receive (m); use (m) cycle-end
   end;
```

FIGURE 9.10

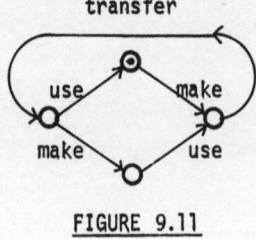

FIGURE 9.11

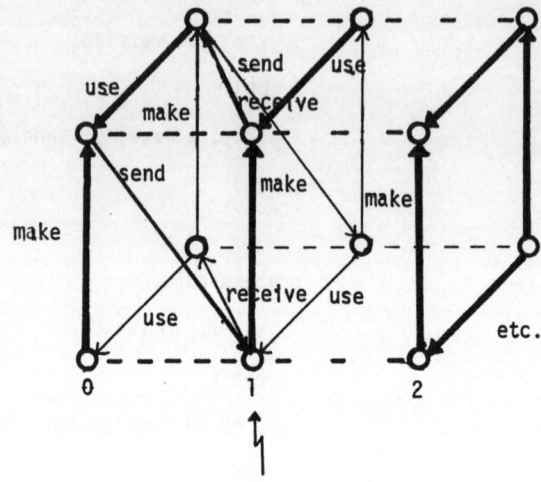

number of messages in buffer

FIGURE 9.12: Synchronization between a producer and consumer obtained by a buffer queue

```
procedure use-resource;
    begin use; ...; use end;
process p_i;
    begin
        cycle work_i; use-resource cycle-end
    end;
```

FIGURE 9.13

```
critical section use_x;
critical section use_y;
process p_1;
   begin
      cycle x.use; y.use ; ...; y.use; x.use  cycle-end
   end;
process p_2;
   begin
      cycle y.use; x.use ; ...; x.use; y.use  cycle end
   end;
```

FIGURE 9.14: Two processes possibly leading to a deadlock

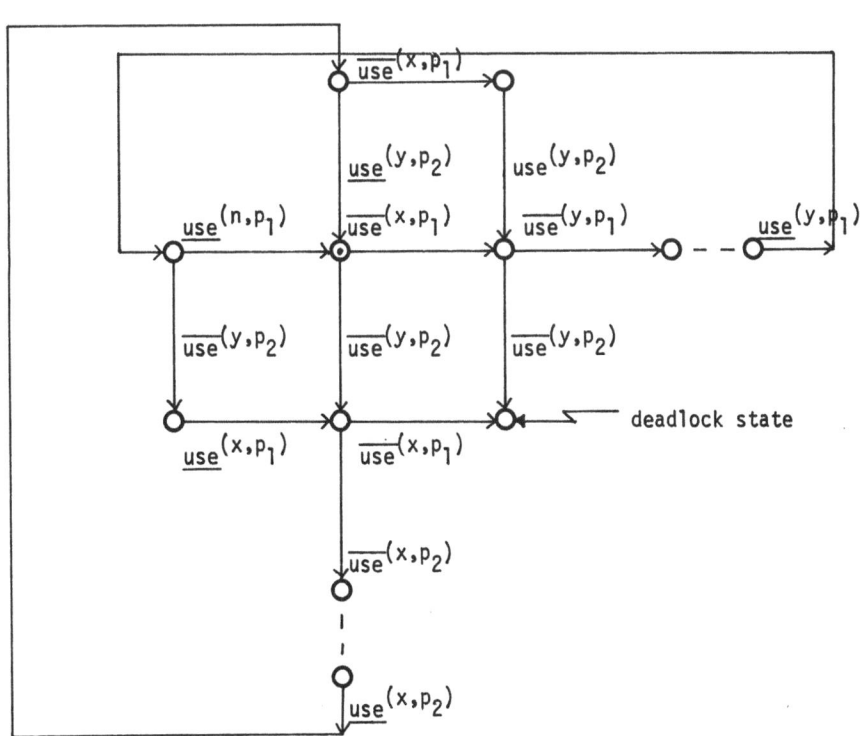

FIGURE 9.15: Possible transitions of the system defined by figure 4.14

The activation conditions of the *producer* and *consumer* are the same as above (replacing the operation *transfer* by *send* or *receive*, respectively). An analysis shows that these conditions and the activation conditions of the *buffer* imply a synchronization between the operations of the system which may be represented by the state transition diagram of figure 9.12.

9.5.3. Mutual exclusion

The discussion of mutual exclusion in section 9.4.1. remains valid when different processes are distinguished. We consider as an example[12] a resource process r with a critical section *use* shared by a number of processes p_i ($i=1,2,\ldots,n$) shown in figure 9.13. The process assignment to operations is as follows :
- $work_i$ implies the process p_i (for $i=1,2,\ldots,n$) ,
- $\overline{use}$ and $\underline{use}$ imply the resource process r and one of the processes p_i (depending on the transition). The activation condition of the resource is

$$CA\frac{(r)}{\overline{use}} \equiv (\text{active}^{(r)}(use)=0) \equiv (N\frac{(r)}{\overline{use}} = N\frac{(r)}{\underline{use}}) \ .$$

Here it is necessary to distinguish between the execution counters for the operations $\overline{use}$ and $\underline{use}$ associated with the resource process (used above) and those associated with the processes p_i (used in the activation conditions of these processes, which are the standard conditions for simple cyclic processes). This distinction is not necessary for the example of cooperation, where the counters of different processes always have the same values.

The activation conditions for mutual exclusion leave much freedom to the system as far as the relative speed of the different processes is concerned. For instance, the operation sequence

$$\underset{work_1}{(p_1)} \quad \underset{.work_2}{(p_2)} \underline{\quad}\underset{.use}{(r,p_2)} \quad \underset{.use}{(r,p_2)} \quad \underset{.work_2}{(p_2)} \underline{\quad}\underset{.use}{(r,p_2)} \quad . \text{ etc.}$$

is allowed by the activation conditions, but usually not desirable since process p_2 alone proceeds. Additional activation conditions may be foreseen for obtaining the desired scheduling (see for example section 9.4.2).

Definition : A schedule is "fair" for a process p iff it is excluded that the system does an unlimited number of transitions not implying process p where the system goes through an unlimited number of states for which the activation conditions imposed by the process p alone would allow a transition that implies the process.

For example, the activation conditions for the readers-writers problem given in section 9.4.1 seems to be unfair for a writer process if the resource is flooded by readers. The $AC \frac{(1)}{write}$ may never become true because there is always some active reader. During all those reading transitions the activation conditions of a writer process, waiting for the *write* transition, will allow this transition. But the activation conditions are not necessarily unfair. Activation conditions never force a transition, they only may prevent them. In this case, a scheduling algorithm is conceivable which lets *read* operations wait when a process waits for writing (see for example section 9.4.2).

Systems with activation conditions for mutual exclusion often lead to system deadlocks unless special precautions are taken[13]. A typical example is given by two processes requesting two critical regions in opposite order, as shown in figure 9.14. If the processes p_1 and p_2 , each enter one critical region no further transition is possible, as shown by the transition diagram of figure 9.15. This deadlock is due to the interplay of the activation conditions of the critical regions for mutual exclusion and the activation conditions of the processes p_1 and p_2 for sequential execution[14]. The deadlock could be avoided by intelligent scheduling.

9.6. THE INDUCTION PRINCIPLE

Definition : A boolean predicate I on the states of the system is "invariant in respect to the initial state $q_0 \in Q$", or shortly "q_0-invariant" iff

$$q_0 \xrightarrow{*} q \text{ implies } I(q) \quad .$$

Definition : A boolean predicate I on the states of the system is "q_0-inductive" iff

$I(q_0)$ and

$[q \rightarrow q' \text{ and } I(q)] \text{ implies } I(q') \quad .$

Proposition : A q_0-inductive predicate I is q_0-invariant.

A property of a system that is to remain valid during the entire operation of the system is naturally a q_0-invariant, where q_0 is the initial state of the system. Such a property is valid for the initial state and all reachable states of the system. The logical verification of a system may therefore be obtained by formulating the desired system properties in terms of state predicates and showing that these predicates are invariant in respect to the initial system state.

The "induction principle" expressed by the proposition above indicates that the invariance of a predicate may be proven by showing that the predicate holds initially and that it remains valid under all possible transitions. Usually, such a proof can be made considering separately each operation of the system[15].

As an example, we prove the lemma of section 9.4 stating that, for any operation o' of the system,

$$\text{active}(o') \equiv N_{\overline{o}} - N_{\underline{o}} \geq 0 \ .$$

Clearly, this holds initially, since initially $N_{\overline{o}} = N_{\underline{o}} = 0$. Using the induction principle, we have to show that if $\text{active}(o') \geq 0$ holds before some transition is executed then it also holds after this transition. If this transition is labelled $\overline{o}$, it increments the execution count $N_{\overline{o}}$ by one ; $\text{active}(o') \geq 0$ will still hold. If the transition is labelled $\underline{o}$, it increments the execution count $N_{\underline{o}}$ by one; $\text{active}(o') \geq 0$ will still hold after this transition since the transition can only be executed when the activation condition $N_{\overline{o}} > N_{\underline{o}}$ holds. If the transition is labelled differently, the execution counts $N_{\overline{o}}$ and $N_{\underline{o}}$, and therefore the value of $\text{active}(o')$, are not affected.

9.7. DISTINCTION BETWEEN "CONTROL STRUCTURE" AND "INTERPRETATION"

Most of the above considerations about the relative synchronization of the different operations within a system are independent of the particular meaning of the operations. The part of the system which determines the order in which the different operations may be executed is sometimes called the "control structure" of the system, when considered in contrast to the actual meaning of the operations, sometimes called their "interpretation" or "semantics". The reason for making such a distinction is that many system properties only depend on the control structure of the system, and are independent of the interpretation of the operations.

For example, the study of program schemas yields many interesting results on the structure and properties of programs, which hold for any possible interpretation or choice of the basic statements in the programs. Another example is the discussion of

mutual exclusion in section 9.4, where the actual meaning of the
operations for which the exclusion is enforced, is not considered
at all. Partial interpretation is introduced when the commutation
between operations is considered, as in section 9.1.5. Whether two
operations commute or not, clearly depends on their meaning.

The distinction between control and interpretation is
indicated in figure 9.16, which may also be viewed as an approach
to the implementation of a system. The control structure determines the order in which operations are to be executed by the interpretation part of the system. The latter usually contains the data on which the operations are performed. Usually, there is also some feedback in the form of test values which is used by the control structure to make certain decisions. For example, the control structure of the statement sequence

$$S_1 \; ; \; \underline{if} \; condition \; \underline{then} \; S_2 \; \underline{else} \; S_3 \; ;$$

may be represented by the diagram of figure 9.17. Here the value
of the *condition*, provided by the interpretation part, is used by
the control part for deciding between the operations S_2 and S_3.

A given control structure for a system corresponds to a
certain set of possible operation sequences (as explained in section 9.2.1). If a particular interpretation is adopted for the
control structure the set of possible operation sequences is usually reduced, due to additional constraints introduced by the interpretation. For example, the above statement sequence with the interpretation

$$S_1 \; : \; x := 5$$

and

$$condition \equiv x > 0$$

yields only the operation sequence $S_1.S_2$, and not $S_1.S_3$ which
is, however, allowed by figure 9.17.

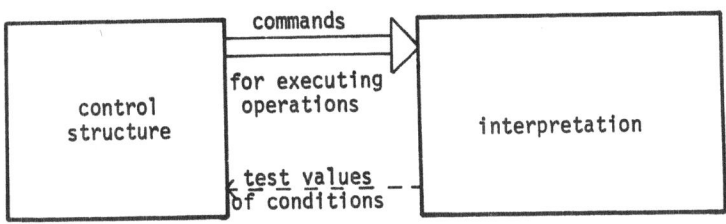

FIGURE 9.16: Distinction between "Control" and "Interpretation"

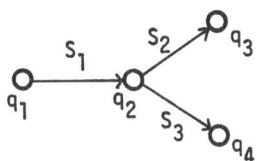

FIGURE 9.17

```
var i,x: integer;
   begin
      x := 1;  i := 1;
      while i < n do begin  i := i + 1;  x := x * i  end
   end
```

FIGURE 9.18: Program for calculating N!

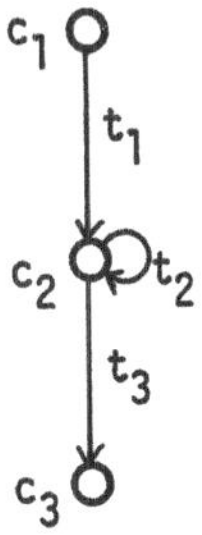

$P_{t_1} \equiv$ true $\qquad F_{t_1}(i,x) = (1,1)$

$P_{t_2}(i,x) \equiv i < n \qquad F_{t_2}(i,x) = (i+1,\ x*(i+1))$

$P_{t_3}(i,x) \equiv i \geq n \qquad F_{t_3}(i,x) = (i,x)$

FIGURE 9.19: Transition system equivalent to the program of figure 9.18

The distinction between control structure and interpretation may be formalized by considering the state space Q of the system to be given by the Cartesian product between a control state space C and an interpretation state space X (which, in turn, usually consists of the Cartesian product of the value spaces of several program variables); i.e.

$$Q = C \times X .$$

9.7.1. *Notation for the case of a finite control structure*

For the case of a finite control state space of the form $C = \{c_1, c_2, \ldots, c_n\}$ and functional operations, we introduce the notion of a "controlled operation", which simplifies some of the following discussions.

Definition : A "controlled operation" t defined as a triplet (o, c_i, c_f) is the subset of those transitions of the operation o that go from a state (c_i, x) to a state (c_f, x') , where $c_i, c_f \in C$ and $x, x' \in X$, i.e. a controlled operation is an operation restricted to given initial and final control states c_i and c_f , respectively.

While the enabling predicate $P_o(q)$ and the transition function $F_o(q)$ of an operation depend on the control part c and interpretation part x of the state $q = (c, x)$ of the system, the corresponding entities P_t and F_t for a controlled operation t can be expressed in a form only depending on the interpretation part x of the state space, since the control part is fixed, i.e.

$$P_t : X \rightarrow \text{boolean}$$
$$F_t : X \rightarrow X .$$

For each pair of control states c_i and c_f, we define the set of possible controlled operations as

$$Tr(c_i,c_f) = \left\{(0,c_i,c_f) \mid \text{there exist } x,x' \in X \text{ such that } (c_i,x) \xrightarrow{0} (c_f,x')\right\}$$

9.8. ASSERTIONS

In the case of a finite control structure, and using the notation of section 9.7.1, we may write an arbitrary predicate on the state space Q in the form

$$I(c,x) = \bigwedge_{k=1}^{n} \left[c=c_k \text{ implies } A_k(x)\right] ,$$

where the A_i are called "assertions". In order to show that I is (c_i,x_0)-inductive, it is sufficient to show that

$$A_i(x_0) \quad \text{and}$$

$$A_k(x) \wedge P_t(x) \wedge x'=F_t(x) \text{ implies } A_{k'}(x')$$

holds for all k,k' and all $t \in Tr(c_k,c_{k'})$.

In the case of a sequential program, the induction principle turns out to justify the well-known method for program verification which associates assertions with certain places in the program text[16]. Each place in the program text corresponds to a control state $c_k \in C$, and a partial correctness proof of a program is equivalent to showing that the predicate

$$I(c,x) \equiv (c=c_f) \text{ implies } A_f(x)$$

is (c_i,x_0)-invariant, where c_i and c_f are the initial and final control states, respectively, x_0 is the initial state of the interpretation part, and A_f is the assertion to hold when (and if) the program terminates. In practice, usually, a predicate stronger than I , saying somethings about the assertions at other places in the program, can be proven to be (c_i, x_o)-inductive, and therefore (c_i, x_o)-invariant.

As an example we consider the program of figure 9.18, which calculates n factorial, and which may be represented by the transition system of figure 9.19. We want to show that

$$(c=c_3) \quad \text{implies} \quad x=n! \quad .$$

This follows in fact from

$$(c=c_2) \quad \text{implies} \quad x=i! \quad \text{and}$$
$$(c=c_3) \quad \text{implies} \quad x=n!$$

which can be easily shown to be (c_1, i, x)-invariant for any integer i and x .

In the case of a shared resource with mutual exclusion for the operations of different processes on the resource, the induction principle turns out to justify the use of an invariant assertion $A_I(x)$ for specifying the consistancy constraints for internal variables x of the resource[17]. The control part of the resource may be represented by a single state c_o , as shown in figure 9.20. Since there is only one control state, the (c_o, x_o)-invariance of A_I is proven by showing that

$$A_I(x_o) \quad \text{and}$$
$$A_I(x) \land P_o(x) \land x'=F_o(x) \quad \text{implies} \quad A_I(x')$$

for all possible operations o of the resource.

In the case of a control structure describing several parallel processes, a control state corresponds to a particular place in the program text of each process. Since each assertion is, in general, associated with a particular control state, the establishment of a correspondence between assertions and places in a program text is not possible like in the case of a sequential program[18].

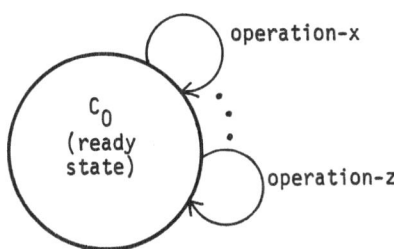

FIGURE 9.20

9.9 SOME FORMALIZED SPECIFICATION METHODS FOR SYSTEMS WITH PARALLELISM

The notions of state and state transitions, as explained in the sections above, seem to be the basis for most methods of system description. The different description methods that have been developed for different purposes seem to be specializations of the general formalism described above. Most description methods for systems with parallelism use either state transition diagrams or a programming language, in which case the execution of a single statement or a procedure may be identified as a transition. In certain methods, a process is a stable entity which is only rarely created or eliminated. In other methods, the degree of parallelism (i.e. the number of parallel processes) in a system varies continuously.

The operation of hardware, as well as software systems may be specified by Petri nets[19]. During the operation of a Petri net, the number of processes, represented by the tokens, usually varies continuously. In most cases, only "safe" Petri nets are considered, for which the number of tokens remains limited. Often it is possible to describe a system as a collection of several finite state automata which interact via input-output or other kinds of couplings[20]. Such descriptions may always be translated into the general context of Petri nets. To characterize the order in which certain operations may be executed, independently of the internal structure of a system, the method of path expressions has been proposed. Specifications based on path expressions may also be translated into Petri net implementations[21].

To add more descriptive power and flexibility, many extensions to Petri nets have been proposed. For example, the introduction of attributes and/or program variables leads to general models[22], which are related to "guarded commands"[23], whereas additional features may be useful for modelling computer and queuing systems, but lead to complex languages.[24]

Another approach to the description of systems with parallelism starts out from the concept of abstract data types or modules, as developed for the structured design of computer software. An abstract data module provides a certain set of interface operations which may be executed in interaction with the other modules of the system. Methods for specifying the interface operations without referring to the internal operation of the module have been developed[25]. This approach to specification may be adapted to systems with parallelism by considering, at a certain level of abstraction, the execution of an interface operation as an indivisible system transition.

Particular synchronization tools, to specify the order in which different operations may be executed in an environment of parallel processes, are conditional critical regions[26], monitors[27] and semaphores[28].

So far, we have ignored real time considerations. The state of the system determines which operations may be executed next, and it is assumed that one of the operations will be executed after some finite time. Therefore, no infinite loops may be involved in the execution of an operation. Real time considerations may be introduced in two steps (as explained in section 3.6) :

(a) Probabilistic real time constraints may be introduced by assigning a transition probability to each of the possible operations in a given system state, and by providing a probabilistic measure of the execution time of each operations. Such a Markov chain model may be used to derive response time and efficiency of communication protocols and interactive applications[29].

(b) Real time constraints are introduced by assigning minimal and maximal execution times for all operations[30]. This is the natural framework for describing time-outs (see section 3.6.1).

FOOTNOTES

1. The presented formalism is strongly influenced by Keller's general model of transition systems [Kell 76] and the approach to synchronization by Robert and Vergus [Robe 77].

2. A more detailed discussion of functionality in parallel system is given in [Coff 73], section 2.2.

3. The same distinction between final and non-final states is made in [Redz 77].

4. Infinite operation sequences of finite state systems are considered in more detail in [Redz 77].

5. This principle has been applied in [Pete 74] to the equivalence of different specification methods for parallel systems.

6. See for example [Dijk 68] or [Brin 73], section 3.4.

7. See for example [Cour 71] or [Brin 73], section 3.4.5.

8. This solution may be compared with the first solution in [Cour 71] using semaphores.

9. For more examples and detailed discussion see [Robe 77] and [Bekk 77].

10. Communication in the form of direct coupling, sometimes called "rendez-vous", is considered in [Boch 78] for finite state modelling of systems and in [Hoar 78] in the context of programming languages. Some algebraic definitions of such communication is given in [Miln 80] and [Miln 82].

11. See for example [Brin 73], section 3.4.4.

12. See also [Brin 73], section 3.3.

13. For detailed discussion of deadlocks, see for example [Coff 73], section 2.3.

14. This view of deadlocks is taken in [Belp 75].

15. Several examples are given in [Kell 76].

16. See for example [Floy 67] or [Hoar 69].

17. See for example [Hoar 74].

18. The association of assertions with the elements of the product control state space of several processes is suggested in [Boch 77d]. The association of separate sets of (partial) assertions with the control states of the different processes, as suggested in [Ashc 75] is not of general applicability (see [Kell 76]).

19. An introduction to Petri nets may be found in [Pete 77].

20. See for example [Boch 77b] or [Boch 78].

21. See for example [Laue 75]. Path expressions are described in [Camp 74].

22. Such as [Kell 76].

23. [Dijk 75].

24. See for example [Noe 73]

25. See for example [Lisk 75], [Parn 77] or [Bart 77]. An introduction to the concept of abstract data types may be found in [Lisk 75].

26. See for example section 3.4 of [Brin 73] and [Kess 77].

27. See for example [Hoar 74]

28. [Dijk 68].

29. See for example [Masu 78] and [Whit 78]

30. A particular model for such real time systems is described in [Merl 76b].

10. A Formal Description Technique for Distributed Systems

This chapter deals with the specification of distributed systems. Many of the concepts discussed here are included in a state machine model being developed by ISO and CCITT as a formal description technique for the specification of OSI communication services and protocols[1]. The concepts are illustrated by examples of service and protocol specifications for a simplified transport layer.

The sections below show how the step-wise refinement of distributed systems, as mentioned in section 2.3, may be supported by formal descriptions. The description method discussed is based on the concepts of "component" and "port". A component performs some data processing and is assumed to be a unit of specification. It may include several concurrent activities. A port is used by a component for the communication with its environment, i.e. other components in the system. A component may use several ports for communication with different parts of its environment, as indicated in figure 10.1.

A refinement of a component, sometimes called an "implementation", is given by defining an internal structure of the component in terms of sub-components and interconnections through ports.

10.1 DISCUSSION OF SPECIFICATION CONCEPTS

10.1.1. *Components and their interactions*

For the specification of a component, the point of view of an external observer is considered. Only the externally visible behavior should be specified; a component is therefore defined by its possibilities for interacting with the other components in the system, which we call the "environment". Many specification methods introduce, however, the notion of a "state" which determines the future behavior of the component. For certain behaviors, it seems to be difficult to write a specification without the explicit or implicit notion of a state. In any case, an implementation of the component is not required to realize such states directly, only the specified behavior must be met.

An interaction between two components occurs when both components invoke the same type of interaction on connected ports. A rendez-vous interaction mechanism is assumed, where the first component ready to execute the interaction must wait for the second to be ready[2]. For most specification methods, including the state machine model of section 10.2, it is assumed that the component first initiating the interaction determines any parameter values, and must complete the interaction before it can proceed to any other activity. However, most concepts discussed here are also applicable in a more general context[3].

Since the specification of a component type should only describe its externally visible behavior, the specification should define the possible interaction types and the order in which these interactions may be executed. This order is usually defined by rules that may take different forms, such as assertions on parameter values, expressions defining full or partial orders of execution sequences, or state machines, as shown in the example of section 10.2[4].

10.1.2 *Ports and interconnections*

The concept of a port may be used to give some structure to the interactions of a component with its environment. A declared port for a given component may be considered as an abstraction of the environment of that component. Let us consider the example of a component **P** with three ports p_1, p_2 and p_3, as shown in figure 10.1. The ports p_i represent an abstract

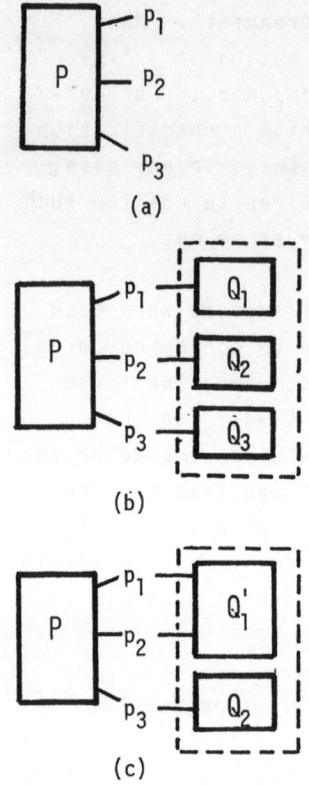

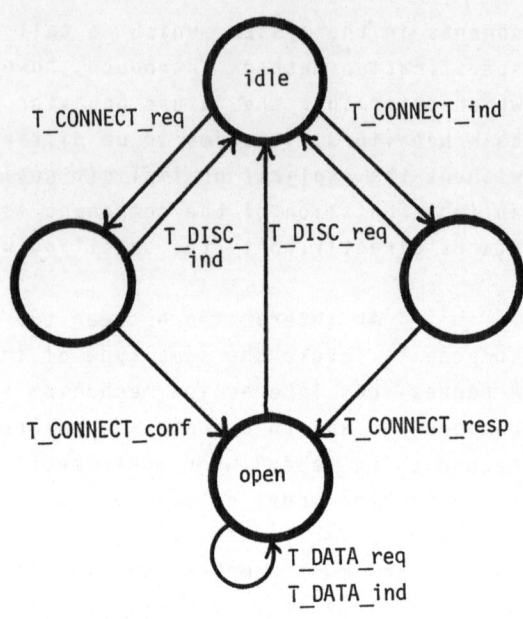

FIGURE 10.3:

State diagram showing the local rules of a transport service access point for a single connection

FIGURE 10.1:

A process and its environment

(a) Abstract view of the environment

(b, c) Different implementations of the same environment specification

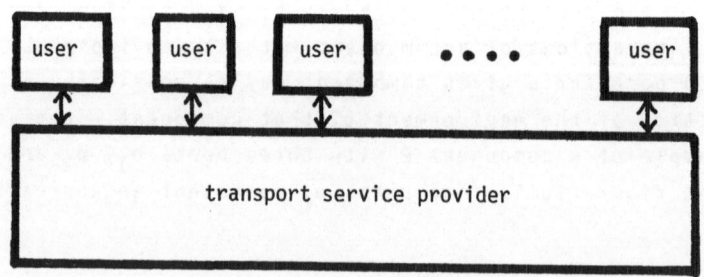

FIGURE 10.2: The transport service providing component and its users

specification of the environment of **P**, as it is seen by the component. The environment may be implemented in different ways, as shown in the figure. The specification of **P**, however, is the same for all these environments.

A given port combines a number of different interaction types and defines "local rules" for their execution, independently from the interactions at other ports. Similarly, the specification of a component, if it has several ports, defines some additional "global rules" which must be satisfied for the executions of interactions at the different component ports. Each interaction of the component is associated with a particular port.

In the context of distributed systems, the notion of a port may also be used for distinguishing different points (in space) of the distributed system, such as the different service access points (see example in section 10.2) which would usually be implemented in different host computers or intelligent terminals.

Apart from the above considerations, the main reason for introducing the concept of a port, is its use in the refinement process. The concept of ports is essential for the specification of component implementations in terms of sub-components, as explained in section 10.3. The interconnection of these sub-components is in fact defined by establishing an identity relation between the ports of different sub-components, as shown in figure 10.4.

10.1.3 *Elements of a specification*

The foregoing discussion leads to the conclusion that the specification of a component, or a complete system, consists of the following elements:

a) The specification of the subcomponents identified within the component (or system). Each subcomponent specification refers to the specifications of the ports that are used by the subcomponent.

b) The specification of the ports (or port types) used by the subcomponents.

c) The interconnection structure which defines how the ports of the subcomponents are interconnected.

The specification of a port type is selfcontained and includes (a) an enumeration of the types of interactions that may occur at the port, including possible parameter values, and (b) the local rules of the port which may restrict the order and parameter values of the executed interactions. The specification of a subcomponent type contains (a) a declaration of the ports and their types, and (b) certain rules which determine the possible order of execution for the interactions at the different ports, including possible parameter values. It is understood that, in addition, the local rules specified for each of the ports will also be satisfied.

10.2 *A TRANSPORT SERVICE SPECIFICATION*

The transport service specification below is given as an example for demonstrating the approach to specifications outlined above. The object of the specification is the *service provider* component shown in figure 10.2, which extends over several communicating computer systems. The stepwise refinement of this service specification is considered in section 10.3 in relation with protocol specifications.

As explained in section 8.1.2, a communication service specification consists of three parts: (a) the enumeration of the interactions by which the user interacts with the service providing component, (b) the local rules determining the possible execution orders for interactions at one end of a connection, and (c) the global rules determining the end-to-end properties of the communication service. The points (a) and (b) correspond to the specification of the ports by which the *user* components (see figure 10.2) interact with the *service provider* component. They

are discussed in sections 10.2.1 and 10.2.2. Point (c), discussed
in section 10.2.3, consists of the rules defined in the *service
provider* specification.

10.2.1 *Ports and interaction primitives*

It is assumed, as shown in figure 10.2, that each user
of the transport service is associated (one by one) with an interface, sometimes called "service access point"[5], for interaction
with the service providing component. The different service access
points of the transport service can be identified by transport
addresses, thus providing for the addressing of the different
users. Each service access point is represented, in the specification, by two interconnected ports[6], a port of the *user*, and a port
of the *service provider*.

The ports of the *service provider* component may be
declared in the following form[7]:

component type
    TS_provider (AP : array [T_address_type] of TSAP (provider));

The component, has one port for each user address (an array of
ports, named *AP*) and the interactions at these ports are defined
by the port type *TSAP* for which the component plays the role of
the *provider*, which means that it may initiate certain interactions and must be responsive to certain other interactions as
specified below.

To simplify the example, it is assumed that each user is
involved in only one transport connection at a time. Then the
possible interactions at a service access point may be specified
as follows:

```
port type TSAP (user, provider)
    interaction by user :
        T_CONNECT_req (to_address : T_address_type;
                       proposed_options : option_type);
        T_CONNECT_resp (proposed_options : option_type);
        T_DISCONNECT_req;
        T_DATA_req (TS_user_data : string_of_octets;
                    last_fr : boolean);

    interaction by provider :
        T_CONNECT_ind (from_address : T_address_type;
                       proposed_options : option_type);
        T_CONNECT_conf (proposed_options : option_type);
        T_DISCONNECT_ind (TS_disconnect_reason : reason_type);
        T_DATA_ind (TS_user_data : string_of_octets;
                    last_fr : boolean );
```

A notation similar to Pascal function declarations is used here for the declaration of the interactions. It is assumed that the data type identifiers used in the definition of the interaction parameters have also been defined. For example, the parameters of the connect request *T_CONNECT_req*, to be initiated by a user component, are the address of the destination user and proposed options for the connection, such as expedited data transfer, etc. In order to keep the example simple, the options are, however, not considered further.

The specification method described in this chapter is based on a state transition formalism as explained in chapter 9. The interactions considered here correspond to the "operations" of chapter 9. Therefore each interaction is atomic, and any interaction activity that may be interrupted must be described by several interaction primitives, corresponding to (at least) the beginning and end of that activity. In the case of the transport service specification, this leads to the following conventions:

a) The interaction activity by which a user requests the establishment of a connection and is informed about the result of this request[8] is modeled by the two interactions *T_CONNECT_req* and *T_CONNECT_conf* (the latter, initiated by the

service providing component, may be replaced by a
T_DISCONNECT_ind in the case of a refusal by the destination
user component).

b) Similarly, the activity by which a user is informed about an
incoming connection request and its response to it, is modeled
by the primitives *T_CONNECT_ind* and *T_CONNECT_resp* (or
T_DISCONNECT_req).

c) The transfer of a single block of user data (sometimes called
"service data unit", which may be of arbitrary length and
interrupted by a disconnection) is modeled by a number of
T_DATA_req interactions (or *T_DATA_ind* interactions, when the
data is delivered) where each interaction transfers a fragment
of the data unit, and the second parameter of the interaction
indicates whether the end of the data unit has been attained.

10.2.2 *Local rules for a service access point*

As discussed in section 10.1, a port is associated with
"local rules" which determine in which order the interactions at
that port may be executed. For specifying such local rules, most
of the specification methods mentioned in section 9.9, and other
methods may be adopted. In the following example a state machine
model[7], is used for this purpose. The local rules for the transport service access points may then be defined as follows.

At any given instant in time, the set of allowed interactions is determined by two variables, which are associated with
an access point:

    state : (closed, open_in_progress, open);
    side : (calling, called);

The variable *state* is considered the "major state" and indicates
whether a connection is established (*open*) or being established.
The operation of a state transition is written in the form

```
    from <present major state>
    when <input interaction>
    provided <condition>
    to   <next major state>
    begin <statement> end;
```

Such a transition is possible when the enabling predicate is true, which is the conjunction of the from, when, and provided clauses[9]. If the transition is made the transition function[10] is executed, defined by the to and begin clauses[9]. The to clause assigns a new value to the major state, and the statement of the begin clause may update the other state variables[11].

The local rules for a service access point may be defined by the following transitions[12], which are graphically represented in figure 10.3:

```
from closed
    when T_CONNECT_req              to open_in_progress
        begin
            side := calling;
        end;

    when T_CONNECT_ind              to open_in_progress
        begin
            side := called;
        end;

from open_in_progress
    when T_DISCONNECT_req           to closed;
    when T_DISCONNECT_ind           to closed;
    when T_CONNECT_resp
        provided side = called      to open;
    when T_CONNECT_conf
        provided side = calling     to open;

from open
    when T_DISCONNECT_req           to closed;
    when T_DISCONNECT_ind           to closed;
    when T_DATA_req                 to open;
    when T_DATA_ind                 to open;
```

The first two transitions read: In the *closed* state, only *T_CONNECT_req* or *T_CONNECT_ind* may occur. In both cases the new major state will be *open_in_progress*, and the *side* variable will indicate whether the user at this access point is the *calling* or *called* party. The fifth transition indicates that a *T_CONNECT_resp* may occur when the major state is *open_in_progress* and the user is the *called* party. It is important to note that transitions are only defined for those interactions that are allowed to happen according to the local rules of the access point. For instance, a *T_CONNECT_resp* is only allowed to occur when the major state is *open_in_progress* and the user is the *called* party, that is, the user has just received a *T_CONNECT_ind*.

10.2.3 Specification of the service provider component

The nature of the specification of a component type is similar to the nature of a port type specification[13]. A component specification consists of a declaration of the different ports used by the component and a "global rule" which must be satisfied by the executions of the interactions at the different ports. In addition, it is understood that the local rules of the different ports are satisfied as well. For the above example, this means that for each port *AP[address]* of the component type *TS*, a *T_CONNECT_resp* may only occur when the user with address *address* has just received a *T_CONNECT_ind*.

Different methods may be used for the specification of the global rule of a component[4]. If the state machine model[7] introduced above is used for this purpose, the resulting service provider specification may look as follows:

```
component type TS_provider
        (AP : array [T_address_type] of TSAP (TS_provider) );
var
   close_in_progress : array [T_address_type] of boolean;
           (* this side has initiated a disconnect *)
   receive_buffer :  array [T_address_type] of TS_buffer_type;
   peer:            array [T_address_type] of T_address_type;
   options :        array [T_address_type (* calling side *)] of option_type;
   TS_reason : array [T_address_type (* disconnecting side *) ]
                                      of TS_disconnect_reason_type;
procedure record_connection (calling_addr, called_addr : T_address_type);
   begin
      close_in_progress [calling_addr] := false;
      close_in_progress [called_addr ] := false;
```

```
            peer [calling_addr] := called_addr;
            peer [called_addr ] := calling_addr;
        end;
    procedure free_connection (addr : T_address_type);
        begin
            peer [peer [addr]] := undefined;
            peer [addr] := undefined;
        end;
(* CONNECTION ESTABLISHMENT PHASE *)

when AP [addr] . T_CONNECT_req (to_address, proposed_options)
    begin
        if ... (* able to provide service *)
        then begin
            record_connection (addr, to_address);
            options [addr] := proposed_options;
            clear (EP[addr].receive_buffer);
            clear (EP[to_address].receive_buffer);
            end
        else AP [addr] . T_DISCONNECT_ind (...);
    end;

any calling_addr, called_addr : T_address_type do
    provided peer [calling_addr] = called_addr
        and AP [calling_addr] . state = open_in_progress
        and AP [called_addr] . state = closed
    (* when the connection request reaches the called side *)
    begin
        AP [called_addr] . T_CONNECT_ind (calling_addr,
                                          options [calling_addr] );
    end;

when AP [addr] . T_CONNECT_resp (proposed_options)
    provided proposed_options in options [peer[addr]]
    begin
        options [peer[addr]] := proposed_options;
    end;

any calling_addr, called_addr : T_address_type do
    provided peer [calling_addr] = called_addr
        and AP [calling_addr] . state = open_in_progress
        and AP [called_addr] . state = open
    (* when the connect response reaches the calling side *)
    begin
        AP [calling_addr] . T_CONNECT_conf (options [calling_addr]);
    end;

(* DATA TRANSFER *)

when AP [addr] . T_DATA_req (TS_user_data, last_fr)
    provided ... (* flow control to the service provider is ready *)
    begin
        append (receive_buffer [peer[addr]], TS_user_data, last_fr);
    end;

any addr : T_address_type do
    provided AP [addr] . state = open
        and fragment_ready (receive_buffer [addr])
        and ... (* flow control to the user is ready *)
    begin
        AP [addr] . T_DATA_ind (next_fragment (receive_buffer [addr])
                                was_last_fragment (receive_buffer [addr]) );
    end;

(* TERMINATION PHASE *)

when AP [addr] . T_DISCONNECT_req
    begin
        close_in_progress [addr] := true;
        TS_reason [addr] := TS_user_initiated_termination;
    end;
```

```
any addr : T_address_type do
   provided AP [addr] . state in [open_in_progress, open]
         and ... (* internal problem of TS_provider *)
      begin
         close_in_progress [addr] := true;
         TS_reason [addr] := ... ;
         AP [addr] . T_DISCONNECT_ind (TS_reason [addr]);
      end;

any addr : T_address_type do
   provided close_in_progress [peer[addr]]
         (* when the disconnect initiation reaches the other end of
                                                    the connection *)
      begin
         if  AP [addr] . state in [open_in_progress, open]
            then  AP [addr] . T_DISCONNECT_ind (TS_reason [peer[addr]]);
         free_connection (addr);
      end;
```

The above specification of the transport service component consists of three parts: (1) the declaration of the variables that determine the state of the component, (2) two definitions of procedures that are used by the transitions, and (3) the possible transitions of the component. Each service access point *AP[addr]* is associated with a *receive buffer* that contains the user data to be delivered at the access point. A transport connection is identified by the addresses of its two end-ponts, *calling_addr* and *called_addr*. Existing connections are recorded in the array *peer*. The transitions are written in a similar form as in section 10.2.2. The transitions starting with a *when* clause are only executed when the specified input interaction is initiated by a user over one of the service access points. The transitions starting with an *any* clause are spontaneous, and are executed when the indicated *provided* condition is satisfied.

For instance, the first transition is executed when the user at the access point with address *addr* initiates a *T_CONNECT_req* primitive providing the indicated parameters of destination address and desired options. In normal circumstances the requested connection is recorded in the state variables of the *TS_provider* component; otherwise a *T_DISCONNECT_ind* output primitive is returned to the user indicating that the connection request can not be granted. It is to be noted that the exchange of the service primitives changes the *state* of the service access point, as specified for the local rules in section 10.2.2. If the request is granted, the *AP[addr].state* has therefore the value *open_in_progress*.

This fact is used to determine when the second transition of the specification may be executed. For any pair of calling and called addresses that represent a recorded connection the second transition may be executed when the calling access point is in the *open_in_progress* state (that is, after the first transition has been executed successfully) and the called access point is still in the *closed* state. This transition then indicates the requested connection to the destination user. Similarly, the next two transitions describe the confirmation returned from the destination to the calling user.

The description of the data transfer phase is straightforward, although a certain number of functions and procedures are used which relate to the *receive_buffers* mentioned above. For the purpose of this specification, it is assumed that the meaning of these functions and procedures is understood. For a complete specification of the transport service, however, their meaning should be specified precisely. Specification methods developed for abstract data types could be useful for this purpose[4].

10.3 STEP-WISE REFINEMENT OF SPECIFICATIONS

10.3.1 *The internal structure of components: examples*

In the preceeding sections, it was assumed that the global rules of a component specification are directly given, for example, in terms of a state transition model. Instead, or in addition, as discussed in this section, the behavior of a component may also be defined by describing a refinement of the component in terms of sub-components and their interconnections. The concept of component substructure is relatively simple (see also section 2.3), and will be demonstrated in the following by some examples which show how the transport service specification given above can be refined into a protocol specification, and then into an implementation description.

As pointed out in section 8.1.3, a protocol specification is a refinement of a service specification where the following sub-components are considered (see also figure 10.4): (a) a component providing the underlying communication service, and (b) components executing the protocol at the different sites, also called "entities". A protocol specification is generally understood to be the specification of certain externally visible behavior characteristics of the protocol entities.

For the case of the transport service, the substructure of figure 10.4 may be expressed in the following linear form:

```
refinement TP_structure for TS_provider;
component
    NS : NS_provider;
    entities : array [N_address_type] of T_entity;
internal connection
    for addr in N_address_type
        entities[addr].N_service = NS.AP[addr];
external connection
    for addr in T_address_type
        entities[Network_prefix(addr)]
            . T_service[Transport_suffix(addr)] = AP[addr];
```
where the type *T_entity* of a transport protocol entity would be declared as
```
    component type T_entity
        (N_service : NSAP(user);
         T_service : array[T_suffix_type] of TSAP(provider));
```

The following hierarchical addressing convention is assumed. Each entity is associated with a single network service access point identified by a network address. A transport address consists of

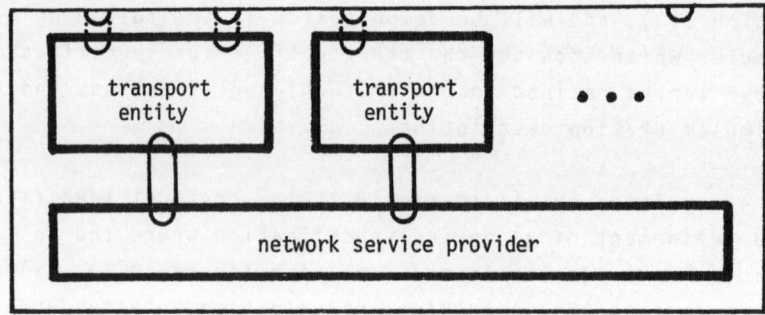

FIGURE 10.4: Refinement of the service provider component of figure 10.2 in view of defining the transport protocol. Notation of a channel (two interconnected ports): here and in figure 10.5 ⌼ ; elsewhere ↔

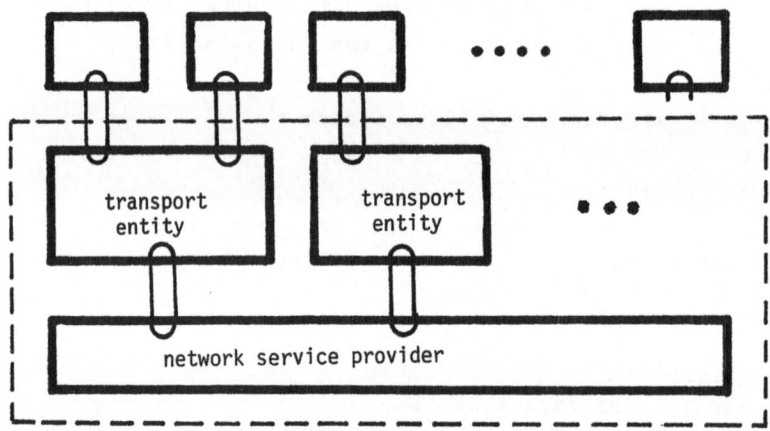

FIGURE 10.5: The refined transport service provider component of figure 10.4 in the environment of figure 10.2

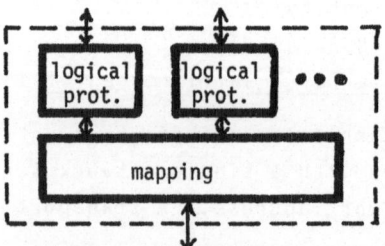

FIGURE 10.6: Possible substructure of the protocol entity of figure 10.4

identified by a network address. A transport address consists of a "transport suffix" and a "network prefix" . The latter is the network address of the entity serving the given transport service access point. Each entity provides the transport service to several access points which are distinguished by the "transport suffix" of the transport addresses.

Given the substructure above, a transport protocol specification is a specification of global rules for the behavior of entities of type *T_entity*. Such a specification may be given using the state transition formalism discussed in section 10.2[14].

Further subdivisions for a protocol entity are often considered. The most important one is a distinction between (a) the logical behavior of the entity in terms of (N)- service interactions and protocol data units (PDUs) exchanged through the underlying communication service with the peer protocol entity, and (b) the mapping of the PDU's into the underlying (N-1)-service interactions. This leads to a substructure of a transport entity as shown in figure 10.6, which contains a single *mapping* component and one *logical protocol* component for each access point serviced. A protocol specification would consist of separate specifications for the two types of sub-components: The *logical protocol* component determines the order of service interactions with the user and PDU's exchanged with a peer component at another site. PDU's and control information are exchanged over the interconnections between these two types of components. The mapping component determines the coding of the PDU's in terms of the service data units exchanged through the underlying layer.

10.3.2 *Comments on component substructure*

As indicated in figure 10.4 and the interconnection syntax of the example above, two kinds of "interconnections" must be distinguished: internal and external ones.

The latter specify which ports of the implementing sub-components represent the (external) ports that are defined in the more abstract specification of the refined component. Therefore the same kind of external connections will be found for any refinement of the component, unless the ports are also refined as discussed below.

The internal connections have no counterpart in the more abstract view of the (non refined) component. An internal connection[6] between the ports of two sub-components supports the communication between the sub-components in terms of the interactions defined for the interconnected port types. Clearly, only ports of identical or "similar" type may be connected[15]. It is important to note that external connections may give rise to internal connections in a larger context, as indicated in figure 10.5.

Refinements, as discussed above, are usually applied in several steps, leading to a more and more detailed system description. As shown by an example in Annex 3, this may lead to a level of detail which allows direct realization in hardware. If software implementation is sought, it seems convenient to convert at a certain level of detail to a description in terms of a programming language, which is used to directly implement the sub-components obtained in the previous refinement steps.

10.3.3 *Port refinements*

In the discussion above, it was assumed that the interaction primitives of the component are the same for the more abstract and more detailed descriptions. It seems to be important to consider also a step-wise refinement of interaction primitives and port types.

A port of a component represents an abstract interface of that component; it defines the possible interactions and rules for their execution, as explained in section 10.1.2. An implementation involving a refinement of a port brings up the following two questions:

a) Is a given interaction of the port, which is a primitive at the abstract level of the specification, realized by several "sub-interactions" at the more detailed level of the implementation?

b) Is a given port composed of several sub-ports? (In this case a non-primitive interaction may involve sub-interactions at several different sub-ports).

The main application of port refinement in communication software design relates to the implementation of the interfaces between protocol layers. In a service specification, these interfaces are defined on an abstract level in terms of the service primitives exchanged between the layers. The protocol specifications are also based on this abstract interface. One of the important design choices during protocol implementation is the determination of a realization of these interfaces in terms of procedure calls, interprocess communication primitives, or other software or hardware constructs.

Annex 3 describes in more detail a possible approach to port refinement, which is demonstrated by a hardware example. It also considers the verification that an abstract component specification is satisfied by a more detailed specification based on sub-components, refined ports, and their interconnection.

FOOTNOTES

1. See for example [FDT 82b]. Much of the discussion in this chapter is based on the concepts described in annexes 1 and 3, where further references are given. The syntax for the examples is borrowed (with modifications) from [FDT 82b] and annex 3.

2. The assumption of such an interaction mechanism simplifies the model without restricting its descriptive power; for example, a message queuing mechanism may be specified by the introduction of an explicit buffering component. However, message queuing introduces possible delays between the "sending" and "receiving", which may lead to more complicated system behavior. Methods for avoiding such complications are discussed in [Boch 79].

3. Since, in general, an interaction is executed when both components invoke the interaction as a rendezvous, both components may, in principle, participate in the determination of the parameter values. Such a situation must be considered, for example, when a connection establishement request and its confirmation are considered a single "interaction", as in Annex 1, section III . Other examples are discussed in Annex 3.

4. The specification methods mentioned in section 9.9 and other methods may be adopted. While chapter 10 concentrates on state-oriented descriptions, global rules for communication services may in fact be better described by sequence-oriented methods [Logr 82, FDT 82c].

5. A service access point may be considered an instance of an abstract interface (see section 8.1.2).

6. The interconnection of two ports is sometimes called a "channel".

7. Here and in the following, a specification language close to the proposed formal description technique of ISO [FDT 82b] is used. Many of the language elements are borrowed from Pascal. The underlined words are reserved identifiers of the language. The concepts of this state machine model are also explained in Annex 1.

8. This whole interaction activity may be considered a single "extended interaction", simply called "interaction" or "service primitive" in section 8. This implies, however that such extended interactions may be interrupted by other interactions, for example the user abandoning his request (see for example Annex 1 or [FDT 82c]).

9. The differents clauses are optional, i.e. not required for every transition.

10. The transition is functional in the sense of section 9.1.2.

11. In general, the statement of the <u>begin</u> clause may also include the initiation of output interactions. However, this is not needed for the specification of local rules.

12. In this example, embedded transition clauses are used. Each pair of <u>when</u> and <u>to</u> clauses represents a "transition".

13. Here and in the following we often simply say component (or port) for a component (or port) <u>type</u>.

14. See for example [FDT 82]. Similar state transition models have also been used in [Boch 77b], Annexes 1 and 2, [Blum 82], [Piat 83], [Boch 82b].

15. It is important to note that during the phase of the compilation of a component refinement description, it is possible to perform certain consistency checks. In particular, the port types and roles can be checked for each connection. Another check would be to detect ports that have not been used for any connection.

References

[Akko 74] E.A. Akkoyunlu, A.J. Bernstein and R.E. Schwarz, "Interprocess communication facilities for network operating systems", Computer (IEEE) 7,6 (June 1974), pp. 46-55.

[Ande 75] G.A. Anderson and E.D. Jensen, "Computer interconnection structures: taxonomy, characteristics and examples", ACM Computing Surveys 7,4 (Dec. 1975), pp. 197-213.

[Ashc 75] E.A. Ashcroft, "Proving assertions about parallel programs", J. Comp. Sys. Sci. 10,1 (Jan. 1975), pp. 110-135.

[Aviz 77] A. Avizienis, "Fault-tolerant computing : progress, problems and prospects", Proc. IFIP Congress 1977, pp. 405-420.

[Barb 77] D.L.A. Barber, "The role and nature of a virtual terminal", ACM Computer Comm. Review 7, 3 (July 1977), pp. 5-22.

[Barb 78] D.L.A. Barber, T. Kalin and C. Solomonides, "An implementation of the X.25 interface in a datagram network", Computer Networks 2 (1978), pp. 340-345.

[Bart 69] K.A. Bartlett et al., "A note on reliable full-duplex transmission over half-duplex links", Comm. ACM 12, 5 (May 1969), pp. 260-261.

[Bart 77] W. Bartussek and D.L. Parnas, "Using traces to write abstract specifications for software modules", UNC Report TR 77-012, University of North Carolina, Dec. 1977; also Proc. ECI Conf., Venise, 1978.

[Bekk 77] Y. Bekkers, J. Briat and J.P. Verjus, "Construction of a synchronization scheme by independent definition of parallelism", Proc. IFIP Working Conference on Constructing Quality Software, North-Holland Publ., 1978, pp. 193-205.

[Belp 75] G. Belpaire, "On programming dependencies between parallel processes", Techn. Report 244, Comp. Sc. Dept., University of Wisconsin, March 1975.

[Bern 81] P.A. Bernstein and N. Goodman, "Concurrency control in distributed database systems", ACM Computing Surveys 13, 2 (June 1981), pp. 185-221.

[Bert 80] H.V. Bertine, "Physical level protocols", in [Gree 82].

[Bert 82] G. Berthelet and R. Terrat, "Petri net theory for the correctness of protocols", in [INWG 82], also to be published in IEEE Trans. COM.

[Blum 82] T.P. Blumer and R. Tenney, "A formal specification technique and implementation method for protocols", Computer Networks 6,3 (July 1982), pp. 201-217.

[Boch 77] G.V. Bochmann and J. Gecsei, "A unified model for the specification and verification of protocols", Proc. IFIP Congress 1977, North Holland, Amsterdam, 1977, p. 229-234.

[Boch 77b] G.V. Bochmann and R.J. Chung, "A formalized description of HDLC classes of procedures", Proc. National Telecommunications Conference, IEEE, 1977, pp. 03A..2-1 to 2-11.

[Boch 77c] G.V. Bochmann, "Standards issues in data communications", Telecommunications Policy, 1,5 (Dec. 1977), pp. 381-388.

[Boch 77d] G.V. Bochmann, "Combining assertions and states for the validation of process communication", Proc. IFIP Working Conference on Constructing Quality Software, North Holland, 1978, pp. 229-232.

[Boch 78] G.V. Bochmann, "Finite state description of communication protocols", Computer Networks 2 (Oct. 1978), pp. 361-372.

[Boch 79] G.V. Bochmann, "Distributed synchronization and regularity", Computer Networks 3 (1979), pp. 36-43.

[Boch 79b] G.V. Bochmann and J. Tankoano, "Development and structure of an X.25 implementation", IEEE Transactions on Software Engineering, SE-5,5 (Sept. 1979), pp. 429-439.

[Boch 80] G.V. Bochmann, "A general transition model for protocols and communication services", IEEE Trans. Comm., COM-28, 4 (April 1980), pp. 643-650.

[Boch 80b] G.V. Bochmann and C.A. Sunshine, "Formal Methods in Communication Protocol Design", IEEE Trans. COM-28,4 (April 1980), pp. 624-631.

[Boch 82] G.V. Bochmann and E. Cerny, "Protocol Assessment", Dendronic Decision Ltd., Montreal, 1982, prepared under contract for DOC, Canada.

[Boch 82b] G.V. Bochmann, L. Henckel and R.P. Zeletin, "Formalized specification and analysis of a virtual file system", Techn. Report HMI-B307 Hahn-Meitner-Institut, Berlin (Febr. 1982).

[Boch 83] G.V. Bochmann and M. Raynal, "Structured Specification of Communicating Systems", IEEE Trans. Computers, Febr. 1983.

[Bogg 80] D.R. Boggs et al., "Pup: an internetwork architecture", in [Gree 82].

[Brin 70] P. Brinch-Hansen, "The nucleus of a multiprogramming system", Comm. ACM 13,4 (April 1970), pp. 238-241, 250.

[Brin 73] P. Brinch-Hansen, "Operating systems principles", Prentice-Hall, Englewood Cliffs, 1973.

[Brin 75] P. Brinch-Hansen, "The programming language Concurrent Pascal", IEEE Transactions on Software Eng., SE-1 (1975), pp. 199-207.

[Burt 72] H.O. Burton and D.D. Sullivan, "Errors and error control", Proc. of the IEEE, Nov. 1972, pp. 1193-1301.

[Camp 74] R.H. Campbell and A.N. Habermann, "The specification of process synchronization by path expressions", in Lecture Notes in Comp. Sc., Vol. 16, Springer, Berlin, 1974.

[Carl 80] D.E. Carlson, "Bit-oriented data link control procedures", in [Gree 82].

[Cave 78] J.K. Cavers, "Implementation of X.25 on a multiple microprocessor system", Proc. Intern. Comm. Conf., 1978.

[Cerf 74] V.G. Cerf and R.E. Kahn, "A protocol for packet network intercommunication", IEEE Transactions on Comm., COM-22, 1974, pp. 637-648.

[Cheri 79] D.R. Cheridon, M.A. Malcolm, L.S. Melen and G.A. Sager, "Thoth, a portable real-time operating system", Comm. ACM 22, 2 (Febr. 1979), pp. 105-115.

[Chun 79] R.J. Chung, and A.M. Rybczynski, "Alternatives for providing highly reliable access to X.25 networks", Proc. Nat. Comm. Conf. 1979.

[Clip 76] W.W. Clipsham, "Security in public packet-switching networks", Proc. IRIA Workshop on protection and security in data networks, June 1976, Cyclades Report SEC 021.

[Coff 73] E.G. Coffmann and P.J. Denning, "Operating systems theory", Prentice-Hall, 1973.

[Cour 71] P.J. Courtois et al., "Concurrent control with readers and writers", Comm. ACM 14, 10 (Oct. 1971), pp. 667-668.

[Cour 77] P.J. Courtois, "Decomposability : queuing and computer system applications", Academic Press, 1977.

[Cunn 77] I.M. Cunningham, W.J. Older and A.K. Trividi, "DATAPAC software architecture", Bell-Northern Research, Febr. 1977.

[Cyps 78] R.J. Cypser, "Communications architecture for distributed systems", Addison-Wesley, 1978.

[Dahl 72] O.J. Dahl and C.A.R. Hoare, "Hierarchical program structures", in Structured Programming, Academic Press, 1972.

[Dant 75] A. Dantine and E. Eschenauer, "Influence on the node behavior of the node-to-node protocol", Proc. 4-th Data Comm. Symp. (ACM/IEEE), 1975, pp. 7-1 to 7-8.

[DATAPAC] The following articles in Proc. International Conference on Computer Communications (ICCC), 1976, pp. 119-156
(a) W.W. Clipsham et al., "Datapac network overview", pp. 131-136.
(b) S.C.K. Young and C.I. McGibbon, "The control system of the Datapac network", pp. 137-142.
(c) D.A. Twyver and A.M. Rybczynski, "Datapac subscriber interfaces", pp. 143-149.
(d) P.M. Cashin, "Datapac network protocols", pp. 150-156.

[Davi 73] D.W. Davies and D.L.A. Barber, "Communication networks for computers", John Wiley & Sons, London, 1973.

[Davi 77] J. Davidson et al., "The Arpanet Telnet protocol : Its purpose, principles, implementation and impact on host operating system design", Proc. Fifth Data Communications Symposium, ACM/IEEE, 1977, pp. 4-10 to 4-18.

[Davi 79] D.W. Davies, D.L.A. Barber, W.L. Price, C.M. Solomonides, "Computer Networks and their Protocols", John Wiley, 1979.

[Delo 80] C. Delobel and W. Litwin, ed., "Distributed Data Bases", North-Holland, 1980.

[Depa 76]   M. Deparis et al., "The implementation of an end-to-end protocol by EIN centres : a survey and comparison", Proc. ICCC, 1976, pp. 351-360.

[Didi 82]   M. Didic and B. Wolfinger, "Simulation of a local computer network architecture applying a unified modeling system", Computer Networks 6, 2 (May 1982), pp. 75-91.

[Dijk 68]   E.W. Dijkstra, "Cooperating sequential processes", in Programming Languages (F. Genuys, ed.), Academic Press, 1968.

[Dijk 68b] E.W. Dijkstra, "The structure of the THE multiprogramming system", Comm. ACM 11,5 (May 1968), pp. 341-346.

[Dijk 74]   E.W. Dijkstra, "Self stabilizing systems in spite of distributed control", Comm. ACM 17,11 (Nov. 1974), pp. 643-644.

[Dijk 75]   E.W. Dijkstra, "Guarded commands, nondeterminacy, and formal derivation of programs", Comm. ACM 18,8 (Aug. 1975), 453-457.

[Ensl 77]   P.H. Enslow, "Multiprocessor organization - a survey", ACM Computing Surveys 9,1 (March 1977), pp. 103-129.

[Farb 75]   D.J. Farber and K.C. Larson, "Network security via dynamic process renaming", Proc. Fourth Data Communications Symposium, ACM/IEEE, 1975, pp. 8-13 to 8-18.

[FDT 82]   "Example of a Transport protocol specification", by G.V. Bochmann, contribution to meeting of ISO TC97/SC16/WG1 ad hoc group on FDT (1982).

[FDT 82b]   ISO TC97/SC16/WG1 ad hoc group on FDT, "A Formal Description Technique based on an extended finite state transition model", working document of Subgroup B (1982).

[FDT 82c]   ISO TC97/SC16/WG1 ad hoc group on FDT, "Interaction primitives in formal specification of distributed systems", working document of Subgroup C (1982).

[Floy 67]   R.W. Floyd, "Assigning meaning to programs", Proc. Symp. in Applied Mathematics, Vol. 19 (1967), American Math. Soc., pp. 19-32.

[Folt 78]   H.C. Folts, "Evolution toward a universal interface for data communications", Proc. Int. Conf. on Comp. Comm., Kyoto, 1978, pp. 675-680.

[Gagn 82]   M. Gagné, "Un compilateur pour la traduction de spécifications de protocoles en Pascal", Document de travail 110, Département d'informatique et de recherche opérationnelle, Université de Montréal, Février 1982.

[Gall 68]   R.G. Gallanger, "Information theory and reliable communication" (chapt. 6.8), Wiley, 1968.

[Garc 81]   J.J. Garcia-Luna and F.F. Kuo, "Addressing and directory systems for large computer mail systems", in Computer Message Systems, ed. R.P. Uhlig, North Holland, 1981, pp. 297-313.

[Gien 78]   M. Gien, "A file transfer protocol", Computer Networks 2 (1978), pp. 312-319.

[Goos 72]   G. Goos, J. Jurgens and K. Lagally, "The operating system BSM viewed as a community of parallel processes", Abteilung Mathematik der TU Munchen, Bericht Nr. 7208, 1972.

[Gree 82] P.E. Green, ed., "Computer Network Architectures and Protocols", Plenum Press, 1982; originally Special Issue of IEEE Trans. COM-28, 4 (April 1980).

[Gutt 77] J. Guttag, "Abstract Data Types and the Development of Data Structures", Comm. ACM, Vol. 28, 6, (June 1977), pp. 396-404.

[Hail 80] B. Hailpern and S. Owicki, "Verifying network protocols using temporal logic", Proc. Trends and Applications, 1980, NBS, Maryland.

[Hech 76] H. Hecht, "Fault-tolerant software for real-time applications", ACM Computing Surveys 8,4 (Dec. 1976), pp. 391-408.

[Hert 78] F. Hertweck et al., "X.25 based process-process communication", Computer Networks 2 (1978), pp. 250-270.

[Hoar 69] C.A.R. Hoare, "An axiomatic basis for computer programming", Comm. ACM 12,10 (Oct. 1969), pp. 576-580.

[Hoar 74] C.A.R. Hoare, "Monitors : an operating systems structuring concept", Comm. ACM 17,10 (Oct. 1974), pp. 549-557.

[Hoar 78] C.A.R. Hoare, "Communicating sequential processes", Comm. ACM 21,8 (Aug. 1978), pp. 666-677.

[Hobb 72] L.C. Hobbs, "Terminals", Proc. IEEE 60,11 (Nov. 1972), pp. 1173-1184.

[Horn 73] J.J. Horning and B. Randell, "Process structuring", ACM Computing Surveys 5,1 (March 1973), pp. 5-30.

[Ichb 79] J.D. Ichbiah et al., ACM Sigplan Notices 14,6 (June 1979).

[IEEE 82] Proposed standard IEEE 802 on local area networks (1982).

[INWG 82] Proceedings of Second Intern. Workshop on Protocol Specification, Testing, and Verification (IFIP WG 6.1), North Holland (1982).

[Jame 78] B. Jamet and G. Mainguenaud, "A multi-line data link control procedure", Proc. ICCC-78 (1978), pp. 289-294.

[Jamm 77] A.J. Jammel and H.G. Stiegler, "Managers versus monitors", Proc. IFIP Congress 1977, pp. 827-830.

[Jard 81] C. Jard and G.V. Bochmann, "An Approach to Testing Specifications", Publ. 430, Département d'informatique et de recherche opérationnelle, Université de Montréal, 1981.

[Jard 82] C. Jard, "Spécification et validation d'un algorithme distribué d'exclusion mutuelle - mise en oeuvre de la simulation: méthode et résultats", Note technique NT/LAA/SLC/93, CNET Lannion, France, July 1982.

[Kahn 72] R.E. Kahn, "Resource-sharing computer communications networks", Proc. IEEE 60,11 (Nov. 1972), pp. 1397-1407.

[Kahn 74] G. Kahn, "The semantics of a simple language for parallel programming", Proc. IFIP Congress 1974, pp. 471-475.

[Karp 69]   R. Karp and R.E. Miller, "Parallel program schemata", Journal of Comp. and Systems Sci. 3, pp. 147-195 (1969).

[Kell 76]   R.M. Keller, "Formal verification of parallel programs", Comm. ACM 19,7 (July 1976), pp. 371-384.

[Kess 77]   J.L.W. Kessels "An alternative to event queues for synchronization in monitors", Comm. ACM 20,7 (July 1977), pp. 500-503.

[Kirs 76]   P.J. Kirstein, "Planned new public data networks", Computer Networks 1,2 (Sept. 1976).

[Klei 75]   L. Kleinrock, "Queuing Systems", Vol. I : Theory, Vol. II : Computer applications, Wiley, 1975-76.

[Knob 75]   D.E. Knoblock et al., "Insight into interfacing", IEEE Spectrum, May 1975.

[Kohl 81]   W.H. Kohler, "A survey of techniques for synchronization and recovery in decentralized computer systems", ACM Computing Surveys 13,2 (June 1981), pp. 149-183.

[Lamp 73]   B. Lampson, "A note of the confinement problem", Comm. ACM 16,10 (Oct. 1973), pp. 613-615.

[Lamp 74]   L. Lamport, "A new solution of Dijkstra's concurrent programming problem", Comm. ACM 17,8 (August 1974), pp. 453-455.

[Lamp 78]   L. Lamport, "Time, clocks and the ordering of events in a distributed system", Comm. ACM 21,7 (July 1978), pp.558-565.

[Laue 75]   P.E. Lauer and R.H. Campbell, "Formal semantics of a class of high-level primitives for coordinating concurrent processes", Acta Informatica 5 (1975) pp. 297-332.

[LeGu 80]   P. Le Guernic, M. Raynal, "Elements d'un langage adapté à la communication entre processus", Actes du Congrès AFCET, Nancy-France, (Nov. 1980), pp. 667-676.

[Lela 77]   G. LeLann, "Distributed systems - towards a formal approach", Proc. IFIP Congress 1977, North Holland Publ., pp. 155-160.

[Lela 78]   G. LeLann and H. LeGoff, "Verification and evaluation of communication protocols", Computer Networks 2,1 (Febr. 1978), pp. 50-69.

[Lind 76]   T.A. Linden, "Operating system structures to support security and reliable software", ACM Computing surveys 8,4 (Dec. 1976), pp. 409-445.

[Lisk 75]   B. Liskov and S. Zilles, "Specification techniques for data abstractions", IEEE Trans. on Software Engineering 1,1 (March 1975), pp. 7-18.

[Logr 82]   L. Logrippo, "Specification of transport service using finite-state transducers and abstract data types", Techn. Report, University of Ottawa, 1982.

[Mart 69]   J. Martin, "Telecommunications and the computer", Prentice-Hall, 1969.

[Mart 70]   J. Martin, "Teleprocessing network organization", Prentice-Hall, 1970.

[Mart 72] J. Martin, "Systems analysis for data transmission", Prentice-Hall, 1972.

[Mart 77] J.G. Martins, "Communication implicite entre des processus répartis sur un réseau hétérogène", Thèse DEA, INPG, Grenoble, Sept. 1977.

[Masu 78] Y. Masunaga, "A probabilistic automaton model of the NRM, HDX HDLC procedure", Computer Networks 2,6 (Dec. 1978), pp. 442-453.

[Mell 77] F. Mellor, W.J. Olden and C.J. Bedard, "A message-switched operating system for a multiprocessor", Proc. COMPSAC 77 (IEEE Chicago, 1977), pp. 772-777.

[Mena 79] D.A. Menasce and R.R. Muntz, "Locking and deadlock detection in distributed databases", IEEE Trans. on Software Eng., SE-5,3 (May 1979), pp. 195-202.

[Merl 76b] P.M. Merlin and D.J. Farber, "Recoverability of communication protocols - implications of a theoretical study", IEEE Transact. on Comm., Sept. 1976, pp. 1036-1043.

[Merl 77] P.M. Merlin and A. Segall, "A failsafe distributed routing protocol", IEEE Trans., Comm., COM-27,9 (Sept. 1979).

[Merl 77b] P.M. Merlin and B. Randell, "Consistant state restoration in distributed systems", IEEE FTCS-8, Int. Conf. Fault-Tol. Comp., Toulouse, France, 1978, pp. 129-134.

[Metc 76] R.M. Metcalfe and D.R. Boggs, "Ethernet : distributed packet switching for local computer networks", Comm. ACM 16,7 (July 1976), pp. 395-404.

[Miln 80] R. Milner, "A calculus of communicating systems", Lecture Notes in CS, No. 92, Springer Verlag, 1980.

[Miln 82] R. Milner, "Four combinators for concurrency", in [PODC 82], pp. 104-110.

[Nayl 75] W.E. Naylor, "A loop-free adaptive routing algorithm for packet switched networks", Proc. Fourth Data Communications Symposium, ACM/IEEE, 1975, pp. 7-9 to 7-14.

[Need 78] R.M. Needham and M.D. Schroeder, "Using encryption for authentication in large networks of computers", Comm. ACM 21,12 (Dec. 1978), pp. 993-999.

[Noe 73]   J.D. Noe and G.J. Nutt, "Macro E-Nets for representation of parallel systems", IEEE Trans. Comp. C-22,8 (Aug. 1973), 718-727.

[OSI 83]   IEEE Proceedings, September 1983.

[OSI TS]   ISO/DP 8072, "Information processing systems - Open Systems Interconnection - Transport service definition", 1982.

[OSI TP]   ISO/DP 8073,"Information processing systems - Open Systems Interconnection - Transport protocol specification", 1982.

[OSI FS]   ISO TC97/SC16/WG5, "Working draft on File Transfer, Access, and Management" (1982).

[OSI RM]   ISO DIS 7498, "Data processing - Open Systems Interconnection - Basic Reference Model", 1982.

[Parn 74] D.L. Parnas, "On a "buzzword" : hierarchical structure", Proc. IFIP Congress 1974, pp. 336-339.

[Parn 77] D.L. Parnas, "The use of precise specifications in the development of software", Proc. IFIP Congress 1977, pp. 861-867.

[Peas 80] M. Pease, R. Shostak, and L. Lamport, "Reaching agreement in the presence of faults", J. ACM 27, 2 (April 1980), pp. 228-234.

[Pete 74] J.L. Peterson and T.H. Bredt, "A comparison of models of parallel computation", Proc. IFIP Congress 1974, North-Holland, Amsterdam, 1974, pp. 466-470.

[Pete 77] J.L. Peterson, "Petri nets", ACM Computing Survey 9,3 (Sept. 1977), pp. 223-252.

[Piat 83] T.F. Piatkowski, Lap-Kin Ip, and Dayun He, "State Architecture notation and simulation", to be published in Computer Networks.

[PLP 82]   "Videotex/Teletext Presentation Level Protocol Syntax (North American PLPS)", Preliminary Standard T.500-1982, Canadian Standards Association ISSN0317-7874, Aug. 1982.

[PODC 82] Proc. ACM Sigact-Sigops Symposium on Principles of Distributed Computing, Aug. 1982, Ottawa.

[Pouz 73] L. Pouzin, "Presentation and major design aspects of the Cyclades computer network", Proc. Third Data Communications Symposium, ACM/IEEE, 1973, pp. 80-87.

[Prob 77] W.G. Probst and G.V. Bochmann, "Operating systems design with computer network communication protocols", Proc. Fifth Data Communications Symposium, ACM/IEEE, 1977, pp. 4-19 to 4-25.

[Ragu 82] K.S. Raghunathan, J.A. Barchanski, and G.V. Bochmann, "Relation between performance parameters for transport and network services", Techn. Report, Dept. d'I.R.O., University of Montreal, 1982.

[Rand 75] B. Randell, "System structure for software fault-tolerance", Proc. International Conf. on Reliable Software, IEEE/ACM, 1975, pp. 437-449.

[Rash 81] R.F. Rashid and G.G. Robertson, "Accent: a communication oriented network operating system kernel", Proc. ACM Symp. on Operating Systems Principles (1981), pp. 64-75.

[Rayn 82] D. Rayner, "A system for testing protocol implementations", in [INWG 82], also to be published in Computer Networks.

[Redz 77] R.R. Redziejowski, "Parallel processes and languages with infinite words", submitted to J. ACM, March 1977.

[Ridd 72] W.E. Riddle, "The modeling and analysis of supervisory systems", PhD thesis, Computer Sc. Dept., Stanford University, March 1972.

[Robe 70] L.G. Roberts and B.D. Wessler, "Computer network development to achieve resource sharing", Proc. SJCC, AFIPS, 1970, pp. 543-549.

[Robe 77] P. Robert and J.P. Verjus, "Toward autonomous descriptions of synchronization modules", Proc. IFIP Congress 1977, pp. 981-986.

[Rudi 78] H. Rudin, C.H. West, and P. Zafiropulo, "Automated protocol validation : one chain of development", Computer Networks 2, 4/5 (1978), pp. 373-380.

[Rybc 77] A.M. Rybczynski and D.F. Weir, "Datapac X.25 service characteristics", Proc. Fifth Data Communications Symposium, ACM/IEEE, 1977, pp. 4-50 to 4-57.

[Sand 76] R.W. Sanders and V. Cerf, "Compatibility or chaos in communications", Datamation, March 1976.

[Sari 82] B. Sarikaya and G.V. Bochmann, "Some experience with test sequence generation for protocols", in [INWG 82], pp. 555-567.

[Schi 81] P. Schicker, "The computer based mail environment - an overview", Computer Networks 5 (1981), pp. 435-443.

[Schl 82] R.D. Schlichting and F.B. Schneider, "Understanding and using asynchronous message passing", in [PODC 82].

[Schw 82] D. Schwabe, "Formal specification and verification of a connection establishment protocol", Proc. 7th Data Comm. Symp. (IEEE/ACM), Mexico, 1982, pp. 11-26.

[Sevc 72] K.C. Sevcick et al., "Project SUE as a learning experience", Proc. FJCC 1972, AFIPS 41, p. 331.

[Shoc 78] J.F. Shoch, "Inter-network naming, addressing and routing", Proc. IEEE Compcon 78, Sept. 1978, pp. 72-79.

[Simo 62] H.A. Simon, "The architecture of complexity", Proc. American Philosophical Society 106 (1962), pp. 468-482.

[Sten 76] N.V. Stenning, "A data transfer protocol", Computer Networks 1, 1976, pp. 99-110.

[Suns 81] C.A. Sunshine, ed., "Communication protocol modeling", Artech House Inc., 1981.

[Thom 78] R.H. Thomas, "A solution to the update problem for multiple copy data bases", Proc. 1979 COMPCON Conf. (IEEE), New York.

[Wang 82] J. Wang, "Delay and throughput analysis for computer communications with balanced HDLC procedures", IEEE Trans. Computers C-31,8 (Aug. 1982).

[Wats 80] R.W. Watson and J.G. Fletcher, "An architecture for support of network operating sytem services", Computer Networks 4 (1980), pp. 33-49.

[Weck 80] S. Wecker, "DNA: The digital network architecture", in [Gree 82].

[Whit 78] C. Whitby-Strevens, "Towards the performance evaluation of distributed computing systems", Chicago, Nov. 1978.

[Wirt 77] N. Wirth, "Toward a discipline of real-time programming", Comm. ACM 20,8 (Aug. 1977), pp. 577-583.

[Wirt 77b] N. Wirth, "Modula : a language for modular multiprogramming", Softw. Pract. Experience 7,1 (Jan-Feb. 1977), pp. 3-35.

[Wulf 74] W.A. Wulf et al., "HYDRA : the kernel of a multi-processor operating system", Comm. ACM 17,6 (June 1974), pp. 337-345.

[Zimm 75] H. Zimmermann, "The Cyclades end-to-end protocol", Proc. Fourth Data Communications Symposium, ACM/IEEE, 1975, pp. 7-21 to 7-26.

[Zimm 80] H. Zimmermann, "OSI Reference Model", in [Gree 82].

Annex

Possible Approaches to Stepwise Refinement, Protocol Specification and Implentation

In order to provide a more detailed discussion of some of the concepts described in chapter 10, we include in this annex the following papers:

ANNEX 1: "A general transition model for protocols and communication services" (Published in IEEE Transactions on Communications, April 1980). This paper presents an extended state transition model, similar in nature to the one used in section 10.2 for the description of local and global rules of service interactions. The application of this model to the formal description of protocols is reviewed, and an extension of the model, using production rules, is used to specify the end-to-end properties of communication services.

ANNEX 2: "Development and structure of an X.25 implementation" (by G.V. Bochmann and J. Tankoano, published in IEEE Transactions on Software Engineering, Sept. 1979). This paper describes the development of an X.25 implementation based on a formal description, which was given using the extended state transition model of Annex 1. The paper describes the systematic translation of the formal description into elements of a Concurrent Pascal program, and discusses the difficulties encountered.

ANNEX 3: "Structured specification of communicating systems" (by G.V. Bochmann and M. Raynal, published in IEEE Transactions on Computers, Febr. 1983). This paper elaborates on the concepts of components, ports and step-wise refinement as discussed in chapter 10, and provides further examples. It also discusses step-wise refinements of port specifications, using a hardware arbiter as example. Similar considerations apply in the context of communication software design for the development of implementations for service access points and other interfaces.

We thank the publisher for the kind permission to include these papers here.

Annex 1

A General Transition Model for Protocols and Communication Services

(Gregor v. Bochmann)

(Invited Paper)

Abstract—Different approaches have been used for the formal specification and verification of communication protocols. This paper explains the approach of using a general transition model which combines aspects of finite state transition diagrams and programming languages. Different ways of structuring a protocol into separate modules or functions are also discussed.

The main part of the paper describes a method for exactly specifying the communication service provided by a protocol. Two aspects of a service specification are distinguished: 1) the local properties which characterize the interface through which the service may be accessed, and 2) the global properties which describe the "end-to-end" communication characteristics of the service. It is shown how the specification method is related to the general transition model for protocol specification. Verification is discussed briefly with emphasis on the use of invariant assertions in the context of finite state as well as programming language protocol descriptions.

The discussed topics are demonstrated with examples based on the HDLC classes of procedures and the X.25 Virtual Circuit data transmission service.

I. INTRODUCTION

DIFFERENT approaches have been used for the formal specification and verification of communication protocols. As explained in another paper of this collection, most of these approaches use finite state transition diagrams or programs written is some high-level programming language or both. The purpose of this paper is threefold.

First, in Section II, we review some experience with a general transition model, which we called a "unified" approach [1] because it involves state transitions and programming language elements. We believe that such an approach is appropriate for the formal specification of protocols, the specification of the services provided, and the verification of correct operation. In Section IV, we point out certain similarities between finite state transition and programming language approaches to verification. Knowledge of the indicated references may be useful, but are not necessary for the understanding of these sections.

Second, we discuss these issues by considering, as an example, the HDLC classes of procedures.

Third—and this is the main part of the paper in Section III—we describe a method for specifying the communication service provided by a protocol. While certain aspects of this method are related to our "unified" approach, we believe that most elements of the method are of general validity and applicability. In fact, the method is related to software engineering methods [2] for specifying software modules. However, certain elements of our method are specific to protocols due to their distributed nature.

II. A GENERAL TRANSITION MODEL

For a given communication layer of a distributed computer system, we assume that the protocol is specified by separate descriptions for both entities executing the protocol, as shown in Fig. 1. We explain in this section the main features of a general transition model [1] which is based on Keller's transition model [3] for parallel programs. We also discuss the relation of this model to other protocol description methods, and the

Manuscript received May 18, 1979; revised December 18, 1979.
The author is with the Department d'Informatique et de Recherche Opérationnelle, Université de Montréal, Montréal, P.Q., Canada, on leave at the Computer Systems Laboratory, Stanford University, Stanford, CA 94305.

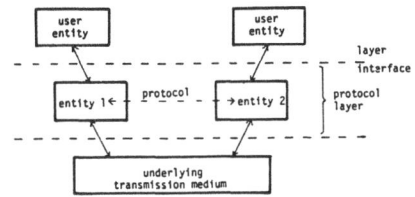

Fig. 1. A protocol layer within a layered system architecture.

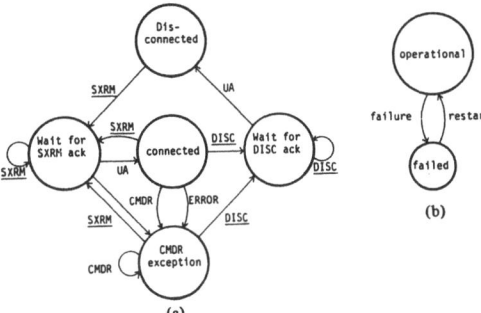

Fig. 2. State transition diagrams for the primary link setup module of an HDLC station. (a) Operational procedure which may be discontinued due to a failure. [The diagram is hierarchically dependent on the *operational* state of diagram (b).] (b) Diagram showing the possible failure and restart transitions.

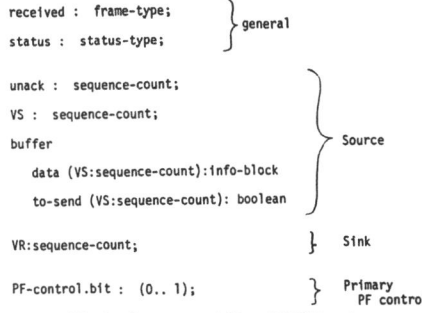

Fig. 3. Program variables of HDLC station.

importance of modularization which may lead to the subdivision of a given communication layer into several sublayers or protocol modules. Without giving the complete definitions which may be found in the literature, these concepts are explained using the HDLC classes of procedures as an example. The complete HDLC specifications, based on this method, may be found in [4]. An experience of using these specifications for the implementation of X.25 link level procedures is described in [8].

A. The Description Method

In our general transition model, an entity is described by the set of possible states in which it may be, and the possible state transitions (which are assumed to exclude one another in time). The possible states are generally described by two components:
1) a finite state transition diagram, and
2) a set of program variables which each may assume certain values.

The state of the entity is characterized by: 1.) a token which indicates the active place in the transition diagram, and 2) the values of the program variables. As an example, Fig. 2 shows the transition diagram of an HDLC module which operates the link setup and disconnection procedure. The state space of a complete HDLC station is defined by this and similar diagrams (one for each of the modules shown in Fig. 5) and the program variables shown in Fig. 3.

The operation of an entity is defined by the possible state transitions. These transitions are indicated in the transition diagram (see, for example, Fig. 2); however, additional information must be provided. For instance, each transition, when executed, may change the values of the program variables and interact with the user entity through the upper layer interface or with the underlying transmission medium through the lower interface (see Fig. 1). A given transition may only be executed when its *enabling predicate*, i.e., a Boolean expression depending on the program variables, is true. This additional information may be given in the form of a table, as shown in Fig. 4. For example, the I transition, which sends an information (I) frame to the peer entity, may only be executed when a data block is *to be sent* and not too many I frames are *unack*nowledged. When executed, the action of the transition sends an I frame and updates the value of the send variable VS.

B. Relation to Other Description Methods

It has been pointed out [5] that most protocols contain certain aspects that are naturally described by finite state (FS) transition diagrams and other aspects that are better described by program variables and executable statements written in some programming language. The HDLC procedures provide a typical example. The link setup and disconnection procedure is described relatively completely by the FS transition diagram of Fig. 2, whereas the data transfer, exemplified by the I and $I_=$ transitions given in Fig. 4, essentially involves program variables and statements. Different approaches have been taken to cope with this situation (see, for example, [6]).

The approach of attempting to write complete descriptions in the FS model is limited because most protocols are so complex that the resulting FS descriptions becomes too large to be useful. However, partial descriptions in the FS model may be very useful. For example, the FS descriptions of X.21 and X.25 are of this kind. We note that even a relatively complete FS description and analysis [7] of the simple "alternating bit" protocol ignores the contents of the exchanged user messages. The partial description approach corresponds to keeping only the FS transition diagram of our general transition model (in the case of the HDLC procedures, for example, keeping Fig. 2 and ignoring Fig. 3 and 4). But it is clear that such a

Transition	Enabling predicate	Action	Meaning
Primary station:			
SXRM	PF-control.bit = 1	send-unnumbered (SXRM) ;	SXRM is SNRM or SARM depending on the mode to be set
UA	received.kind = UA	init (source) ; init (sink) ; init (transmission) ;	initialize the source and sink components
DISC	PF-control.bit = 1	send-unnumbered (DISC) ;	
CMDR	received.kind = CMDR	init (transmission) ;	
ERROR	Status in [invalid-control-field, invalid-info, invalid-size, invalid-NR]	init (transmission) ;	frame received contained an error to be resolved by a higher level recovery procedure at Primary
OTHER	...	init (transmission) ;	in certain states, the reception of certain kind of frames is simply ignored (not shown in the transition diagrams
I	buffer.to-send (VS) and VS ≠ (unack + window) mod modulus	send-info (VS,VR,buffer.data (VS)); VS := (VS+1) mod modulus ;	when there is an I frame to be sent, which lies within the send window, send it
I=	received.kind = I and received.NS=VR	unack := received.NR; VR := VR+1; init (transmission)	if I-frame is in sequence, pass data to user

Fig. 4. Definition of the transitions shown in Fig. 2(a) and of the *I*-frame receiving $I_=$ and sending I transitions.

description, and a protocol analysis based on it, must be complemented with additional information.

On the other hand, the FS aspects may be eliminated from the description of a protocol in the general transition model by replacing each FS transition diagram, which contains one token, by a variable which indicates the place of the token in the diagram, together with appropriate enabling predicates and update actions for the transitions. Such a transformation is straightforward, and is usually performed in order to obtain an implementation of the protocol.

C. Modularization

Most protocols implemented in a given layer of a hierarchical system are so complex that a conceptual subdivision into several sublayers or functions is very useful. In this case, each sublayer or function corresponds to a module within each entity executing the protocol. The different modules of an entity are relatively independent of one another. In the examples which we have considered, i.e., the link level HDLC procedures [4], the X.25 packet level procedures [8], and the ML Protocol [9] providing transport and session layer functions, the following concepts were sufficient to naturally describe the interactions between the modules within one entity, and different entities through a layer interface. We note that all, except the second concept, are also applicable to FS models.

Complete Independence: Each module is described by a separate transition model.

Shared Variables: The modules are independent, except that the transitions of one module may update the program variables of the other module, thus influencing its behavior. Fig. 5 shows a possible modular decomposition of an HDLC primary station. In this example, a shared variable is used to indicate a time-out condition to the *P/F-bit control* module,

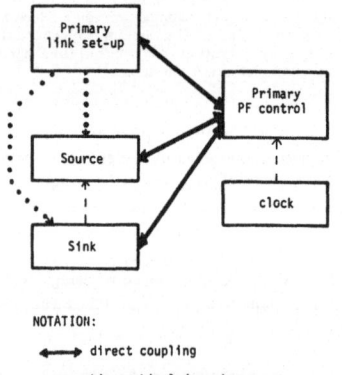

Fig. 5. Modules of an HDLC primary station and their relation.

and the variable *unack* of the *source* module is accessed by the *sink* module when a piggybacked acknowledgment arrives.

Hierarchical Dependence [4]: A module *B* is hierarchically dependent on a module *A* if *B* enters its initial state whenever *A* enters a particular state, which we call the *activating state* for *B*, and the transitions of *B* are only possible while *A* remains in the activating state. In the example of Fig. 5, hierarchical dependence is used to describe the fact that the data transfer executed by the *source* and *sink* modules is only active when the *link setup* module is in the *connected* state (see Fig. 2).

Direct Coupling [4], [7]: This concept introduces a strong synchronization between certain transitions of different modules. Two transitions of different modules are directly coupled if they can only be executed jointly (only when both respective enabling predicates are true). This mechanism may be used to describe the local interaction of an entity through the upper layer interface with its user or through the lower interface with the underlying transmission medium (see Section III). In a more general form, where a given transition is directly coupled alternatively to several transitions of the other module, this concept was also used for describing the interaction between the *P/F-bit control* module and the other modules of an HDLC station [4], as indicated in Fig. 5. In fact, each sending and receiving transition of the other modules must be coordinated with a transition of the *P/F-bit control* module which checks the validity of the P/F-bit sent or received.

III. SPECIFICATION OF COMMUNICATION SERVICE

The specification of the communication service provided by a given protocol layer (see Fig. 1) defines what the user entities have to know about the protocol layer they use, without being concerned with the details of the protocol. We distinguish the local and the global properties of a communication service. The local properties of the service are those which characterize the local interaction of one user entity with an entity providing the service, ignoring what happens at the other end of the communication link. Given that we consider a *communication* service, the local properties leave an important aspect unspecified, namely, the relation between what happens at the two ends of the communication link. Since the global properties specify this relation, they may be called the "end-to-end" properties of the communication service. We note that the distinction between local and global properties is not "exclusive" since the specification of the global properties of a service usually implies (i.e., includes) its local properties. We include in the following only some simple examples. A complete service specification along the lines discussed here may be found in [14].

A. Local Properties

In this subsection, we concentrate on the local properties of a communication service. These properties clearly determine the local interface through which a user entity accesses the service. The properties may be considered to be the abstract specification for the local interface, which must be satisfied in each local system. At the end of the section, we comment on how this abstract interface may be refined in order to give rise to a particular interface implementation.

1) A Directly Coupled Interface: We assume that both entities that interact through the interface are described by a general transition model, as explained in Section II. We describe the interaction between the two entities by direct coupling. In particular, certain transitions of the service providing entity are directly coupled with certain transitions of the user entity. If we do not want to specify the operation of the user entity (which is usually the case), we may simply give a list of *interface transitions* which may be executed by the user entity subject to some (unspecified) enabling predicates, and which are directly coupled with transitions of the service providing

interface transition of user entity	coupled transition of HDLC station (see figures 2 and 4)
↓Open$_{request}$	SXRM starting in *disconnected* or *connected* state
↑Open$_{indication}$	SXRM starting in *CMDR exception* state
Open$_{confirmation}$	UA starting in *Wait for SXRM ack* state
↓Close$_{request}$	DISC starting in *connected* state
↑Close$_{indication}$	DISC starting in *CMDR exception* state
Close$_{confirmation}$	UA starting in *Wait for DISC ack* state
↓D(data:info-block)	a transition appending the *data* parameter into the *buffer* variable of the source module
↑D(data:info-block)	I$_\infty$ where the *data* parameter is equal to *received.data*
Fail	failure

Fig. 6. Interface transitions for the HDLC link layer service and their coupling with the transitions of the service providing HDLC station.

entity. For example, for the entity using the HDLC link layer service, we may define the interface transitions given in Fig. 6. We note that the flow control at the interface is automatically present since a pair of directly coupled transitions may only be executed when the corresponding enabling predicates in both entities are true and no other transition is in progress. Parameterized transitions may be used for passing value parameters between the two entities, such as the *data* parameter in the case of the ↓D and ↑D transitions.

2) Abstraction: While the conceptual operation of the interface may be described by directly coupled transitions, as explained above, we discuss in the following three further abstractions which lead to simpler interface descriptions. The first two abstractions are based on the fact that the user entity does not need to (and should not) know the operation of the protocol which provides the service. The same considerations apply also in the general context of software engineering for the specification of the service provided by a software module. The last abstraction is particular to the context of communications.

Ignoring the Operation of the Protocol: The order in which the interface transitions may be executed by the user entity is clearly determined by the direct coupling and the order in which the transitions of the service providing entity may be executed. Let us consider the example of the layer interface for the HDLC protocol. We may deduce from the information in Figs. 6 and 2 that the interface transitions may be executed in the order shown in Fig. 7. (This diagram is obtained from the diagram of Fig. 2 by merging the *Connected* and *CMDR exception* states, and replacing the transition labels according to the table of Fig. 6. We note that this derivation is generally not so simple because the interaction between the two protocol entities may limit the transition possibilities.)

Combining Interface Transitions into "Service Primitives": Continuing with the example above, we see in Fig. 7 that certain interface transitions are always followed by the same next transition. We may therefore combine these transitions into a single one, thus simplifying the overall transition

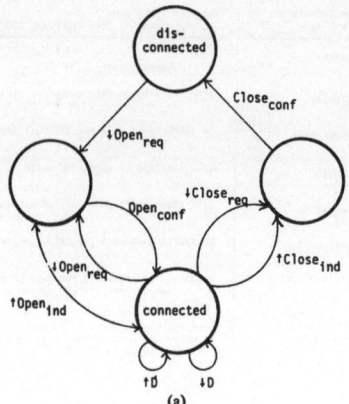

(a)

Fig. 7. Local service interface transition diagram based on Figs. 2(a) and 6.

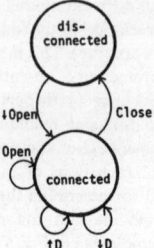

Fig. 8. Simplified local service interface transition diagram.

diagram. Adopting the following combinations

↓Open$_{request}$	Open$_{confirmation}$	≡ ↓Open
↑Open$_{indication}$	Open$_{confirmation}$	≡ ↑Open
↓Close$_{request}$	Close$_{confirmation}$	≡ ↓Close
↑Close$_{indication}$	Close$_{confirmation}$	≡ ↑Close

leads to the interface transition diagram of Fig. 8. We call the remaining (partially combined) interface transitions *service primitives*.

Ignoring the Source of Initiation: The symbols "↑" and "↓" in the names of the service primitives have been introduced to explicitly indicate whether the execution of the primitive is initiated by the service providing entity ("↑") or the user entity ("↓"). In the case of the data transmission primitives ↑D and ↓D, this distinction is clearly important. In the case of the link setup or disconnection primitives, however, this distinction is not always important, in which case one may make abstraction from it. In particular, the diagram of Fig. 8 does not require this distinction; neither does the specification of the global properties of the service discussed in the next section. We therefore drop the symbol "↑" or "↓" whenever this distinction is of no importance.

If we consider the exchange of parameter values between the interacting entities during the execution of a service primitive, the situation may become more complicated. In the case of a primitive for establishing a virtual circuit through a packet-switched data network, for example, a *distant subscriber address* parameter value is provided by the initiating entity, while a *response* parameter value is returned by the other entity. Independently of which entity initiates the primitive, this fact may be described by the following notation:

VC-Establishment (→x: distant subscriber address, ←y: response code).

3) Discontinuation of Service Primitives: As shown in Fig. 7 and 8, the concept of hierarchical dependence (see Section II-C) may be used to indicate that the normal link layer service is only available as long as the physical circuit is *operational*. Since a *Fail* interface transition may occur any time in the *operational* state, link establishment primitives, for example, will be "interrupted" by a failure which occurs after an Open$_{req}$ transition and before the corresponding Open$_{conf}$ transition (see Fig. 7). We say that the service primitive is *discontinued*. In Fig. 8, this possibility is not shown explicitly, but it must be taken into account. We conclude that whenever the layer interface description involves some hierarchical dependence, the possibility of discontinuation for the dependent service primitives must be considered.

Another example of discontinuation is given by the virtual circuit data transmission service where, according to X.25, the transfer of a complete user sequence (i.e., variable length data block) between the DTE and the network may be "interrupted" by a reset or circuit clear.

4) Interface Implementation: It is clear that many details must be added to the abstract interface specification suggested in this section in order to obtain an interface implementation. However, these details may be chosen differently for each local implementation, whereas the abstract interface properties discussed in this section must be valid for every actual interface. In particular, the mechanisms for implementing flow control and the distinction between which entity initiates a service primitive may be implemented in quite different ways. For instance, the use of message queues between the service providing entity and its user would be a particular way of implementing the interface.

B. Global Properties

An interface description, as discussed in Section III-A, defines the service primitives and the order in which these primitives may be executed at a local interface between a user and a service providing entity. Here we concentrate on the global properties of a communication service, which are those aspects that make the service useful for *communication*. The local service interface description for the HDLC protocol, for example, states that sending and receiving of user data blocks is possible in the *connected* state (see Fig. 8). Only the global properties state that the first block received at one end is equal to the block first sent at the other end.

The global properties of a communication service usually have two aspects: 1) restrictions on the order in which the service primitives at the two ends of the link may be executed, and

2) restrictions on the possible parameter values exchanged. An example of the second aspect is given above; an example for the first aspect is the fact that (usually) the number of possible receive executions at one end is always smaller or equal to the number of send executions performed at the other end.

Speaking about the execution order of service primitives at different locations brings up the problem of how such an order can actually be observed or enforced. We assume, for the present purposes, that the execution order at different locations can be determined by some hypothetical observer or with sufficiently well synchronized real time clocks.

We use the following notation. Given two service primitives A and B, "$A \Rightarrow B$" means that the beginning of the execution of A is earlier (in real time) than the end of the execution of B (that is, there may be a causal influence of A on B). The notation "$A \Leftrightarrow B$" means that $A \Rightarrow B$ and $A \Leftarrow B$ holds (that is, there is some instant (in real time) when both service primitives are in progress). We say that A and B are *simultaneous*.

For many purposes, instead of considering the execution order to be defined in respect to the real time, it may be adequate to consider that the execution order defined by the global properties of the service determine some partial order of events which represents some "logical time" as discussed by Lamport [10].

A Possible Notation: A possible notation for specifying the global properties of a communication service are production rules of a particular form. We adopt the usual convention of writing the nonterminal symbols in brackets $\langle ... \rangle$, and writing the possible productions after the symbol "::=". Each production is defined in terms of (possibly other) nonterminals and terminals which are written in the form $\{ \begin{smallmatrix} X \\ Y \end{smallmatrix} \}$. X and Y are sequences of service primitives which describe a possible pair of corresponding execution sequences at the respective ends of the communication link.

As an example, Fig. 9 contains a possible specification of the global properties of an HDLC link layer service. Rule 2, for instance, states that an ⟨Open Sequence⟩ consists of *Open* primitives executed simultaneously at both ends of the communication link followed by a ⟨Data Sequence⟩ with possibly further repetitions. The ⟨Data sequences⟩ are defined by rules 3 and 4, and rule 1 defines the possible global execution sequences which consist of a repetition of an ⟨Open Sequence⟩ followed by a pair of simultaneous *Close* primitives executed at the two ends of the link. (We note that the rules of Fig. 9 imply the "local" transition rules given in Fig. 8 which apply separately at each end of the communication link.)

Restrictions on the possible parameter values may be stated for each of the production rules. In the case of Fig. 9, the only parameters exchanged are the user data sent and received (see rule 4 of Fig. 9). In the case of the establishment of a virtual circuit, using the service primitive given in Section III-A2), the following rule may apply:

$$\langle \text{VC Open} \rangle ::= \left\{ \begin{array}{l} \text{VC-Establishment } (x, y) \\ \text{VC-Establishment } (x', y') \end{array} \right\}$$

where $y = y'$, $x =$ subscriber address of the entity executing the "lower" part, and $x' =$ subscriber address of the entity executing the "upper" part.

(1) ⟨Link Seq⟩ ::= empty
    ::= ⟨Link Seq⟩ ⟨Open Seq⟩ $\left\{ \begin{array}{c} \text{Close} \\ \updownarrow \\ \text{Close} \end{array} \right\}$

(2) ⟨Open Seq⟩ ::= $\left\{ \begin{array}{c} \text{Open} \\ \updownarrow \\ \text{Open} \end{array} \right\}$ ⟨Data Seq⟩
    ::= ⟨Open Seq⟩ $\left\{ \begin{array}{c} \text{Open} \\ \updownarrow \\ \text{Open} \end{array} \right\}$ ⟨Data Seq⟩

(3) ⟨Data Seq⟩ ::= ⟨Fifo Seq 12⟩ ∥ ⟨Fifo Seq 21⟩, i.e. arbitrary interleaving of data transfer in both directions

(4) ⟨Fifo Seq 12⟩ ::= $\left\{ \begin{array}{cccc} \downarrow D(x_1) & \downarrow D(x_2) & \cdots & \downarrow D(x_n) \\ \downarrow & \downarrow & & \downarrow \\ \uparrow D(x'_1) & \uparrow D(x'_2) & \cdots & \uparrow D(x'_m) \end{array} \right\}$

where $0 \leq m \leq n$ and
$x_i = x'_i$ for $i = 1, 2, \ldots m$

⟨Fifo Seq 21⟩ ::= ... (similarly)

(5) Discontinuation due to a failure: The execution sequences defined above for entity 1 and entity 2 may be "interrupted" by a local *Fail* transition, such that the last primitive executed by an entity may be discontinued. If $A \rightarrow B$ holds between executions of two service primitives the following is true: A is completely suppressed due to the failure implies that B is discontinued or completely suppressed.

Fig. 9. Global properties of the link layer communication service.

C. Elements for a Communication Service Specification

We conclude from the foregoing discussion that the specification of a communication service for a given protocol layer should contain the following elements.

1) An informal explanation of the service provided and the functions included in the layer: this part is given in natural language. It should give an overall understanding of the purpose and operation of the layer.

2) A list of service primitives available at the layer interface: this parts describes precisely each of the service primitives individually.

3) Local properties determining in which order the service primitives may be executed at one end of the communication link without regard to the other end.

4) Global properties relating the execution order and exchanged parameter values at both ends of the communication link: this is the essential part of the service specification.

5) Grade of service considerations: they specify quantitative properties such as throughput, delay, etc., and also indicate in which situations and with which probabilities certain malfunctions, such as undetected errors and failures, may occur. (In contrast to this, points 2)-4) above concentrate on qualitative properties of the service which are always satisfied.)

We believe that any communication service specification that does not contain the equivalent of the elements 2)-5) must be considered incomplete. Elements 2)-4) are discussed in the foregoing sections. We believe that formal methods, similar to those described here, may be useful for specifying these elements in a more precise manner.

IV. PROTOCOL VERIFICATION

Instead of giving a review of protocol verification (which may be found elsewhere [6]) or describing any particular approach to verification, we give in the following some remarks which show the relation of the previous sections with the problems of protocol verification, and which show also, we hope, that many approaches to verification are basically very simple.

A. What Should be Verified?

The term "protocol verification" usually means to ascertain that the entities executing a given protocol together with the underlying transmission medium (see Fig. 1) actually provide the specified communication service to the user entities in the layer above. It is therefore necessary to determine the service actually provided (based on the specification of the underlying transmission service and the definition of the communicating entities) and compare it with the communication service specified. Let us assume that we want to verify that the service actually provided is equal to the service specified. The proof may be divided into two parts.

1) Partial correctness: to show that every execution sequence of service primitives (at both ends of the communication link, and including specific parameter values) that is actually possible satisfies the constraints imposed by the service specification.

2) Effective progress: to show that every execution sequence of service primitives that satisfies the service specifications is actually possible, and that no situations of deadlock or starvation or infinite loops without progress exist.

B. Various Kinds of Assertions

The use of "assertions" is a well-known technique for the verification of sequential programs and has been extended for use with parallel programs. Similar techniques also apply to the verification of protocols. The basic idea consists of defining an invariant assertion, or briefly "invariant," i.e., a Boolean expression depending on the state of the system which is always true (i.e., as long as no state transition is in progress). Since this technique was developed for verifying programs, it seems natural to use it for verifying protocols that are defined in terms of program variables and executed statements. In this case, the invariants typically involve the program variables of both entities and the state of the underlying transmission medium (i.e., the "messages" in transit) [5], [11].

It is interesting to note that certain approaches to the verification of protocols based of FS description techniques may be shown to be based on a particular form of invariant assertions. For example, the equations given in [7] for the "adjoint states" of a protocol are such that the following assertions are always true when the underlying medium is empty (i.e., no "message" in transit). If $a_i(i = 1, 2, \cdots, n)$ are the possible states for entity 1, and s_1 and s_2 are the actual states of entity 1 and entity 2, respectively, then the assertion

$$s_1 = a_i \text{ implies } s_2 \text{ is an element of Adj } (a_i)$$

holds for every possible state a_i. This is not surprising since the definition of "adjoint state," roughly speaking, is as follows. The adjoint states $Adj(a_i)$ of a given state a_i are those states of entity 2 in which entity 2 may possibly be when entity 1 is in state a_i.

Another example is the detection of incompleteness or overspecifications as described by Zafiropulo et al. (see, for example, [12]). Their main idea is as follows. Given an FS protocol definition, an invariant assertion of the following form is derived for each possible state $a_i(i = 1, 2, \cdots, n)$ of entity 1:

$$s_1 = a_i \text{ implies the messages } \ldots \text{ may now be received by}$$

the entity 1, but no other messages.

Given such assertions, it is easy to check whether the definition of entity 1 includes all necessary receiving transitions and no unnecessary ones. It is sufficient to verify, for any given state a_i, that the definition foresees the handling of exactly those received messages which are mentioned in the corresponding assertion.

In the case of a protocol definition in terms of the general transition model described in Section II where the state of an entity is defined by an FS transition diagram and certain program variables, invariant assertions are in general of the following form:

$$s_1 = a_i \text{ and } s_2 = b_j \text{ implies Assertion}_{ij}$$

where a_i and b_j are possible states of the entities 1 and 2, respectively, and Assertion$_{ij}$ is a Boolean expression depending on the program variables of both entities and possibly also on the state of the underlying transmission medium [13].

As an example, we give the following invariant assertion which may be derived from the definitions of the HDLC procedures given in the Figs. 2–4 and the assumption that each frame received without error notification is an exact copy of a frame sent by the other entity.

$s_1 =$ connected and $s_2 =$ connected implies

$$\left[\begin{array}{l} \text{entity2.received.kind} = I \text{ and} \\ \text{entity2.received.NS} = \text{entity2.VR} \\ \text{implies} \quad \text{entity2.received.data} = \\ \quad \text{entity1.buffer.data (entity2.VR)} \end{array} \right]$$

This assertion is important for the verification of correct data transfer of the HDLC procedures. It specifies conditions under which a data block received by entity 2 is equal to the corresponding data block in the buffer of entity 1. Given the definitions of the service primitives ↓D and ↑D (see Fig. 6) and the transition $I_=$ (see Fig. 4), this invariant assures that the data blocks received by the user from entity 2 are the same as those submitted by the user to entity 1. This is what rule 4 of the service specification in Fig. 9 postulates.

We conclude that the above invariant assertion proves the partial correctness of the HDLC protocol, as far as rule 4 of the service specification is concerned. However, it does not imply effective progress, which would mean that each data block submitted to entity 1 will eventually be delivered to the user by entity 2. For proving this, we must rely on the underlying transmission service not to make "too many" transmission errors. A more detailed discussion of a simple protocol verification example in the context of the general transition model is given in [1].

V. CONCLUSIONS

In the framework of distributed system architecture involving a hierarchy of different protocol layers, the clear delimitation between the different layers becomes an important issue. The delimitation between a given layer and its user is given by the layer interface which is characterized by the communication service provided through that interface. For the description of the layered architecture of a distributed system, the service specifications for the individual layers seem to be the main tool. For instance, one objective for a layered system architecture is the possibility to change the protocol adopted in a given layer without affecting the other layers of the system. During such a change, the protocol of that layer clearly changes, while the service provided must remain unchanged.

Because the communication service definitions play such an important role in the design of distributed systems, great care should be taken for their exact specification. This paper presents a possible formal approach to the specification of communication services. While a finite state approach seems to be useful for many aspects of communication protocol specification and verification (although not all), we feel that, for the specification of communication *services*, the finite state approach alone is insufficient. It seems that important service characteristics are naturally described by constraints on parameter values which are exchanged over the interface during the execution of the service primitives. The two aspects of "order of execution" and "exchanged parameter values" seem to correspond to the two aspects of our general transition model described in Section II, namely, "state transitions" and "program variables."

ACKNOWLEDGMENT

I would like to thank J. Gecsei for suggesting many improvements on the manuscript.

REFERENCES

[1] G. V. Bochmann and J. Gecsei, "A unified model for the specification and verification of protocols," in *Proc. IFIP Congr. 1977*, pp. 229–234.
[2] D. L. Parnas, "The use of precise specifications in the development of software," in *Proc. IFIP Congr. 1977*, pp. 861–867.
[3] R. M. Keller, "Formal verification of parallel programs," *Commun. Ass. Comput. Mach.*, vol. 19, pp. 371–384, July 1976.
[4] G. V. Bochmann and R. J. Chung, "A formalized specification of HDLC classes of procedures," in *Proc. Nat. Telecommun. Conf.*, Los Angeles, CA, Dec. 1977, pp. 03A..2-1-2-11; reprinted in *Advances in Computer Communications and Networking*, W. W. Chu., Ed. Dedham, MA: Artech House, 1979.
[5] N. V. Stenning. "A data transfer protocol," *Comput. Network*, vol. 1, pp. 99–110, Sept. 1976.
[6] G. V. Bochmann and C. Sunshine, "Formal methods in communication protocol design," this issue, pp. 624–631.
[7] G. V. Bochmann, "Finite state description of communication protocols," in *Proc. Comput. Network Protocols Symp.*, Univ. Liège, Liège, Belgium, Feb. 1978, pp. F3-1–F3-11; and *Comput. Networks*, vol. 2, pp. 361–372, Oct. 1978.
[8] G. V. Bochmann and T. Joachim, "Development and structure of an X.25 implementation," *IEEE Trans. Software Eng.*, vol. SE-5, pp. 429–439, Sept. 1979.
[9] G. V. Bochmann and F. H. Vogt, "Message link protocol—Functional specifications," *ACM Comput. Commun. Rev.*, vol. 9, pp. 7–39, Apr. 1979.
[10] L. Lamport, "Time, clocks and the ordering of events in a distributed system," *Commun. Ass. Comput. Mach.*, vol. 21, pp. 558–565, July 1978.
[11] G. V. Bochmann, "Logical verification and implementation of protocols," in *Proc. 4th Data Commun. Sympo.*, ACM/IEEE, 1975, pp. 8-15–8-20.
[12] P. Zafiropulo *et al.*, "Towards analyzing and synthesizing protocols," this issue, pp. 651–661.
[13] G. V. Bochmann, "Combining assertions and states for the validation of process communication," in *Constructing Quality Software*, P. G. Hibbard and S. A. Shuman, Ed. Amsterdam: North-Holland, 1978, pp. 229–232.
[14] ——, "Specification of the services provided by the MLP," Univ. Montreal, Montreal, P.Q., Canada, Tech. Rep., 1979.

Annex 2

Development and Structure of an X.25 Implementation

(G. v. Bochmann and J. Tankoano)

Abstract—This paper describes experience with an implementation of the X.25 communication protocols for accessing public data networks. The implementation effort is characterized by: 1) the development of a formalized protocol specification on which all further implementation work is based, and 2) the use of Concurrent Pascal as the implementation language. The main features of the formalized protocol specification are given, and a method for deriving a protocol implementation based on parallel processes, *monitors*, and *classes* is explained. The overall structure of the system and the step-wise refinements leading to the complete implementation are discussed. Some comments on the possible implementation on multiple microprocessors are also given.

Index Terms—Communications software, Concurrent Pascal, formal specification, process structuring, protocol implementation, step-wise refinement, structured programming, X.25 protocol.

I. Introduction

X.25 [1] is a standard access protocol for using virtual circuits (VC's) provided by public data networks. This paper describes certain aspects of the experience gained from the implementation of this protocol in a host computer [2]. For the implementation of most communication protocols, the following points must be considered:

1) ensuring the compatibility of the implementation with the remote communication partner,

2) implementing several parallel activities, which is usual for real-time systems, and

3) a step-wise refinement of the system design, which is a useful discipline for any software development project.

We have used a high-level implementation language [3] which provides the concepts of abstract data types (i.e., *class*), parallel processes, and *monitors* (for process interaction). These concepts support points 2) and 3) above. In view of point 1), we have used a formalized specification of the X.25 protocol. Part of our project was the development of this specification. More precise and more algorithmical in nature than the original specification of the protocol, given in natural language, it has been used as the basis for deriving the implementation in a more or less straightforward manner, as described in Section III.

Section II describes the main features of the formalized X.25 specification as used in our project. (The complete specification is contained in [2].) Section III explains how such a formalized specification may be transformed into an implementation, taking one component of the X.25 link level as an example. In Section IV, we describe the overall structure of our X.25 implementation as far as the organization of parallel activity is concerned, and the interfaces between the different system parts, including the user of the VC communication facility provided. In Section V, we make some remarks on the step-wise refinement of our system, and discuss in some detail the problems of buffer management and message coding. We finish with some general conclusions from our implementation experience. The complete text of our formalized specification of X.25, and its implementation in Concurrent Pascal, is contained in [2].

We assume in the following some familiarity with the X.25 protocol [1], the concepts of classes, processes, and monitors as realized in Concurrent Pascal [3], and the unified protocol specification method of Bochmann and Gecsei [4].

II. A Formalized Specification of X.25

The X.25 specification contains three procedure layers:

1) the physical layer, specifying bit transmission between the subscriber and network equipments,

2) the link layer, specifying frame formats, transmission error detection, and error recovery procedures, and

3) the packet layer, specifying packet formats and procedures for the use of VC's.

A basic decomposition of the X.25 protocol is shown in Fig. 1, where the different modules communicate by exchanging packets or frames, respectively. The *VC control* modules implement the packet level procedures separately for each VC, and the *Packet sender* and *receiver* modules implement the link level procedures. These procedures have been considered for the formalized specification. The other modules of Fig. 1 have essentially a (de-) multiplexing function, and are relatively simple. The *Frame input* and *output* modules also handle transmission error detection and transparency coding, as well as physical input/output. We note that the X.25 link level (we consider the original LAP A standard [1]) distinguishes primary and secondary functions which, relatively independent of one another, perform the sending and receiving of frames,

---

Manuscript received July 12, 1978; revised February 16, 1979. This work was performed at the Université de Montréal, P.Q., Canada, and was supported by the Ministère de l'Education du Québec and the Canadian International Development Agency.

G. V. Bochmann is with the Département d'I.R.O., Université de Montréal, Montreal, P.Q., Canada. In 1978 he was on leave at the Département de Mathématiques, Ecole Polytechnique Fédérale, Lausanne, Switzerland.

T. Joachim is with the Centre National du Traitement de l'Information, Upper Volta.

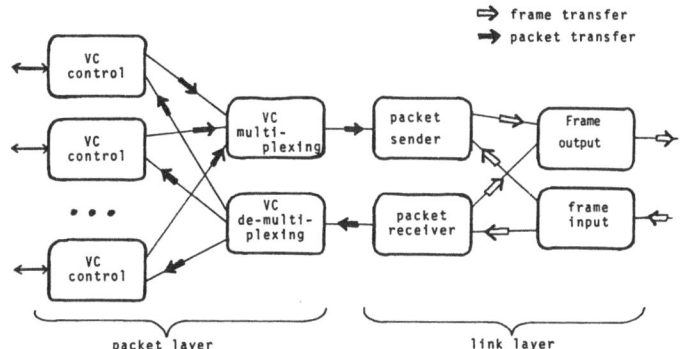

Fig. 1. Decomposition of an X.25 implementation into modules interacting by exchange of messages.

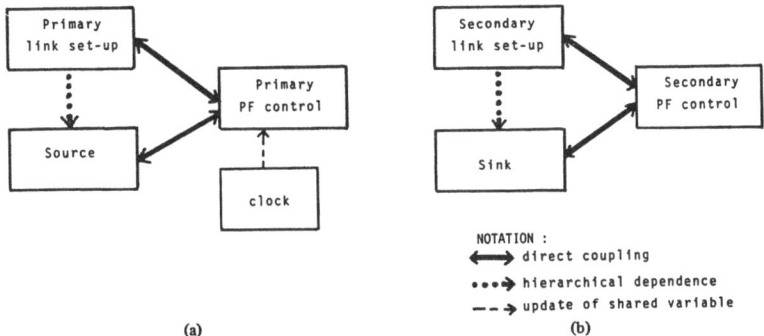

(a) (b)

Fig. 2. (a) Component structure of the *Packet sender* module. (b) Component structure of the *Packet receiver* module.

respectively. This is reflected by separate *Packet sender* and *receiver* modules.

A. The Link Layer

The link level procedures describe a particular class of HDLC procedures. A formalized specification of HDLC procedures, in general, has been described elsewhere [5]. Our formalized specification of the X.25 link level is based, as far as possible, on that specification, and therefore uses the same specification formalism.

The HDLC procedures may be considered [5] to be composed of several different interrelated components, as shown in Fig. 2. The link between the computer and the network is set up (and disconnected) separately for each direction of frame transmission by the *Link setup* components. The *Source* and *Sink* components perform the frame transmission during the *connected* state; and the *PF control* components determine the exchange of poll/final (PF) bits [1]. The *Clock* component provides a time-out mechanism for retransmission.

In the formalized specification, each component is characterized by program variables, a transition diagram, and enabling predicates and actions for each transition. All transitions exclude one another in time, and a given transition may only be executed when its enabling predicate, which depends on the variables, is true. When executed, the transition action may update the variables and thus enable or disable other transitions of the same and other components (for more detail, see [4]). As an example, we show in Fig. 3 the specification of the *Primary link setup* component. The transition diagram of Fig. 3(a) shows the possible transitions. Fig. 3(c) shows, for each transition, when it may be executed and what its action is. Enabling predicates, as well as actions, may involve variables of other components, which are written in the form "<component name>.<variable name>". The local variables of the *Link setup* component are listed in Fig. 3(b).

There are certain differences between our formalized specification of the X.25 link level procedures and the specification of HDLC given in [5]. They may be attributed to the following two factors.

1) The X.25 procedures operate in a particular configuration including a primary and a secondary station, and in asynchronous response mode only.

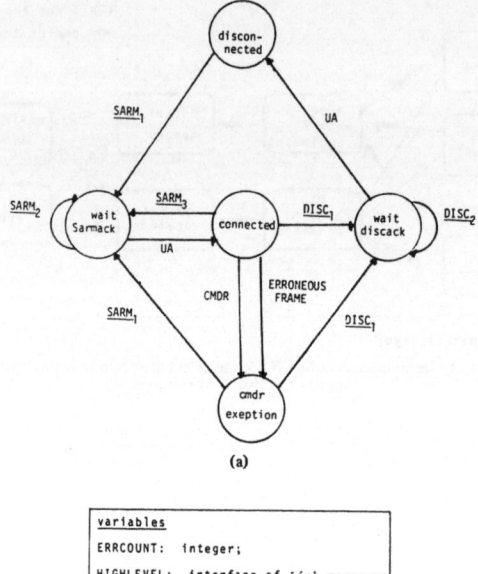

Fig. 3. Specification of the *Primary link setup* component. (a) Transition diagram (underlined transition names indicate a sending transition; nonunderlined names a receiving transition). (b) Local variables. (c) Definition of the transitions.

2) One objective of the specifications in [5] was to include only those aspects that are necessary to ensure the compatibility between the communicating system parts. For the X.25 specification, we have included additional aspects, not essential for compatibility. These aspects include points described in the standard, points adopted for the subscriber equipment by analogy with the specifications for the network equipment, and an interface to a higher level link manager module.

A comparison between the two formalized specifications may be made comparing Fig. 3(c) and (d). Finally, Fig. 3(e)

TRANSITION	ENABLING PREDICATE	ACTION	MEANING
SARM	PF-control.bit = 1	send-unnumbered (SARM) ;	
UA	received.kind = UA	init (source) ; init (sink) ; init (transmission)	initialize the source and sink components
DISC	PF-control.bit = 1	send-unnumbered (DISC)	
CMDR	received.kind = CMDR	init (transmission) ;	
ERROR	status C [invalid-control-field invalid-info, invalid-size, invalid-NR]	init (transmission) ;	frame received contained an error to be resolved by a higher level recovery procedure at Primary

(d)

2 3 4 5 Set Asynchronous Response Mode (SARM) Command
   The SARM unnumbered command is used to place the addressed secondary in the Asynchronous Response Mode (ARM)
   No information field is permitted with the SARM command A secondary confirms acceptance of SARM by the transmission at the first opportunity of a UA response Upon acceptance of this command the secondary receive state variable is set to zero
   Previously transmitted frames that are unacknowledged when this command is actioned remain unacknowledged

2 4 3 1 Link Setup
   The DCE will indicate that it is able to set up the link by transmitting contiguous flags (active channel state)
   The DTE shall indicate a request for setting up the link by transmitting a SARM command to the DCE
   Whenever receiving a SARM command the DCE will return a UA response to the DTE and set its receive state variable V(R) to zero
   Should the DCE wish to indicate a request for setting up the link or when receiving from the DTE a first SARM command as a request for setting up the link the DCE will transmit a SARM command to the DTE and start timer T1 (see Section 2 4 7) The DTE will confirm the reception of the SARM command by transmitting a UA response

When receiving the UA response the DCE will set its send state variable V(S) to zero and stop its timer T1 If timer T1 runs out before the UA response is received by the DCE the DCE will retransmit a SARM command and restart timer T1
   After transmission of SARM N2 times by the DCE appropriate recovery action will be initiated
   The value of N2 is defined in Section 2 4 7

2 3 5 6 Rejection Condition
   A rejection condition is established upon the receipt of an error-free frame which contains an invalid command / response in the control field an invalid frame format an invalid N(R) count or an information field which exceeded the maximum information field length which can be accommodated
   At the primary this exception is subject to recovery / resolution at a higher function level

2 4 5 5 If the DCE transmits a CMDR response it enters the command rejection condition This command rejection condition is cleared when the DCE receives a SARM or DISC command Any other command received while in the command rejection condition will cause the DCE to retransmit this CMDR response The coding of the CMDR response will be as described in Section 2 3 4 8 In the case of an invalid N(S) bits 4 5 6 and 7 of octet 3 will be set to zero

(e)

Fig. 3(cont'd). (d) Definition of the transitions, taken from [5] (the same transition diagram (a) applies, but there are no local variables). (e) Some pieces of text from the X.25 standard; relevant to the *Link setup* component.

shows some pieces of text describing the use of the SARM command (one of the topics relevant to this component) extracted from the standard specification [1].

B. The Packet Layer

We found that the same specification techniques used for the link layer could be easily applied to the description of the packet level procedures. We adopted the decomposition of the layer into the components shown in Fig. 4, with a hierarchical dependence [5] between the different components. The *restart* component is the hierarchically highest component on which all VC's depend; the components of only one VC are shown. A timer component seems to be necessary for a realistic system, although this aspect has been ignored in the standard.

As in the case of the link layer, each component is described by variables, transition diagrams, and transitions. Most of the transition diagrams given in the annex of the standard have been adapted, and completed with an *error* state and corresponding transitions. As an example, we show the transition diagram of the *Reset* component in Fig. 5.

III. IMPLEMENTATION TRANSFORMATIONS

We now explain how the formalized protocol specification discussed above may be transformed into an implementation in terms of processes, monitors, and classes. As mentioned above, a system component is characterized by variables, a transition diagram, and enabling predicates and actions for each transition. A straightforward realization of a component could be obtained using conditional critical regions, for which an efficient implementation, however, is not always easy to obtain [6]. We have chosen an implementation pattern where a component is generally implemented by a monitor and some processes. The monitor contains the component variables, a variable representing the state of the transition diagram, and procedures which, when called, effect the component transitions. The processes represent different external events and call these procedures. The transitions of the *Primary link setup* component, for example, are activated by two processes representing the reception and sending of frames over the network access circuit, as shown in Fig. 6.

This implementation approach works for independent components, such as the *Primary* and *Secondary link setup* components of the X.25 link layer. In the case of component dependences, we have adopted the following implementation patterns.

1) Variables shared between several components: the monitor parts of all components are merged into a single monitor to ensure mutual exclusion between the transitions of different components.

2) A component X is hierarchically dependent on a com-

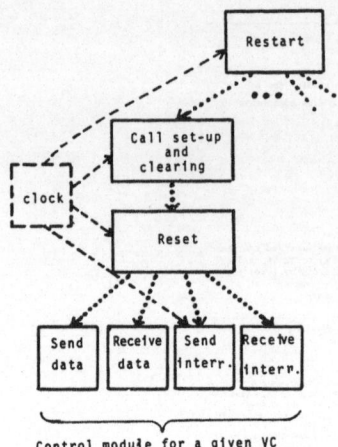

Control module for a given VC

Fig. 4. Component structure of the *VC control* modules (see explanations in Fig. 2).

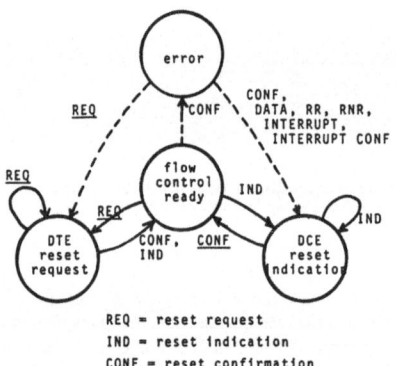

REQ = reset request
IND = reset indication
CONF = reset confirmation

Fig. 5. Transition diagram for the *Reset* component (X.25 packet level).

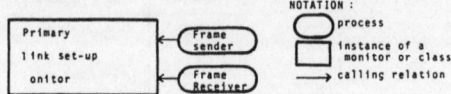

Fig. 6. The *Primary link setup* component realized by a monitor and two processes activating the transitions defined in Fig. 3.

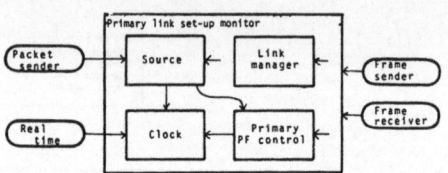

Fig. 7. The realization of the *Packet sender* module in terms of monitors, classes, and processes (see explanation in Fig. 6).

ponent Y (i.e., transitions of X are only possible when Y is in a particular state; see [5]): the monitor part of X is realized as a class declared as local variable or parameter inside the monitor part of Y. The process part of X accesses this class via the monitor part of Y.

3) Two components X and Y are directly coupled (i.e., certain transitions of X may only be executed in parallel with certain transitions of Y; see [5]): the monitor part of one component is realized as a class declared inside the monitor part of the other component, similarly to the case above.

As an example, Fig. 7 shows the inner structure of the packet sender module. In addition to the *Primary link setup* component, already shown in Fig. 6, this figure also shows the realization of the other components of the module (see Fig. 2), and the *Link manager* monitor (see Section IV). To explain the relations shown in the figure, we note that a sending transition, for instance, is activated by the *Frame sender* process calling an operation of the *Primary link setup* monitor. The latter performs a link setup, reset, or disconnection transition, if appropriate (depending on its own state and the *Link manager*), and otherwise calls an operation of the *Source* class which, in turn, may perform a sending transition. Any transition performed is coordinated with the *PF control* class which sets the poll/final bit of the frame to be sent. Appendix A shows the detailed coding of the *Primary link setup* monitor in Concurrent Pascal.

The transformation rules for obtaining a protocol implementation from its formalized specification should be straightforward in order to avoid programming errors. This is the case for the rules discussed so far. However, we found that the following two aspects of the transformation involved more complex decisions, and are therefore more subject to errors.

1) The nondeterminism inherent in the transition diagram must be eliminated, which implies an ordering of the transitions and some rearrangement of the enabling predicates in order to obtain efficient test sequences. The transition actions may also be rearranged in order to eliminate redundancy.

2) To avoid busy waiting in the case when no transition is enabled, a calling process must *wait* in the monitor until another process changes the component state. This change must be *signaled* to the waiting process. It is not always easy to decide when, and to which process, a signal must be sent (for an example, see Appendix A).

An example of nondeterminism is given by the transitions SARM and DISC possible in the *connected* state of the *Primary link setup* component [see Fig. 3(a)]. While the choice between these two transitions is left completely open by the formalized specification of [5] [see Fig. 3(d)], the choice is largely determined by the enabling predicates in our formalized specification [see Fig. 3(c)]. However, a system state is possible for which both transitions are enabled. In our implementation (see the Appendix), we have given a priority to the DISC transition.

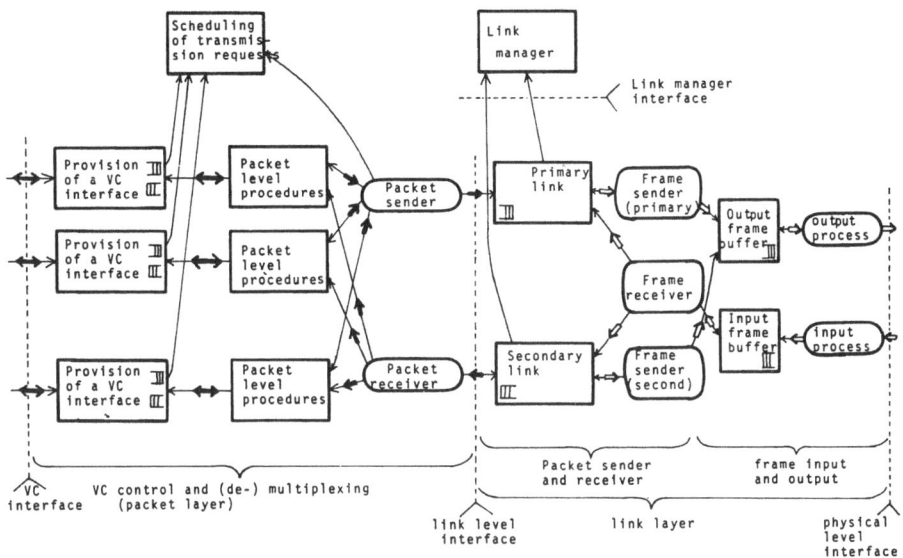

Fig. 8. Structure of the X.25 implementation in terms of monitors and processes (see explanations in Figs. 1 and 6).

IV. THE STRUCTURE OF THE X.25 IMPLEMENTATION

The general structure of the X.25 implementation is shown in Fig. 8. The physical layer of X.25 is implemented in the line controller hardware, and is not shown.

The structure of the link layer is obtained by applying the transformations discussed above to the structure of Fig. 1. The three *Frame sender* and *receiver* processes activate the transitions of the primary and secondary link components. The piggybacking of acknowledgments is performed in the *Output frame buffer*, which also performs the multiplexing of frames from the primary and secondary link components over the output circuit. The demultiplexing of incoming frames on to the primary and secondary link components is performed by the *Frame receiver* process. This process activates the receiving transitions of both components. Two separate *receiver* processes could have been used to allow for full parallelism between the sending and receiving of packets. The *Input* and *Output* processes activate the frame input and output, and perform the transmission error detection, frame delimitation, and transparency functions. In our implementation, these functions are mainly realized in software by the Concurrent Pascal system kernel [7] via IO commands executed by the *Input* and *Output* processes. Clearly, these functions would be more efficiently implemented by a separate hardware processor.

The operation of the link layer is supervised by a *Link manager*. It determines whether the link to the network should be established, disconnected, or reset, and coordinates the operation of the primary and secondary components. The latter, in turn, report to the link manager those errors which cannot be recovered by the link level procedures. The interface between the *Link manager* and the *Primary link* component, for instance, is described in Fig. 3(b), and its use is shown in Appendix A.

The interface between the link and packet layers is very simple. It consists of two primitives for sending and receiving a packet, respectively. We note that the calling processes may be delayed due to flow control considerations (see Section V-B below).

The transformation principles described above were also applied to the *VC control* module of the packet level. As in the case of the link layer, a single process, the *Packet receiver* (see Fig. 8), performs the demultiplexing of incoming packets into the different VC's, and activates the receiving transitions of all *VC control* monitors. For the multiplexing of outgoing packets, an approach different from the link layer was adopted. Instead of having independent packet sending processes, one for each VC, a single *Packet sender* process looks after all VC's and receives requests for packet transmission through a *Scheduling* monitor. This monitor is the place where different priorities may be introduced for the different VC's. The control of each VC is partitioned into a module responsible for observing the X.25 packet level procedures, and a module which provides a VC interface to the next higher layers of the computer system. In particular, the latter module provides flow control functions, automatic answering of clear, reset, and interrupt indication packets, and a time-out function for call, clear, and reset requests and interrupts [8].

We have tried to design a reasonable VC interface to the higher layers following the X.25 specifications as closely as possible. The resulting interface may be characterized by the following primitives:

    restart-request
    call-request (···)
    wait-for-incoming-call (···)
    accept-call
    clear-request
    reset-request
    send-interrupt (···)
    send-data (···)
    receive-data (···)
    get-new-status.

Each of these primitives, called by the higher layer, returns VC status information, which includes

1) information about the present state of the interface, such as

    restarted by DTE or DCE,
    connected by DTE or DCE,
    disconnected by DTE or DCE,
    reset by DTE or DCE,
    interrupt sent by DTE or received from DCE,
    time out, i.e., the primitive returned control to the higher level before the system received an appropriate packet from the network (DCE) in response to a request from the system;

2) flow control, i.e., indication that received data are available, or no buffer space is available for sending more data;

3) error indications, such as

    procedure errors of the network
    invalidity of a request from the higher layer in the present interface state.

V. STEP-WISE REFINEMENT AND IMPLEMENTATION CHOICES

A. General Remarks

Our X.25 implementation effort may be considered as an exercise in step-wise refinement. The first step is the establishment of the formalized protocol specification described in Section II. Further steps, some of which are described in Sections III and IV, lead towards the implemented system which is described in full in [2]. In Sections III and IV, we have described the choices that lead from the system structure of Fig. 1, which consists of message-driven modules, the operation of which is described by the formalized protocol specification, to the structure of Fig. 8, which is based on the monitor, class, and process primitives available in the implementation language.

However, there are many more implementation choices to be made. They mainly concern the implementation of classes and monitors for which, so far, only the interfaces have been defined. Examples are the *Link manager* component, which in our system is implemented as a monitor and process interacting with the operator, and the buffer management described below. For both modules, the interface has been used in the formalized protocol specification. A complete list of all program components is given in Appendix B.

Our effort for obtaining the X.25 implementation may be subdivided into the following steps, each of which took about one man month of work:

to derive the formalized specification of the link and packet level procedures (given the specification in [5]),

to design the structure of the system, such as shown in Figs. 7-9 and in Appendix B (this includes the development of the implementation transformations described in Section III),

to write the program components in Concurrent Pascal, and

to test and debug the system.

B. Buffer Management and Flow Control

Buffer queues for the intermediate storage of packets or frames between any pair of cooperating processes have been foreseen in the system as indicated in Fig. 8. These queues control the information flow within the system, and synchronize the relative speeds of the different processes in the system, since a process accessing a queue has to wait until it is not empty or not full respectively. The only exception is the *Input* process which is not delayed when the *Input frame buffer* is full. Instead, the last frame is lost.

In order to avoid unnecessary copying of data packets from one queue to another during the processing of the packets within the system, the frames coming in from the network, as well as the data packets from the higher system layers, are stored within a centrally managed buffer space and subsequently referred to by pointers. Therefore, the information exchanged between the system components shown in Fig. 8 includes these pointers, together with other control information, but not the copies of data packets.

In order to simplify the avoidance of deadlocks, a fixed number of packets or frames, respectively, is allocated as the maximum length for each of the queues. The total space required may be determined according to the equation

$$\left.\begin{array}{c}\text{total number}\\ \text{of blocks}\end{array}\right\} = \sum_i \text{maximum number of blocks in queue } i$$

$$+ \sum_j \begin{array}{l}\text{number of blocks not in a queue and}\\ \text{being processed by process } j.\end{array}$$

The structure of the buffer management facility is shown in Fig. 9, which shows the central buffer manager (a monitor) and the different buffer queues (classes). The queue of the *Primary link* is completed by a class providing additional management facilities needed for packet retransmission. The central buffer manager may also be directly accessed, to obtain a new block, change or read the information stored in a block, or free a block.

C. Message Coding

For compatibility with the remote communication partner, a protocol specifies the exact layout of information fields within the exchanged messages. This message format must be implemented by the communications software, and involves the specification of memory layout of structured data, bit packing, etc. It is not possible to describe these details in a single soft-

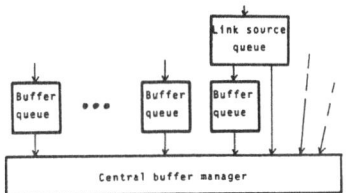

Fig. 9. Structure of the buffer management facility (see explanation in Fig. 6).

ware module, since each protocol layer, separately, specifies the layout of the corresponding message header. An implementation language with facilities for specifying memory layout of packed data structures would be convenient for this purpose.

Our implementation language did not provide this facility; therefore, the coding and decoding of the packet and frame headers are implemented in several different procedures. The central buffer manager provides operations for reading and writing selected octets of a given data block. These operations may also be used by higher level protocols. Specific procedures are included in the *Packet sender* and *receiver* processes (for packet header (de-)coding), and in the *Frame receiver* and *Output frame buffer* (for HDLC header (de-)coding).

VI. Concluding Remarks

A. The Use of a Formalized Protocol Specification

As explained in Sections II and III, we have developed a formalized specification of X.25 which served as the basis for the implementation. We would have appreciated a more formalized specification of the X.25 standard which could have saved us this effort. A formalized protocol specification not only has the advantage of simplifying the implementation, but is also useful during the protocol design, verification, and evaluation phase (see, for example, [9]).

B. The Use of a High-Level Implementation Language

We conclude from our experience that the following properties of the implementation language were most valuable for the project.

1) Facilities for step-wise refinement, in particular, the *class* concept.

2) Facilities for describing parallel activities. We used the *processes* and *monitors* of Concurrent Pascal; however, we would have appreciated a language construct (see, for example, [2]) closely related to the *component* structure described in Section II-A.

3) The facilities for type definition and checking, common to most Pascal-like languages.

Other aspects of our language implementation were not entirely satisfactory, such as, for example, its low efficiency and the inability to interwork with the standard computer operating system.

An advantage of using a high-level implementation language is the reduction of the programming and testing effort required. The testing of each protocol layer was done in two phases. First the system was embedded, on the same computer, in a testing environment, also written in Concurrent Pascal. Second, the system was checked with an X.25 protocol tester equipment which was connected to the computer via the data network access line. Both phases were effective.

We believe that a high-level language implementation such as ours is useful even when the high-level programming language is not implemented on the target computer, or when the efficiency or operating system interfaces of the implementation are insufficient. Efficiency may be increased by reprogramming the critical procedures in machine language, or the whole program may be used as a "blueprint" for an implementation in a suitable language. We note that Belsnes [10] comes to similar conclusions, describing an implementation of X.25 in Simula.

C. The VC Interface

In Section IV, we described in some detail the VC interface, which is the interface between the X.25 network access module and the remaining part of the computer system. In deriving this interface from the X.25 packet level specifications, we were astonished by the great complexity of the resulting interface. We wonder whether an interface to an end-to-end transport service [11] would be simpler in nature. A criterion for the delimitation of major system modules is the simplicity of the resulting interfaces. The experience with our X.25 implementation has not convinced us that the X.25 VC is a natural system interface.

D. Implementation on Multiple Microprocessors

In a microprocessor-based implementation of X.25, the different protocol layers may be distributed over several microprocessors [12], [13]. To avoid memory bus congestion, each microprocessor usually has its own local memory, which contains the program code and processed data, and may exchange messages via a system bus with the other microprocessors in the system. A system described in terms of processes and monitors, such as shown in Fig. 8, is suitable for distribution over a multimicroprocessor system. A possible distribution method, called "split process organization" by Cavers [12], proceeds as follows. First each monitor of the system is allocated to a suitable microprocessor. Then the processes are allocated. Processes accessing the monitors in one microprocessor are allocated to that microprocessor. Processes accessing monitors in more than one microprocessor are split into subprocesses, one for each microprocessor involved and allocated to it. The subprocesses communicate by message exchange via the system bus. This organization is particularly appropriate when most processing in the system is done in the monitors, and the processes have essentially the role of passing information. This is the case in the X.25 system of Fig. 8.

Annex 3

Structured Specification of Communicating Systems

(G. v. Bochmann and M. Raynal)

ABSTRACT

      Specification methods for distributed systems is the underlying theme of this paper. A model of communicating processes with rendez-vous interactions is assumed as a basis for the discussion. The possible interactions by a process, and the interconnection between several sub-processes within a process are specified using the concept of ports, which are specified separately. Stepwise refinement of process specifications and associated verification rules are considered. The stepwise refinement of port specifications and associated interactions is considered as well. After the presentation of an introductory example, the paper discusses the basic concepts of the specification method. They are then applied to more complex examples. The stepwise refinement of ports and interactions is demonstrated by a hardware interface for which an abstract specification and a more detailed implementation is given. Proof rules for verifying the consistency of detailed and more abstract specifications are discussed in some detail.

© 1983 IEEE, reprinted with permission from IEEE Transactions on Computers, Febr. 1983

1. Introduction

Much work has been done in recent years in the area of design methods for distributed systems. This includes the development of languages for distributed systems, the choice of appropriate interaction mechanisms (message transmission, rendez-vous interactions, remote procedure calls etc.), communication protocol design for long distance and local computer networks, as well as for the communication between several VLSI components within a single computer system. As in the case of non-distributed software systems, the notion of step-wise refinement seems to be an important design tool for distributed systems. Some difficulty is encountered, however, if some sort of undivisible interaction primitives are assumed.

The specification method discussed in this paper indicates how the step-wise refinement of distributed systems may be described with the concept of process substructure and the concept of interactions that may be refined. The method is based on the concepts "process" and "port". A process is an entity that performs some data processing and is assumed to be the unit of specification. A port is a part of a process and serves for the communication of that process with its environment, i.e. other processes in the system. A process may possess several ports for communication with different parts of its environment. The specification of the properties of a process or port is given at an abstract level, in the sense that only the externally visible behavior of a process or port is descibed (i.e. its communication behavior), but not the way this behavior is realized by an internal structure of the process or port. Process and port implementations are specified separately as the elements for one step in the step-wise refinement of a system description.

The specification of a port consists of two parts : (a) an enumeration of the types of interactions that may occur at the port, and (b) additional properties of the port which may in particular restrict the order and parameter values of the executed interactions.

The specification of a process also consists of two parts : the specification of the communication properties of its ports (as described above), and (b) additional properties of the process which may in particular relate the interactions taking place at the different ports of the process. An implementation of a process is given by defining an internal structure of the process in terms of sub-processes and interconnections between their ports.

This paper discusses the different aspects of this specification method : In section 2 an introductory example is given which illustrates the method and the concepts used. In section 3, the elements of the specification method and its underlying model are defined in more detail. The approach of step-wise refinement, in particular the refinement of port specifications, is discussed in detail in section 4. Section 5 contains an overall discussion of the problems of design verification which allows to check the consistency between a process implementation with its specification.

2. An example

The following example is given as an illustration for the specification method discussed in this paper. It introduces the main specification elements, which are processes and ports. These elements are more formally defined in section 3. The specification method favors a top-down design where first the specification of a process is given and then its refinement (implementation) in terms of communicating sub-processes is considered. Because of such possible refinements, a process is not necessarily sequential, but may involve several parallel activities.

2.1. The specification of a *multiserver*

Our example consists of a finite number of user processes which use the service provided by another process which is of type *multiserver*. Two operations are provided for interaction with the multiserver process. They are called *request* and *response*. A *request* contains a question which is answered by a *response*. For each user, a *request* interaction initiated by the user must always preceed a *response* interaction.

The concept of a port is introduced to structure a process and its possiblities for interaction with the environment. Independently of its realization, a port is defined by a set of interactions and the constraints on their execution. For the example considered here we have the following port type definition.

<u>port type</u> service-access <u>is</u>
   <u>operation</u> request (X : question);
          response (Y : answer);
   <u>constraint</u>
     (/request)i --> (/response)i --> (/request)$i+1$
<u>end</u> service-access;

Here it is assumed that data type definitions are given for the parameters used in the port definition. They could for example be of the form

  <u>type</u> question <u>is</u> <u>array</u> [1..100] <u>of</u> char;
         answer <u>is</u> <u>array</u> [1..200] <u>of</u> char;

The notation $(p/a)i$ --> $(q/b)j$ specifies that the i-th interaction of type a at the port p must preceed the j-th interaction of type b at the port q. For the specification of a port constraint, as in the definition above, the name of the port is implicitly given; therefore we simply write $(/a)i$ for the i-th interaction at the port. We note that this sequence-oriented notation is just taken as an example. The concepts discussed in this paper could as well be used when the constraints are specified by methods oriented towards programming languages or state machines [FDT 82b].

In the following are consider a *multiserver* process which has a number of ports (one for each user process) through which the user processes obtain access to the question answering service. This service is realized by the interactions of type *request* and *response*, as explained above. Without going into more detail, we assume that the answer to a question is a function of that question, and that the interactions over the different ports do not interfer with one another. More formally, these properties may be specified as follows :

<u>process type</u> multiserver <u>is</u>
   users : <u>array</u> [user-id-type] <u>of</u> service-access ;
   <u>constraint</u>
     <u>for</u> u <u>in</u> user-id-type <u>holds</u>
       (users[u]/response)i.Y = FUNCTION-OF((users[u]/resquest)i.X)
<u>end</u> multiserver;

Here we assume that the index data type of the array is defined as
   <u>type</u> user-id-type <u>is</u> 1 .. n :
and the function *FUNCTION-OF* defines the answering service of the *multiserver*. This function is not specified here. The given constraint defines the non-interference between the different ports.

The nature of the specification of a process type is similar to the nature of a port type specification. (In the following we often simply say process (or port) for a process (or port) _type_). In the case of a process specification, the set of declared ports of the process are associated with a constraint which must be satisfied by the executions of the interactions at the different ports. In addition, it is understood that the port constraints of the different ports are satisfied as well. For each port _users[u]_, for example, the i-th interaction _request_ must preceed the i-th interaction _response_. Each process cooperating with the _multiserver_ uses a port of type _service-access_. To show the flexibility of the specification method, we continue the explanation of the example by distinguishing two types of user processes, in particular, we assume that a _simple-user_ process will only submit a subset of the possible questions. The user processes may be specified as follows :

```
process type user is
    service : service-access :
end user;

process type simple-user is
    service : service-access :
    constraint (service/request)i.X in simple-question
end simple-user;
```

As before, the specification of a user process describes the interactions of a process with its environment. The specification of a _simple-user_ includes an additional constraint for the parameter value of the _request_ operation. Such restrictions are considered in [Buck 77]. In simpler cases, it could be specified by a data type definition of the form

type simple-question _is_ question _range_ ...

which is analogous to the definition of sub-types in ADA [Ichb 79].

For the specification of process types, only the interactions of that process are considered, but not the internal structure of the specified process. In the example above, nothing is said about the internal operations of the user processes. It is assumed here that they are really the sink for the information provided by the _multiserver_ process. In reality, a user process may consist of a terminal handling process, a terminal and an operator that consults the database of the _multiserver_ for some clients requesting information. The interactions between the operator and the clients is not defined in the specifications given in our example.

The interconnection of processes of type _user_, _simple-user_ and _multiserver_, as shown in figure 1, is called a system of cooperating processes. In general, such a system may again be considered a process at a higher level of abstraction. Some language elements are needed for specifying the interconnection structure of the processes. The system shown in figure 1 may be specified as follows :

```
system is
    S : multiserver ;
    SU : array [1..nSU] of simple-user ;
    U : array [(nSU+1)..n] of user ;
connection
    for u in 1..nSU : SU[u].service = S.users[u];
    for u in (nSU+1)..n:U[u].service = S.users[u]
end system;
```

An interconnection between processes is established by connecting their ports.

(It is necessary, however, that the ports are of the same type). An interaction occurs when the two processes invoke the same type of interaction on the interconnected ports. A rendez-vous kind of interaction mechanism is assumed, as discussed in more detail in section 3.1.

2.2. A refinement of the *multiserver* process

It is important for a specification method to support the step-wise refinement of specifications. In the case of the specification method discussed in this paper, a decomposition method is used similar to the example shown in figure 1.

Continuing our example, we assume that a *multiserver* process consists of two sub-processes, as shown in figure 2 : a *server* process that provides the answering service over <u>one</u> port, and a *multiplexer* process which provides the appropriate multiplexing between the different users.

The specification of each of these subprocesses may be given in the following form :

```
process type server is
    user : service-access :
    constraint
        (user/response)i.Y = FUNCTION-OF((user/request)i.X)
end server;

process type multiplexer is
    singles : array [user-id-type] of service-access :
    multiplexed : service-access :
    constraint
        for s in user-id-type holds ∀i ∃i'
            ((singles[s]/request)i = (multiplexed/request)i'
        and (singles[s]/response)i = (multiplexed/response)i')
end multiplexer;
```

In the case of the *server*, the constraint specifies the correspondence between the i-th question and the answer. In the case of the *multiplexer*, the constraint specifies that all requests from a given user *s* are forwarded to the *service* process and that the obtained answer is returned to the user, without interference with the activity of the other users.

Given the above specification of the sub-processes, we may now give a refined specification of the *multiserver* process as shown in figure 2. The specification below defines instances of the *service* and *multiplexer* process types, and defines the interconnection between these sub-process instances :

```
process implementation imps for multiserver is
    M : multiplexer :
    S : server ;
    internal connection M.multiplexed = S.user;
    external connection users is M.singles
end imps;
```

Here the abbreviation   users <u>is</u> M.singles   stands for
  <u>for all</u> u <u>in</u> user-id-type : users[u] <u>is</u> M.singles[u].

While a process type specification has the major parts "port declarations" and "constraints", a specification of a process implementation, which is a refinement of a given process type specification, has the major parts "declarations of the sub-processes" and the "interconnection of their ports". As the example shows, two kinds of interconnections are distinguished : The *external connections* specify how the ports of the process type specification are realized by the implementation, while the *internal connections* define connections between the ports of the sub-processes that are not visible at the higher level of abstraction (as represented by the process type specification).

It is clearly possible to define several different implementations for a given process type. They would differ from one another by the types of the sub-processes used and by the interconnection structure between the sub-processes. The same kind of external connections must be defined by all implementations, since they connect the external ports which are defined, together with their type, in the process type specification. This approach has certain similarities with the step-wise refinement of abstract data type specifications [Lis 74, Gutt 77, Wulf 77]. As in the case of such specifications, we have to address the problem of asserting the coherence between a process type specification and its implementation. We come back to these questions in the sections 4 and 5. We note that the example above and most related work [Chen 81, Hoar 78, Miln 80, Misr 81, Jorr 81] assume that the same type of ports are used in the process type specification and its implementation. In section 4, we consider the refinements of ports which eliminates this restriction of the specification method.

3. The concepts used for specification

In this section we examine in more detail the concepts used for specification. This amounts to defining an underlying model for the specification method. In section 3.1, we first examine the concepts of processes and their interactions; then in section 3.2, we consider the concept of a port and the interconnection mechanism associated with it. In section 3.3 we introduce the concept of a role which is taken by a process in respect to a given port. Section 3.4 discusses the specification method based on processes, ports and their interconnection.

3.1. Processes and their interactions

For the specification of a process type, the point of view of an external observer is considered. Only the externally visible behavior should be specified; a process is therefore defined by its possibilities of communicating with its environment, i.e. interacting with the other processes in the system.

An interaction between two processes occurs when both processes invoke the same type of interaction on ports that are connected. It is assumed that a rendez-vous kind of interaction mechanism [Hoar 78, Miln 80] is used. The first process ready to execute the interaction must wait for the second to be ready. (The assumption of such an interaction mechanism simplifies the model without restricting its descriptive power; for example, a message queuing mechanism may be specified by the introduction of a buffering process).

In this paper we do not make the assumption that interactions are necessarily atomic. In fact, we assume, as discussed in [Lamp 79], that the execution of an interaction consumes some time. This assumption seems more realistic than an "event model" [Kell 76] where it is assumed, for specification purposes, that different interactions exclude one another in time. We note, however, that a transition between the two models may be defined : It is sufficient to define for each non-atomic interaction p two atomic events $begin(p)$ and $end(p)$. Defining a total order over the events $begin(pi)$ and $end(pi)$, it is possible to define an arbitrary ordering of the interactions pi, including the possibility of simultaneity [Grei 77, Shaw 78, Andl 79].

Since the specification of a process type should only describe its externally visible behavior, the specification should define the possible interaction types and the order in which they may be executed. As shown by the example in section 2.1, the interaction types are defined by a name and the type of the exchanged parameters. (The reason for associating the interactions with ports will be discussed in section 3.2). In general, the constraint part of the specification of a process type defines restrictions on the possible interactions and the possible execution order. The specification of such restrictions may take different forms, such as assertions on parameter values, or expressions defining full or partial orders of execution sequences. Different specification techniques may be considered for this purpose. Whichever technique is chosen, it must be suitable for the two kinds of restrictions mentioned above. In the case that a total order of the interactions is specified, the specification of a process type is analogous to the specification of a module or abstract data type, as discussed in [Bart 77] and [Rayn 81].

3.2. Ports and their connections

The concept of a port [Balz 71, Silb 81] allows to give some structure to the interactions of a process with its environment. The ports defined for a given process type may be considered as an abstraction of the environment of that process. Let us consider the example of a process P with three ports $p1$, $p2$ and $p3$, as shown in figure 3 (see figure 10.1 in chapter 10).

The ports pi represent an abstract specification of the environment of P, as it is seen by the process. The enviroment may be implemented in different ways, as shown in the figure . The specification of P, however, is the same for all these environments.

A port binds together a number of different interaction types and defines some constraints on their executions (see example of section 2.1). Similarly, a process, if it has several ports, defines some additional constraints that must be satisfied for the executions of interactions at the different process ports. Each interaction of the process is associated with a particular port.

For the specification of distributed systems, the notion of a port may also be used for distinguishing different points (in the distribution space) of the distributed system. The specification of a communication service, for example, is usually given in terms of a (distributed) process that provides a certain number of ports (called "access points") through which the user processes may access the communication service [Boch 80b].

Apart from the above considerations, the main reason for the introduction of the port concept is its use in the refinement process. As already discussed in section 2.2, the concept of ports is essential for the specification of process implementations in terms of sub-processes. The interconnection of these sub-processes is in fact defined by establishing an identity relation between the ports of different sub-processes. The connected ports must be of the same type (i.e. allow the same type of interactions with the same port constraints). It is possible to define more complex connection patterns where the ports of more than two processes are identified by one connection [Rayn 81]. An example of such a connection can be found in section 4.3.

3.3. The role concept

The concept of a port as explained above may appear incomplete. In fact, for an interaction that involves the transfer of parameter values from one process to another, it may be necessary for a complete specification to indicate which process determines the value. (We note that the interaction is executed when both processes invoke the interaction as a rendez-vous; therefore both processes may, in principle, participate in the determination of the parameter values). The role concept is introduced to make this aspect more precise : In the definition of an interaction, each parameter is associated with the name of a role, and only the process that has this role attribute associated with the port will have to provide the parameter value for the interaction in question; the other process is implicitly the receiver of the parameter value. When for the purpose of implementation two ports of different processes are connected, it is clearly necessary that the two connected processes have complementary roles for the connected ports. We note that this concept has certain similarities with the definition of protection attributes [Jone 76] which apply to operation names, instead of to parameters as in our case.

To further explain the concept, we consider the following example :

```
port type p is
    role side1, side2 :
    operation  op1 (X by side1 : integer) ;
               op2 (Y by side2 : character) ;
               op3 (T by side1 : integer, U by side2 : boolean) ;
    constraint ....
end p;
```

We suppose that two processes $Q1$ and $Q2$ have declared the ports $p1$ and $p2$ of type p with the roles *side1* and *side2*, respectively, and suppose that the two ports are connected. In the case of a joint execution of the *op1* interaction, the process $Q1$ will provide the integer parameter value and the process $Q2$ will receive it; in the case of *op2* the actions of $Q1$ and $Q2$ are interchanged. In the case of *op3*, $Q1$ determines the integer value of the parameter T, while $Q2$ determines the boolean value of U.

It is important to note that the roles played by the processes in respect to interaction parameters is independent of the question which process initiates the interaction. For example, the execution of *op1* could be initiated by $Q1$ or $Q2$. The distinction of an initiating process is usually made in a more detailed specification or an implementation of a system. For example, when guarded commands [Dijk 75] are used for the description of the processes, the initiating process is usually the one for which the interaction is not part of a guard. (The initiation is usually in a deterministic context). We note that in CSP [Hoar 78], in contrast to ADA [Ichb 79], the distinction between initiation and parameter determination does not exist : Only the reception of interaction parameters may appear in guards. Several proposals for eliminating this restriction have been made [Bern 80, Silb 81, Boch 80c].

3.4. Specification of ports and processes

The example of section 2 showed the similarity of the specifications for ports and processes : The specification of a port type consists of a list of interactions (possibly with roles) and constraints on their execution; the specification of a process type consists of a list of ports and constraints on the execution of the interactions that are defined for those ports. The latter constraints are sometimes called "global constraints" since they involve the interactions on several ports. In addition the process satisfies, for each of its ports, the constraints specified for the corresponding port type. These constraints are sometimes called "local constraints" since they are local to a port. The syntax used in this paper for the specification of process types adopts the "ADA style", anof the specification language used in this paper adopts a kind of "ADA style". The syntax for a process type specification is as follows :

```
process type <name> is
    <list of port declarations>:
    constraint
    <port constraints on execution order>
end <name>;
```

For the description of an implementation of a process type, as a step in the refinement process, the following syntax is used :

```
process implementation <impl-name> for <name> is
    <sub-process declarations>;
    internal connection <interconnections of sub-process ports>;
    external connection <interconnections to the external ports >
end <impl-name>;
```

In the remaining part of this section we give another example which illustrates the specification of processes with roles. The example is a process that provides some communication service with queuing between two ports $p1$ and $p2$. User processes that are connected to these ports may exchange messages in both directions through the service. A specification of the port and process type is given below.

```
port type sr-point is
    role caller, callee ;
    operation send (X by caller : message) :
              receive (X by callee : message) ;
    constraint
         (/send)i --> (/receive)j or (/receive)j --> (/send)i
end sr-point;

process type service is
    p1(callee), p2(callee) : sr-point ;
    constraint (p1/send)i.X = (p2/receive)i.X
           and (p1/receive)j.X = (p2/send)j.X
end service;
```

The constraints of the *service* specifies that the received messages are those that were sent, and that the order of reception is the same as the order of sending; the communication service is reliable, no messages are lost nor dammaged. In the case that additional coordination is desired (such as rendez-vous, limited buffering, etc.), supplementary constraints must be give For instance, the additional constraints

$(p2/receive)i \longrightarrow (p1/send)i+n$ *and* $(p1/receive)j \longrightarrow (p2/send)j+m$

would specify a maximal buffering of n in one direction, and m in the other.

We note that the declaration of the ports in the definition of the *service* process type includes a definition of the role of the *service* process at the ports. The specification for the port p1 implies that the connected user process provides the message parameter for the *send* interaction, and the *service* process for the *receive* interaction.

4. Step-wise refinement of a specification

The proposed specification method allows a step-wise refinement of specifications. The example of section 2 shows on the one side, how the specification of the external behavior of a process or port can be given independently of an implementation, and on the other side, how a specification can be refined by giving a particular implementation. Such an implementation is given by defining a decomposition of the process into several sub-processes and a connection pattern between the ports of the sub-processes. This kind of step-wise refinement is considered in previous work [Chen 81, Misr 81, Jorr 81]. It implies that the interaction primitives that are exchanged between the process and its environment are the same for the more abstract specification as for the more detailed refinement. We think that it is important to allow for a step-wise refinement of the interaction primitives as well. Therefore we discuss in section 4.2 an approach to the step-wise refinement of port specifications. The use of this approach is illustrated in section 4.3 by the example of an arbiter [Seit 80, Boch 80b], and the implications for the verification of the refinement step are discussed in section 5.

We note that the approach to refinement discussed in this paper can be used in as many steps of refinement as desired. As shown by the arbiter example of section 4.3, this may lead to a level of detail which allows direct realization in hardware. If software implementation is sought, it seems convenient to convert at a certain level of detail to a specification by a programming language, which is used to implement the sub-processes obtained in the last step of the refinement. An example for this can be found in [Owic 79].

4.1. The internal structure of processes

We give in this subsection some comments on the internal structure of a process implementation. First, there are two kinds of connections : internal and external ones (see example in section 2.2). The former interconnect ports of the sub-processes and are purely a matter of implementation choice. The latter specify which ports of the implementing sub-processes represent the (external) ports that are defined in the higher-level specification of the process. Therefore the same kinds of external connections will be found in each implementation of the process. Second, it is important to note that during the phase of the compilation of a process implementation description, it is possible to perform certain consistency checks. In particular, the port types and roles can be checked for each connection, as discussed in the sections 3.2 and 3.3. Another check would be to detect any port that has not been used for any connection.

4.2. Port refinements

A port of a process represents an abstract interface of the process

which defines the possible interactions and the constraints for their executi(
as explained in section 3.2. A refinement of such a port, which must be defin(
for an implementation, brings up the following two questions :

(1) Is a given interaction of the port, which is a primitive at the abstract
    level of the specification, also a primitive at the more detailed level o
    the implementation ?

(2) Is a given port composed of several sub-ports ? (In this case a
    non-primitive interaction may involve several interactions at several
    different sub-ports).

To illustrate the first question, we consider the port specificatio
below.

```
port type resource is
    role user, server;
    operation use-resource (X by user : question,
                            Y by server : answer) ;
    constraint (/use- resource)i --> (/use-resource)i+1
    end resource;
```

This port defines the interaction *use-resource* which represents a procedural
access by a *user* process to of a process playing the *server* role. The *user*
process provides the *question* value of the first parameter and receives from
server the *answer* value of the second parameter. Comparing this port
specification with the *service-access* port defined in section 2.1, we see tha
the latter may be considered an implementation of the former, where the
use-resource interaction is implemented by the sequential composition of the
interactions *request* and *response*. (The syntax for the specification of such
port implementation is demonstrated by the next example).

To illustrate the second question (implementation with sub-ports),
to give an example of the syntax for port implementations, we consider the po
specification below.

```
port type reservation is
    role requesting, responding :
    operation   reserve;
                release;
    constraint (/reserve)i --> (/reserve)i+1       (1)
           and (/release)i --> (/release)i+1      (2)
           and (/reserve)i --> (/release)i        (3)
           and (/release)i - -> (/reserve)i+1     (4)
end reservation;
```

The port type *reservation* offers two types of interactions *reserve* and *releas*
The execution constraints are expressed using two temporal relations "-->"
(preceeds) and "- ->" (may influence) [Lamp 79]. (The expression "A --> B" me
that the execution of the interaction A ends before the execution of the
interaction B begins; and "A - -> B" means that A has begun when B ends). The
temporal relations are used in the specification of the constraints to indica
that the execution of the interactions may extend over a certain time period,
and their execution may possibly overlap. In fact, the (i+1)-th *reserve*
interaction may begin before the i-th *release* interaction ends, but it may nc
end before the latter (see line (4)). The lines (1) through (3) define the us
sequential ordering of interactions.

Let us now consider the port specification given below, which reflects the properties of a hardware circuit (i.e. a single wire) in a digital system.

port type circuit *is*
    role active, passive ;
    operation up:
              down :
    constraint $(/up)i \rightarrow (/down)i \rightarrow (/up)i+1$
end circuit;

The two interactions of the *circuit* are *up* and *down* (i.e. "set" and "reset", or set to 1 and set to 0) with the constraint that their execution alternates.

In the following we give an implementation of the *reservation* port type by two sub-ports R and A of type *circuit*. The implementation is based on the so-called "four-cycle signaling scheme" which is illustrated in figure 4.

The sub-port R carries the *reserve* and *release* requests (implemented by the *up* and *down* interactions, respectively) from the process with the *requesting* role to the process with the *responding* role, while A returns the acknowledgements of the *responding* process. The order in which these signals may be invoked is defined by the four-cycle signaling scheme, as shown in figure 4. (We note that a temporal logic description of this scheme may be found in [Boch 82]). A formal notation for the description of this port implementation is given below. It also demonstrates a possible syntax for such specifications.

port implementation four-cycle *for* reservation *is*
    R (active=requesting), A (active=responding) : circuit ;
    constraint
        $(R/up)i \rightarrow (A/up)i \rightarrow (R/down)i \rightarrow (A/down)i \rightarrow (R/up)i+1$;
    mapping reserve *is* R.up $\rightarrow$ A.up;
    mapping release *is* R.down $\rightarrow$ A.down
end four-cycle;

The *constraint* part of the specification defines the four-cycle signaling scheme, and a *correspondence* part which defines the implementation of the interactions by giving for each interaction of the *reservation* port a mapping into a sequence of interactions of the sub-ports R and A. The declaration of the sub-ports also defines the relation between the roles of the sub-ports and the roles of the port. We note that this relation is not the same for the two sub-ports, since R carries information from the *requesting* to the *responding* process (the *active* role is *requesting*), while A carries information in the opposite direction (the *active* role is *responding*). We note that the mapping definition which defines the correspondence between the port and sub-port interactions is particularly simple in this example. In general, it may involve sets of sub-port interaction sequences, and/or mapping of parameter values similar to the mappings found in the stepwise refinement of abstract datatypes [Wulf 77, Gutt 77].

The above example demonstrates the refinement of a port into two sub-ports of simpler structure. It is an example of a step-wise refinement process that leads from a more abstract port specification to a more detailed specification that shows how the abstract port may be implemented. Such port refinements are important for the design of communicating systems for the following reasons :

(1) The communication between the different parts of a system is usually first described by defining an "abstract interface" which defines the logical

interactions that may take place [Boch 80b]. Subsequently, during the
system implementation, this abstract interface is refined by giving an
implementation in the form of software procedure calls, interprocess
communication primitives, or hardware constructs.

(2) The *constraint* part of the port type, or port implementation specification
gives a complete view of the constraints that are imposed on the
communication between two processes at the given level of detail. We
believe that a separate specification of these constraints leads to a
clearer structure of the system specification.

(3) We note that the port refinement may lead to a specification level that is
directly implementable in hardware, as the above example demonstrates. (*
reservation port is implemented by two hardware *circuits*).

Once an implementation of a port is described, the question rises
whether the implementation is correct. This is discussed in section 5.3. Befor
however, we give a more complete example for the refinement of a process
specification, using the port implementation given above.

4.3. An example of refinement

The following example serves two purposes : (a) to illustrate the us
of port refinements as discussed in section 4.2, and (b) to serve as an examp:
for the discussion of verification in section 5.

4.3.1. The abstract specification

We consider the example of an *arbiter* which assures mutual exclusion
to the access of a shared resource between two user processes. As in [Seit 80
Boch 82], from where this example is taken, the *arbiter* is associated with two
transfer-device-i (i=1,2) processes which transfer the operational parameters
from the two respective users to the resource. The communication between the
arbiter and the other processes in the system is realized through ports of typ
reservation using the interactions *reserve* and *release*.

As shown in figure 5, the *arbiter* communicates with the other
processes through the five ports *user[1], user[2], transfer[1], transfer[2]* a:
resource. In respect to the first two ports, it plays the *responding* role, wh
it plays the *requesting* role in respect to the others. When a user process
executes a *reserve* interaction the arbiter establishes a rendez-vous between
user, the resource, and the corresponding transfer process, such that the lat
may transfer the operational parameters from the user to the resource (as
indicated in the figure by the pointed lines). A similar rendez-vous occurs
during a *release*.

This informal description may be defined more precisely with our
specification language as follows :

```
process type arbiter is
    user (responding),
    transfer (requesting) : array [1..2] of reservation :
    resource (requesting) : reservation ;
    constraint
        for i in 1..2 holds
            ((user[i]/reserve)j <---> (transfer[i]/reserve)j and   (1)
            (user[i]/reserve)j <---> (resource/reserve)j and       (2)
            (transfer[i]/reserve)j <---> (resource/reserve)j and   (3)
            ... similarly for release ...);
        for i in 1..2 holds
            ( i <> j implies not
            ((user[i]/reserve)k --> (user[j]/release)k'            (4)
            and (user[j]/reserve)k' --> (user[i]/release)k))       (5)
end arbiter;
```

This specification uses the abbreviation "A <---> B" which is equivalent to "A --> B and B --> A" which means that A and B overlap in time. The lines 4 and 5 of the specification define the mutual exclusion property, while the lines 1, 2, and 3 define the three-way rendez-vous during the *reserve* interaction of a user.

4.3.2. Refined specification - implementation

The implementation of the *arbiter* process considered here uses as sub-processes elementary hardware components. The components used are the combinational circuits AND and OR, the more complex Muller C-elements (for which the output remains constant until both inputs assume the opposite value), and a primitive mutual exclusion element ME. The interested reader may find more details in [Seit 80] and [Boch 82]. Here we concentrate our discussion on the sub-process and connection structure of the implementation, and the refinement of the *reservation* ports. The structure of the implementation is shown in figure 6.

The implementation uses two ports of type *circuit* to realize a *reservation* port of the abstract specification. For example, UA1 and UR1 implement the *reservation* port user[1]. The correspondence between the pairs of *circuits* shown in figure 6, and the abstract *reservation* ports is defined by the *four-cycles* implementation discussed in section 4.2. We note that the circuits URi, TRi and SR carry requests (for the TRi and SR the *arbiter* plays the *active* role, whereas for the URi, it is the user), while the other circuits UAi, TAi and SA carry the corresponding acknowledgements.

More formally, the implementation may be defined as follows :

```
process implementation arb-impl for arbiter is
    OR : array [1..2] of OR-gate :         --- these elementary
    AND : array [1..2] of AND-gate :       --- processes have ports
    Ca, Cb : array [1..2] of C-element ;   --- named "input" and
    ME : ME-element ;                      --- "output" of type
    OR3 : OR-gate :                        --- circuit
    internal connection
        for i in 1..2 begin
            MEO[i] is ME.output[i] = AND[i].input[1];
            MEI[i] is ME.input[i] = OR[i].output ;
            SR[i] is Cb[i].output = OR3.input[i]
        end;
```

```
    external connection
       for i in 1..2 begin
               user[i] using four-cycle is
                  (OR[i].input[2] = AND[i].input[2] = Cb[i].input[2],   (1)
                   Ca[i].output = OR[i].input[1]) :                      (2)
               transfer[i] using four-cycle is
                  (Cb[i].input[1], AND[i].output = Ca[i].input[1]);      (3)
               resource using four-cycle is
                  (Ca[1].input[2] = Ca[2].input[2], OR3.output)          (4)
        end
end arb-impl:
```

For clarity purposes, the internal connections are given a name which is also used in figure 6. As in the example of section 2.2, the external connections define the ports of the abstract process specification. In this case, however, these ports are implemented by a refinement. Therefore the specification of the external connections define the correspondence between the abstract ports and the ports of the implementation, as well as the implementation model used, i.e. the port implementation *four-cycle*.

As explained in section 3.1, a connection between two ports imposes synchronized execution of the interactions by the two connected processes. The above example shows how such a synchronization can be extended to more than two ports. For instance, the three-port connection of line (1) between the ports $OR[1].input[2]$, $AND[1].input[2]$, and $Cb[1].input[2]$ imposes a synchrony between these three circuits, and defines in addition the correspondence with the sub-port R of the *four-cycle* implementation of the abstract *reservation* port $user[1]$.

5. Verification of specification consistency

We discuss in this section the steps that are required to verify that the definition of a process implementation is consistent with the more abstract specification of the process. We first discuss in section 5.2 the case of a process implementation with an internal structure of sub-processes, but no port refinement. Port refinements are considered separately in section 5.3. In the first sub-section some comments on the underlying semantic model are made. No formal definition of the semantics of process specifications is given. Such a definition would depend on the scope and generality of the language adopted for the specification of process and port constraints. These considerations are beyond the scope of this paper. We think, however, that the following considerations are valid for most semantic models that could be adopted.

5.1. Comments on the semantic model.

The following definitions and comments are made in order to clarify the meaning of the specifications of processes and their implementations, and define the framework in which a semantic model for processes and their interactions can be given which would be the formal basis for proofs of consistency between specifications at different levels of detail.

a) Interaction type : the type of interaction defines the possible parameter values that are exchanged over a connection during the occurrence of an interaction of that type.

b) Interaction occurrence : an interaction occurrence is defined by the following informations :
- the connection (within the system) where the interaction occurs; this may be an external port of the process considered or an internal connection between the ports of (several) sub-processes of an implementation.
- the time period during which the interaction is executed (beginning and ending point in real time).
- the interaction value that occurs, i.e. the parameter values exchanged. (We note that these values must adhere to the corresponding interaction type).

c) Execution histories : an execution history is a set of interaction occurrences. (We note that this definition excludes the possibility of including in the same history two identical interaction occurrences, i.e. identical interactions (with same parameter values) during the same time period and on the same connection). In the case of a model with atomic interactions, the interaction occurrences of an execution history may be put into a (in part arbitrary [Lamp 78]) order. One obtains a semantic model based on execution sequences.

d) Safeness properties : safeness properties of a process specification or implementation are usually stated by defining conditions that are satisfied by all possible execution histories in which the process can be involved.

e) Liveness properties : for the consideration of liveness properties of a process specification or implementations, it seems natural to distinguish between the process that initiates an interaction occurence over a given connection and its counterpart. This distinction is related to guarded commands [Dijk 75, Hoar 78] that may be part of a process implementation and determine a choice among several possibilities for future behavior. Liveness properties may also be described by the concept of a *process state* which defines the possible future execution histories of the process [Miln 80, Owic 81].

f) Sometimes it is necessary to make certain assumptions about the safeness and liveness properties of the environment in which the process evolves [Misr 81, Boch 82].

5.2 Consistency of subprocess structures.

We consider in this subsection a process specification and an implementation of that specification in terms of several sub-processes without port refinements, i.e. each (external) port of the process is a port of one of the sub-processes.

A process type specification defines the following properties of the execution histories in which a process of that type can be involved. Such a process may be part of a larger system.

A) Interaction type constraints : the values of each interaction occurrence in a history correspond to the interaction type associated with the external connection where the interaction occurs.

B) Port constraints (one for each port of the process) : the sub-history of those interaction occurrences (of a history) that occur at a given external connection of the process satisfies the constraints explicitly specified in the port type definition corresponding to that connection. (Such sub-histories are special cases of "projections" as considered in [Merl 82, Lam 81]).

C) Global constraint : A history satisfies the constraints explicitly defined in the process specification.

The definition of a process implementation, similarly, implies the following properties of the execution histories possible for this implementation :

D) Subprocess constraints (one for each sub-process of the implementation) : the sub-history of those interaction occurrences of a history that occur over (external and/or internal) connections to which the sub-process is connected satisfies the properties A), B) and C) of that process. (We note that a suitable port/connection name substitution must be made corresponding to the connection structure of the implementation before the property C) of the sub-process can be applied to the execution history of the implementation).

To show the consistency of a process implementation with the specification of the process, we have to prove that properties A), B) and C) of the process specification can be implied from the sub-process contraints D of the implementation. Since there are no port refinements, and the type compatibility of connected ports is compile-time checked, the properties A) and B) follow directly from the corresponding properties of the sub-processes. The property C) is in general more difficult to prove.

For the example of the *multiserver* process given in section 2.1, the consistency proof is outlined as follows. The global constraint C) of the *multiserver* specification (to be proven) has the form :
for each (external) connection $users[u]$ <u>holds</u>
$\forall i \ (users[u]/response)i.Y = \text{FUNCTION-OF}((users[u]/request)i.X)$

This property can be implied from the global constraints of the sub-processes *server* and *multiplexer* implementing the *multiserver* (see section 2.2); these constraints are re-written as follows with the appropriate renaming of the port/connection names used in the implementation :
$(S.user/response)i.Y = \text{FUNCTION-OF}((S.user/request)i.X)$
and for each connection $users[u]$ <u>holds</u>
$\forall i \ \exists i' \ ((users[u]/request)i = (S.user/request)i'$
<u>and</u> $(users[u]/response)i = (S.user/response)i')$

This example is particularly simple. In more typical cases, the proof involves induction and invariant properties that hold throughout the execution of the system. The proofs of the input/output properties of a procedure, based on its implementation in an algorithmic language, is the corresponding consistency problem for sequential programs. Related work can be found in [Apt 80, Misr 81, Chen 81]. A constructive approach for deriving the specification a sub-process from the specification of the process and the other sub-processes is explored in [Merl 82].

5.3 <u>Consistency and port refinements</u>.

We consider in this subsection in addition to the problem of section 5.2 that the process implementation uses one or several port implementations, explained in section 4.2.

5.3.1. Consistency of port implementations.

A port type specification defines the following properties of the port histories of the interactions occuring over the port (which are sub-histories of global system execution histories with appropriate renaming) :

$\tilde{A}$) Operation type constraint : the values of each interaction occurrence in a history correspond to the interaction type specified.

$\tilde{B}$) Port constraint : A history satisfies the explicitly specified constraints.

A port implementation defines, similarly as a process type specification, three properties $\tilde{A}$), $\tilde{B}$) and $\tilde{C}$) for a port implementation history (i.e. an execution history of the interactions occurring over the sub-ports of the implementation) where the port constraints (property $\tilde{B}$) are those of the declared sub-ports of the implementation, and the global constraint (property $\tilde{C}$) is the constraint explicitly defined for the implementation.

In addition, a port implementation defines a "correspondence" which is, in the more general case, a mapping (possibly one to many) from occurrences of port interactions to (finite) port implementation sub-histories. We assume that the inverse of this mapping is not ambiguous, by which we means that for each port implementation sub-history, it can be determined whether it is the implementation (i.e. image of the correspondence mapping) of a port interaction occurrence or not; and that it is the implementation of at most one interaction occurrence.

The correspondence mapping can be naturally extended to a mapping from port histories (sets of port interaction occurrences) to port implementation sub-histories, where the resulting history is the set union of the sub-histories corresponding to the different operation occurrence in the port history.

A port implementation should satisfy the following consistency conditions :

(1) Inverse functionality of correspondence : the extended correspondence mapping should have an inverse function over the set of those implementation histories that satisfy the conditions $\tilde{A}$), $\tilde{B}$) and $\tilde{C}$) of the implementation.

(2) Realization of port constraints : the image, under the inverse correspondence mapping, of an implementation history satisfying $\tilde{A}$), $\tilde{B}$) and $\tilde{C}$), should satisfy the port constraints (property $\tilde{B}$) of the port type specification.

As an example, we consider the *four-cycle* implementation of the *reservation* port type discussed in section 4.2. The global port implementation constraint (property $\tilde{C}$)

$(R/up)i \longrightarrow (A/up)i \longrightarrow (R/down)i \longrightarrow (A/down)i \longrightarrow (R/up)i+1$

and the given correspondence rule imply that the i-th *reservation* interaction occurrence of a port history corresponds to the i-th sequence of $(R/up) \longrightarrow (A/up)$ in the corresponding implementation history; and the i-th *release* to the i-th sequence of $(R/down) \longrightarrow (A/down)$. Therefore the inverse functionality of the correspondence mapping is guaranteed. This also shows that

$(/reserve)i \longrightarrow (/release)i$

holds; and applying the global constraint once more for $i + 1$ one obtains

$(/release)i$ --> $(/reserve)i+1$ --> $(/release)i+1$

which implies the constraints of the port type *reservation* which is implemente

5.3.2. Consistency of process implementations.

We now consider the consistency conditions that should be satisfied a process implementation using port implementations. As in the case without po refinements discussed in section 5.2, the general consistency condition is tha the properties A), B) and C) of the process specification can be implied from the sub-process constraints (property D) of the implementation. Considering th structure of the implementation, this consistency condition can be implied fro the following conditions :

(a) For each port not using any refinement : properties $\tilde{A}$) and $\tilde{B}$) (see sectio 5.3.1) are satisfied.

(b) For each port using an implementation :
  (b1) For each sub-port of the implementation : properties $\tilde{A}$) and $\tilde{B}$) (see section 5.3.1) are satisfied.

  (b2) The global port implementation constraint (property $\tilde{C}$) can be impli from the sub-process constraints.

(c) The global process constraint (property C, see section 5.2) can be shown be satisfied by all (abstracted) execution histories obtained by the applicati of the inverse correspondance functions of the port implementations, from the implementation execution histories satisfying the sub-process constraints.

We note that the conditions (b1) and (b2) for a given refined port together with the consistency conditions of the port implementation (see secti 5.3.1) imply that the properties $\tilde{A}$) and $\tilde{B}$) are satisfied for the given port. Therefore the conditions (a), (b) and (c), together with the consistency conditions (1) and (2) for the port implementations, imply the general consistency condition mentioned above.

The verification of the conditions (a) and (b1) is made by the port type compatibility checking at compile-time. The verification of the condition (b2) and (c) is in general more difficult and must be compared with the verification of property (C) in the absence of port implementations (see secti 5.2). Often the verification involves the establishment of invariant propertie that are needed for deriving both conditions (b2) and (c).

As an example we consider the arbiter specification and implementation discussed in section 4.3. A detailed verification of the consistency conditions is given in [Boch 82]. We limit the discussion here to the major points of the verification. It is important to note that the verification of the port implementation constraint (condition (b2)) involves several sub-processes of the implementation. As figure 6 shows, the constraint that the *UA1* circuit of the *user[1]* port, for example, is not set up before th *UR1* circuit of the same port goes up, involves the propagation of the *UR1* circuit signal through the sub-processes *OR1*, *ME*, *AND1* and *Ca1*; and also relie on the assumption that the same port implementation constraint is satisfied by the processes in the environment of the arbiter connected to the ports *transfer[1]* and *resource*. As a consequence condition (b2) can only be verified

by considering the interplay between the different parts of the process
implementation and its environment, which is formalized in [Boch 82] by an
invariant and a reachability analysis based on the properties of the
sub-processes, their interconnection structure and assumptions on the
environment. From this invariant and reachability analysis, it is then
straightforward to derive the constraints of the port implementations. The same
invariant is also the basis for deriving the global constraints (especially the
mutual exclusion) of the arbiter specification (condition (c)). We note,
however, that the global constraints of the arbiter specification in [Boch 80b]
are not given in terms of an abstracted *reservation* port specification, but in
terms of the sub-port operations of the implementation. This simplifies the
proof since it is not necessary to consider the inverse correspondence function
to make the abstraction from the detailed interactions of the implementation
sub-ports to the more abstract interactions of the *reservation* port used in the
arbiter specification of section 4.3. With the correspondence discussed in
section 5.3.1, it is however not difficult to derive the global constraints of
the arbiter specification given in section 4.3 from the global properties of the
arbiter specification given in [Boch 80b].

6. Conclusions

A method for specifying communicating systems is discussed and
demonstrated by several examples. The method is based on the concepts of
communicating processes and process interactions that are associated with
communication ports. The step-wise refinement of a process specification is
considered by the definition of an internal structure of the process, consisting
of sub-processes and connections. Internal connections identify the ports of the
sub-processes, and external connections define the ports of the abstract process
specification in terms of some internal ports of the sub-processes.

The described specification method combines this process refinement
approach with a method for the refinement of ports and their interactions, which
is analogous to the refinement of sequential software modules, where an
operation at the higher level of abstraction is implemented in general by
several operations at the more detailed level. This port refinement method is
important for considerations of subsystem interfaces, their abstract
specification and implementation.

The stepwise refinement of process specifications as discussed in this
paper is similar some approaches described in the literature [Chen 81, Misr 81,
Jorr 81]. These approaches do not foresee the refinement of interacitons and
port specification. Such refinement is considered in the literature on stepwise
refinement of a abstract datatype specifications [Wulf 77, ...?]. These
references, however, consider the refinement of the operations defined for a
given module in the context of sequential process or shared resources where the
operations of the module are called upon by the active agents of the system. The
approach to port refinement, as discussed in this paper, may be considered a
generalization of the refinement of abstract data types to the context of
distributed systems.

The structured specification method described in this paper seems
applicable to the areas of software as well as hardware design. It addresses in
particular the question of system structure and the communication between the
different system parts, which is an important aspect in the design of
distributed system. It is to be noted that the described method only considers
static implementation structures. This seems to be suitable for description at
the hardware (or physical subsystem) level, and for many software applications
in systems for communication and real-time control.

While this paper concentrates on the __structure__ of communicating
systems, it is clear that appropriate specification techniques must be availab
for defining the __constraints__ that determine the possible interactions and thei
order of execution for the specified system. For the examples of this paper we
have used certain specification language elements which have been used on
different occasions, such as temporal ordering of interactions, constraints on
parameter values expressed by assertions, etc. Other specification languages,
involving for instance the notion of process states [Kell 76, FDT], could also
be used. A complete specification method could therefore be based on the proce
and port structure discussed in this paper and a semantic model which provides
the framework for formally defining the execution histories considered in
section 5. This semantic model would also be the basis for the specification
language by which process and port constraints can be expressed. However, such
considerations go beyond the scope of this paper.

__REFERENCES__: For a complete list of references see [Boch 83].

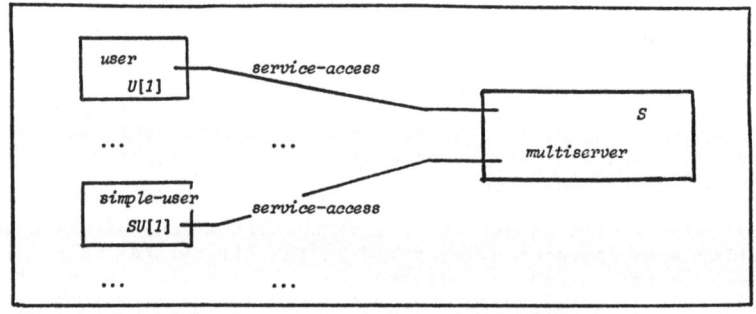

Figure 1 : A system of cooperating processes

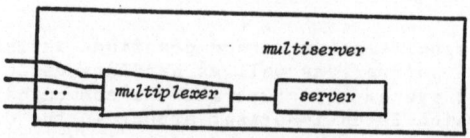

Figure 2 : The internal structure of a *multiserver* process

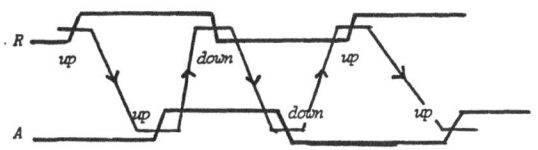

Figure 4 : Four-cycle signaling scheme

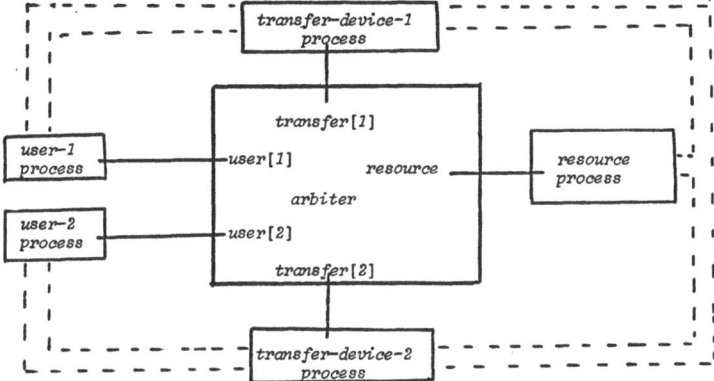

Figure 5 : Structure of the system with an arbiter

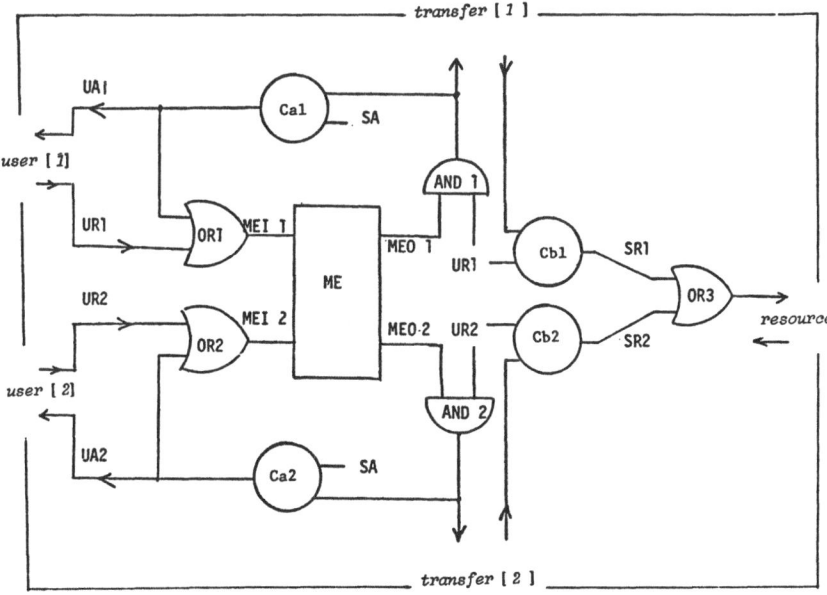

Figure 6 : Internal structure of the *arbiter*

Microcomputer System Design

An Advanced Course

Trinity College Dublin, June 1981

Editors: M. J. Flynn, N. R. Harris, D. P. McCarthy

1982. VII, 397 pages
(Lecture Notes in Computer Science, Volume 126)
ISBN 3-540-11172-7

Contents: Perspective on microcomputers. – Integrated circuit physics and technology. – Comuter aided design for microcomputer systems. – Properties of instruction set processor. – Customized microcomputers. – High level sequential and concurrent programming. – Microcomputer operating systems. – Notes on distributed systems of microprocessors. – LILITH: A personal computer for the software engineer.

Springer-Verlag
Berlin
Heidelberg
NewYork
Tokyo

In order to use microcomputers effectively, system designers require a broad knowledge of computer hardware, interfacing, software, and design tools.

Covering both theory and practice the microcomputer system design course destribed in this volume integrates the hardware and software sides of microcomputers. It includes the revised notes of a course which spanned development from silicon technology to software. It brought together current techniques in LSI/VLSI design, computer structures and languages, showing their application to, and implications for, microcomputer system desgin.

Operating Systems

An Advanced Course

By **M. J. Flynn, J. N. Gray, A. K. Jones, K. Lagally, H. Opderbeck, G. J. Popek, B. Randell, J. H. Saltzer, H. R. Wiehle**

Editors: **R. Bayer, R. M. Graham, G. Seegmüller**

Springer Study Edition
Reprint. 1979. 100 figures, 14 tables. X, 593 pages
ISBN 3-540-09812-7
(Originally published in the series *Lecture Notes in Computer Science,* Volume 60, 1978)

From the reviews: "Despite its description as 'An Advanced Course' this book is much more akin to a set of conference proceedings; the 'course', given in July 1977 and again in April 1978, takes the form of a series of presentations bordering on, or even consisting of, research topics in a number of areas connected with the entire spectrum of operating systems...
The course organisers, the editors of this book and its several contributors are to be congratulated. There is a minimum of the repetition which so often mars such a product, and yet the internal linkages between the various facets are present. I found much that was new, and appealing, in terms of new techniques, new results and especially valuable, new ways of looking at familiar situations. The main emphasis is on the abstract modelling of three aspects of current advances in operating systems; the invocation, allocation and control of resources; improvements in reliability by co-operation between software and specific functions of the hardware; and the provision of efficient and secure interprocess communications, especially where the communicating processes are under distinct local managements."
The Computer Journal

Contents: Introduction. – Models: The Object Model: A Conceptual Tool for Structuring Software. Computer Organization and Architecture. – Issues and Results in the Design of Operating Systems: Naming and Binding of Objects. Issues in Kernel Design. Protection Mechanisms and the Enforcement of Security Policies. Synchronization in a Layered System. Reliable Computing Systems. Notes on Data Base Operating Systems. Common Carrier Provided Network Interfaces. Design Issues for Secure Computer Networks. – Future Outlook and Research Problems: On System Specification. Research Problems of Decentralized Systems with Largely Autonomous Nodes.

Springer-Verlag
Berlin
Heidelberg
New York
Tokyo